SOUTHERNERS ACTING
Southern

SOUTHERN LITERARY STUDIES
Scott Romine, Series Editor

SOUTHERNERS ACTING Southern

ON CELEBRITIES AND THEIR STAR PERSONAS IN THE IMAGINED SOUTH

TISON PUGH

LOUISIANA STATE UNIVERSITY PRESS BATON ROUGE

Published by Louisiana State University Press
lsupress.org

Copyright © 2025 by Louisiana State University Press
All rights reserved. Except in the case of brief quotations used in articles or reviews, no part of this publication may be produced or transmitted in any format or by any means without written permission of Louisiana State University Press.

DESIGNER: Barbara Neely Bourgoyne
TYPEFACE: Whitman

Cover illustration based on a ca. 1957 photograph of singer Elvis Presley promoting the film *Jailhouse Rock*.

LIBRARY OF CONGRESS CATALOGING-IN-PUBLICATION DATA
Names: Pugh, Tison, author.
Title: Southerners acting southern : on celebrities and their star personas in the imagined South / Tison Pugh.
Description: Baton Rouge : Louisiana State University Press, 2025. | Series: Southern literary studies | Includes bibliographical references and index.
Identifiers: LCCN 2025001222 (print) | LCCN 2025001223 (ebook) | ISBN 978-0-8071-8398-4 (cloth) | ISBN 978-0-8071-8401-1 (paperback) | ISBN 978-0-8071-8466-0 (pdf) | ISBN 978-0-8071-8465-3 (epub)
Subjects: LCSH: Southern States—Civilization. | Entertainers—Southern States. | Southern States—In popular culture. | Southern States—Intellectual life.
Classification: LCC F209 .P885 2025 (print) | LCC F209 (ebook) | DDC 975—dc23/eng/20250203
LC record available at https://lccn.loc.gov/2025001222
LC ebook record available at https://lccn.loc.gov/2025001223

In memory of Phyllis Lefeaux . . .
  whose southernness, as it outshone all others, was never an act

CONTENTS

LIST OF ILLUSTRATIONS ix

ACKNOWLEDGMENTS xi

Introduction: Southern Stars and Southern Myths 1

1. Louis Armstrong's Smile versus New Orleans's Confederate Monuments 14
2. Truman Capote's Queer Celebrity and the Decadently Sentimental South 27
3. Elvis Presley, Graceland, and Celebrity Shrines 41
4. Great Actors, Southern Accents, and Tennessee Williams's Star Factory 54
5. Andy Griffith, *The Andy Griffith Show,* and the Paradox of Yokel Stereotypes 70
6. Tina Turner: Southern by Birth, Swiss by Choice 83
7. Dolly Parton: The Hillbilly Queen of Crossover Self-Censorship 96
8. Which Floridians Are Southerners? Tom Petty, Gloria Estefan, and the Vagaries of Pop-Star Southernness in the 1980s 109
9. On Southern Women's Book Clubs: Oprah Winfrey, Reese Witherspoon, Jenna Bush Hager, and the Performance of a Literary Star Persona 123

Contents

10. Ellen DeGeneres's Queer Voice of Southern (Un)Kindness 144
11. Tyler Perry: Atlanta's Entrepreneur and Queer Auteur 156
12. Matthew McConaughey Crowns Himself Texas's Philosopher King 169
13. Aziz Ansari: Comic Star of the Postsouthern South 181
14. Miley Cyrus's Queerly Authentic Southern Innocence 195

    Coda: Southern Stargazing as the Universe Expands 209

NOTES 213

WORKS CITED 235

INDEX 253

ILLUSTRATIONS

1. Ava Gardner, from *One Touch of Venus* 2
2. Louis Armstrong and Barbra Streisand in *Hello, Dolly!* 22
3. Truman Capote's author photograph for *Other Voices, Other Rooms* 29
4. Elvis Presley in *Change of Habit* 43
5. Katharine Hepburn and Elizabeth Taylor in *Suddenly Last Summer* 67
6. Andy Griffith in *No Time for Sergeants* 75
7. Tina Turner in *Mad Max: Beyond Thunderdome* 90
8. Dolly Parton in *9 to 5* 101
9. Tom Petty in a promotional image for his *Southern Accents* tour 113
10. Gloria Estefan in her "Bad Boy" music video 119
11. Oprah Winfrey during the inaugural episode of her book club 128
12. Reese Witherspoon in *Legally Blonde* 133
13. Jenna Bush Hager promoting her book club 142
14. Ellen DeGeneres in *Ellen* 151
15. Tyler Perry in *Diary of a Mad Black Woman* 164
16. Matthew McConaughey in *Dazed and Confused* 171
17. Aziz Ansari in *Parks and Recreation* 184
18. Miley Cyrus twerking with Robin Thicke 204

ACKNOWLEDGMENTS

This project began in earnest while I was watching the much-beloved sitcom *Parks and Recreation*, featuring Aziz Ansari as southerner Tom Haverford, a transplant to the fictional town of Pawnee, Indiana. Ansari's southern-inflected role and performance inspired my article "Aziz Ansari: Star of the Postsouthern South," copyright © 2020 Mississippi State University. This article first appeared in *Mississippi Quarterly: The Journal of Southern Cultures* 73.4 (2020): 457–77, published by Johns Hopkins University Press. I then noticed that the issue of southern celebrity emerged in some of my earlier work, including studies of Truman Capote in *Truman Capote: A Literary Life at the Movies* (University of Georgia Press, 2014) and of Miley Cyrus in *The Queer Fantasies of the American Family Sitcom* (Rutgers University Press, 2018). The chapters on Ansari, Capote, and Cyrus in this volume draw from these previous works.

NOTE

All songs, song lyrics, and audio recordings cited in this volume were listened to through the streaming service Spotify, with lyrics and transcripts confirmed by online searches. All other sources are documented in endnotes. All italics in quoted materials are original to the source.

SOUTHERNERS ACTING
Southern

INTRODUCTION
Southern Stars and Southern Myths

Blessed with extraordinary beauty, screen legend Ava Gardner, a native of Grabtown, North Carolina, enjoyed a steady rise into Hollywood's elite in the 1940s, but her career nearly collapsed before it began owing to her southern accent. As she recalled of her early days in the entertainment industry soon after being discovered, "I was terribly afraid that my North Carolina accent made me . . . 'very, very Southern.' During my screen test, [the studio representative] listened attentively. . . . I don't think he understood more than three words out of the twenty I'd spoken. Finally, he said smiling, 'I think a photographic test would be better.'"[1] The photographs succeeded in capturing her rare beauty. Gardner diligently practiced her diction and elocution, and, soon enough, a star was born, as she was cast in an array of now-classic movies: *The Killers* (1946), *Showboat* (1951), *Mogambo* (1953), among many more. In a key irony related to the vexed nature of southern stardom so central to this book, Gardner's southern roots almost derailed her career before it began. Only her stunning looks, to the extent that she played the title role in *One Touch of Venus* (1948), warranted her sufficient opportunity to shuck off the vestiges of her regional heritage in favor of a more all-American appeal. (See figure 1.)

And so should Ava Gardner be considered a southern star? On one hand, according to readily verifiable biographical facts of her upbringing in Grabtown, of course she is. On the other hand, according to the hazy constellations of paratextual markers that constitute her star persona, including her personal

FIG. 1. As this image from *One Touch of Venus* captures, Ava Gardner's remarkable beauty saved her film career, after her southern accent sabotaged early screen tests.

identity and acting roles, the casting decisions and marketing blitzes of studio executives, media coverage and celebrity gossip, and fan responses ranging from adoring to dismissive, among many other such factors, she need not necessarily be considered a southern star. By veering sharply away from her southern roots in creating and maintaining her star persona of international glamor, she redefined herself away from her roots. Quite simply, Hollywood executives encouraged Gardner to leave Grabtown, North Carolina, far behind in pursuing her acting career and stardom, and so she did.

As this example demonstrates, many stars from the South downplay or simply do not accentuate this foundational characteristic of their identities, preferring to present themselves as geographically unmarked Americans rather than as southerners. Such a strategy is particularly important for actors, most of whom would eschew being typecast as such southern stereotypes as the redneck, the gentleman, the belle, and most troublingly, the slave. For examples of southern celebrities mostly uninterested in stressing their geographic roots and thus in underscoring southern aspects of their star personas, we might consider Morgan Freeman, who hails from Memphis, Tennessee; George Clooney, who hails from Lexington, Kentucky; or Viola Davis, who hails from St. Matthews, South Carolina. Little in their celebrity personas stresses their southern heritage, even if they occasionally play southern roles: Freeman in *Driving Miss Daisy* (1989), Clooney in *O Brother, Where Art Thou?* (2000), and Davis in *How to Get Away with Murder* (2014–20) and *Ma Rainey's Black Bottom* (2020). Ironically, in *O Brother, Where Art Thou?* Clooney, playing an escaped convict in Mississippi, sings the song "A Man of Constant Sorrow," which includes the lyrics, "I bid farewell to ol' Kentucky / The place where I was born and raised." This song aptly summarizes Clooney's segue from his regional roots to his current cosmopolitanism, but it was mostly overlooked as an ironic commentary on his career. *A star from the South, it would appear, need not necessarily be a southern star.*

As the history of the South in particular and the United States as a whole vibrantly attests, southernness, in all its rich complexity, historical lineages, and conflicting mythologies, often catalyzes a reaction from newcomers and new acquaintances, whether positive, negative, or neutral in tone, and southernness continues to connote and denote a host of meanings throughout the United States and beyond. Southerners have long negotiated these tensions throughout our daily lives, whether by resisting them, reinforcing them, or ignoring them altogether. The cultural weight of southernness is magnified for actors, musicians, comedians, and other celebrities who hail from the South because their heritage thus becomes a potential inflection point in their star persona and their reception by their fans. Of course, like Gardner, not all stars from the South *act* like southerners or even lean into their southern roots, but a notable subset of southern celebrities across multiple media platforms accentuates their regional roots to build their star personas. This book seeks to explore this fascinating and illuminating facet of southern stars and southern stardom. Certainly, when one thinks of many of the celebrities born and raised in the U.S. South, including the stars addressed in these pages—Louis Armstrong, Truman Capote, Elvis Presley, Tennessee Williams, Andy Griffith, Tina Turner, Dolly Parton, Tom Petty, Gloria Estefan, Oprah Winfrey, Reese Witherspoon, Jenna Bush Hager, Ellen DeGeneres, Tyler Perry, Matthew McConaughey, Aziz Ansari, and Miley Cyrus, among others—their southernness springs to mind as a defining aspect not only of their autobiographical history but of their continuing appeal. By the roles they play, the stories they tell, the songs they sing, and the social media identities they curate, these stars build on the longstanding yet conflicting mythologies of the South to establish their personalities for fans, agents, and, perhaps most important, producers.

Of course, no objective scale exists for measuring stars' views of their childhood hometowns, yet it is equally obvious that some performers stress their regional roots more than others do. Certainly, most of his fans—and even many of his detractors—would know that comedian Jeff Foxworthy hails from the U.S. South (Atlanta, Georgia) owing to his redneck jokes ("You might be a redneck if . . ."). In contrast, it is less likely that audiences would know, for example, that Kevin Hart hails from Philadelphia, or that Lily Tomlin hails from Detroit, or that Sarah Silverman hails from Bedford, New Hampshire, because their humor is much less grounded in the traditions of their regional roots. Further relevant to this point, Foxworthy's fellow southern comedians include Wanda Sykes (Portsmouth, Virginia) and Chris Rock (Andrews, South Carolina), yet neither of these stars notably emphasizes this aspect of their lives in their comedy or in their film and television roles. In this regard Sykes and Rock contrast with Jack McBrayer, who built his comedy career playing Kenneth Parcell, a naïve southern rube, in the sitcom *30 Rock* (2006–13), as well as with such earlier stars as Andy Griffith and Jim Nabors, who did so in their respective sitcoms *The Andy Griffith Show* (1960–68) and *Gomer Pyle, U.S.M.C.* (1964–69). Comedians may joke about such topics as family life, childhood, adolescence, and their elementary and high school educations without foregrounding the geographic locations of these events. An amusing anecdote that took place at one's grandmother's house, or in a third-grade classroom, does not require a setting within a particular city and state, even though they must have transpired at a specific location. Foxworthy, McBrayer, and other southern comedians of their ilk, in contrast, lean into, tweak, subvert, and otherwise toy with southern tropes and southern stereotypes to create their unique personas and comic styles. (Indeed, as many southerners and ex-southerners who find themselves alienated from the prevailing mores of the region would agree, it is somewhat of a cosmic joke that we were born here.)

Because stardom stands as the ultimate ambition of many, likely most, entertainers, they must create, tend to, and nurture their star personas to maintain their public appeal. In his foundational work in the field of celebrity studies, simply titled *Stars*, Richard Dyer writes, "Stars are like characters in stories, representations of people."[2] Simultaneously people and representations of people, stars are inherently interpretable media constructions subject to scrutiny for the inherent contradictions and paradoxes of their self-presentation. In his follow-up volume *Heavenly Bodies: Film Stars and Society*, Dyer elaborates on his earlier points: "The star phenomenon consists of everything that is publicly available about stars. A film star's image is not just his or her films, but the promotion of those films and of the star through pin-ups, public appearances, studio hand-outs and so on, as well as interviews, biographies, and coverage in the press of the star's doings and 'private' life. Further, a star's image is also what people say or write about him or her. . . . Star images are always extensive, multimedia, intertextual."[3] Star personas are molded both by the celebrities themselves and by their publicity teams, but also by the public who comments on them, whether in adulation, indifference, or exhaustion. Further explicating the cultural work of stars and celebrity personas, Sean Redmond comments, "Stars and celebrities are often supericonic figures, who embody model identity positions that speak to certain psychic, cultural and economic needs"; he also states that stars and celebrities embody "desires and aspirations . . . that fans and consumers are invited or positioned to hold and share."[4] Fans define key aspects of their own identities through their fandom, and so a star's persona can, in a very real sense, bear exponential effects in the magnification and amplification of cultural tropes, whether divisively longstanding or daringly innovative.

Concerning southern stars and their personas, three intertwined yet divergent concerns of critical career importance emerge: stereotypes, typecasting, and authenticity. Briefly, the exaggerations and distortions of stereotypes construe an entire group of people as adhering to particular mannerisms, singularities, and cultural codes. Typecasting, which could be described as the institutional enforcement of stereotypes onto certain actors, threatens to limit these performers to a circumscribed subset of roles, curtailing the range of options available to them as creative talents. In contrast to stereotypes and typecasting stands authenticity, in which stars build stronger connections to their audience because there seems to be little distinction between the star and the human being—that they are, in fact, themselves, even if playing themselves. As will be seen throughout this volume, southern stars must negotiate the tensions of stereotypes, typecasting, and authenticity, all the while presenting themselves both to regional fans in the South and to a wider fan base outside of it.

To expand on these points in relation to stars and southern star personas, the South has long suffered the sting of the nation's stereotypical view of its denizens, and so southern entertainers embark on their careers aware of the ways in which a national audience might (mis)view them. Yet as much as stereotypes should be decried unanimously in their cruel assumptions about real people, southern performers often cagily manipulate southern stereotypes to their benefit, whether sincerely or with a winking nod, and thus win over new fans for their very embodiment of otherwise troubling stereotypes. The ethics of stereotypes in real life is simple—one should not use them, for one should never make blanket assumptions about any human being simply for belonging to a particular racial, ethnic, or other such group—but in the creation and dissemination of media, performers and creators must grapple with the more challenging ethics of stereotypes in their representations of themselves and others. Certainly, the vast variety of stereotypes—from the positive to the anodyne to the negative—affords a wide arena for entertainers to construct themselves for the enjoyment of their fans.

Whereas southern stars can manipulate, to some degree, the utility of stereotypes in fashioning their public image, typecasting, by definition, is enforced on them when casting agents and other industry executives limit them to particular roles for which they are deemed particularly appropriate. By the very strength of their previous performances, some actors inadvertently lock themselves into similar roles long into their future. Pamela Robertson Wojcik explains the convoluted intersections of typecasting with actors' careers, cultural stereotypes, and casting decisions: "insofar as the actor represents human characters, film acting relates to changing conceptions of identity and identity politics, and thus the actor will inevitably negotiate stereotypes and represent identities inflected by race, gender, ethnicity, class, and national difference. Rather than something imposed on actors and audiences from without . . . typecasting occurs at many varied levels, and is equally something spectators and fans enact or impose on actors."[5] Whereas few southern actors would choose to be typecast as southerners owing to the limitations it would likely place on their careers, southern singers, particularly country music singers, often lean into their regional roots as part of their personas: Loretta Lynn, Dolly Parton, Garth Brooks, and Toby

Keith need not fear the repercussions of southern stardom and typecasting as much as such southern-born actors as Johnny Depp, Julia Roberts, Renée Zellweger, and Jamie Foxx might. On this issue, Billy Bob Thornton reminisced ruefully on the struggles of negotiating Hollywood's dismissive view of southern actors and the roles for which they are typically judged appropriate: "There is some prejudice against actors from the South. I didn't really get auditions when I was coming up in Hollywood. They either wanted me to play a hillbilly or a killer, sometimes at the same time! Sometimes they'd even say I wasn't Southern enough. *Really*, I am not Southern enough? They wanted me to talk like Big Daddy [in Tennessee Williams's *Cat on a Hot Tin Roof*]."[6]

In complementary contrast to stereotyping and typecasting stands the potential of authenticity, in which southern stars who accentuate their southern heritage can enhance their appearance as "real people," those who "remember where they came from," and thus forge more genuine connections with their fans. As Kate Egan and Sarah Thomas aver, one of the foremost features of virtually all star personas is authenticity: "In star studies, authenticity largely remains characterized in terms of the ordinary, the natural, the intimate or domestic . . . and as a major quality sought by all audiences—even if it is achieved by artificial means."[7] Few phrases better capture the concept of the celebrity persona than "artificial authenticity"—an oxymoronic coinage that illustrates the ways in which celebrities must curate their very selves to expand and maintain their consumer appeal. As any number of celebrity scandals have revealed over the years since comic actor Roscoe "Fatty" Arbuckle's murder trial in the 1920s, some star personas present an outward façade of authentic likeability only to reveal the darker sides of their personalities when unmasked to the world. Celebrity authenticity, no matter how many times it is debunked in jawbreakingly stunning fashion, remains a core quality of many stars' likeability. Simply put, so many fans want to believe the best of their favorite performers, no matter the blinders needed to maintain the view.

Ironically, the term "artificial authenticity" could also be applied to the South itself. It is, of course, a real place, an actual region of the United States of America, but it is simultaneously a landscape whose mythologies play an outsized role in creating its many, often conflicting, cultural meanings. Geographically, it is amorphous: under various maps and governments during the founding and frontier years of the United States, its core states have included

Alabama, Arkansas, Florida, Georgia, Kentucky, Mississippi, Louisiana, North Carolina, South Carolina, Tennessee, and Virginia, with border states such as Maryland, Missouri, Oklahoma, Texas, and West Virginia floating in and out of its borders according to historical circumstances and cultural realignments. One often hears of the so-called "Solid South," in the fact that the southern states have often voted in lockstep with one another in favor of a variety of conservative politicians and social mandates; at the same time, the South is constituted of various regions and subregions—most predominantly, urban and rural—but also the unique patches that defy any expectations of uniformity.[8]

Whatever its geographic borders, however, the South matters profoundly to the United States' cultural imaginary as a region both representative of and estranged from the wider nation, as Jennifer Rae Greeson eloquently explains: "A concept of the South is essential to national identity in the United States of America. Wherever U.S. citizens were born, wherever we presently live, whatever our personal experience of the southeastern states—for all of us, knowing the South is part of knowing what it means to be an American. This South that we hold collectively in our minds is not—could not possibly be—a fixed or real place. It both exceeds and flattens place; it is a term of the imagination, a site of national fantasy."[9] The South is and it is not, it communicates and it impedes communication, it is a site of fantasy but one that metes out brutally real effects on countless lives. As a field, star studies, it must be admitted, is inherently a lighter affair than historical accounts of the U.S. South and its racist past and present, but southern star studies further enlighten these dynamics by delving into the ways in which the region's tropes persist in the present. Tara McPherson proposes the necessity of this type of southern analysis: "Studying the role of the South in the national imaginary and in the works of individual southerners illuminates the role of the imagination in social life, mining the links between imagination and representation."[10] Both imaginary and real, the South's "artificial authenticity" persists in efforts to understand the region's culture within its borders and its pervasive influence beyond them.

And as southern stars cultivate their personas through regional stereotypes and myths, it is equally important to examine the ways in which the South cultivates and updates its myths through its stars. "The South" is not a singular consciousness acting with purpose and clarity of intent, but the South is composed of millions of residents—citizens, governmental leaders, immigrants, recent transplants, visitors, among others—who do indeed act with purpose and clarity of intent, and many of these people foster the connections between the region and its celebrities for a host of reasons: to celebrate local talent, to increase tourism and thus tax dollars, to redress the region's racist history (or sadly, to reinforce it), and so on. The mythologies of the South are longstanding and hoary but never fully static, and southern celebrities allow the southern states to present a new (or antiquated) vision of themselves to the wider U.S. culture. As the 1960s feminist axiom proclaimed that "The personal is the political," so too does the personal and public construction of celebrity effect social, cultural, and political consequences, even if indirectly.

Following these lines of thought, the following chapters address the star personas of a range of southern celebrities, each of whom has inflected their performances with southern cadences or otherwise captured a defining, perhaps delimiting, perhaps paradoxical, aspect of southern culture in their self-presentation. The first chapter, "Louis Armstrong's Smile versus New Orleans's Confederate Monuments," details the ways in which, in New Orleans's efforts to rewrite its troubling racial politics, Louis Armstrong was conscripted to serve as its icon. His smiling performance persona ultimately toppled the city's many monuments to Confederate soldiers, in a striking example of the ways in which the South rewrites its history through its celebrities. As explored in the chapter "Truman Capote's Queer Celebrity and the Decadently Sentimental South," Capote, with the publication of his breakthrough novel *Other Voices, Other Rooms* in 1948, savvily deployed southern gothic tropes to market both his fiction and himself. Throughout his career he presented himself as both an insider and an outsider to the South's mores, warmly recalling childhood memories in one media appearance or publication and condemning its hidebound traditions in another, all the while insisting midcentury American audiences confront his decadent performance of queerness.

Whereas so many celebrity tourist sites fade into cultural obsolescence after the death of their namesake, Elvis Presley's Graceland continues to flourish. The following chapter, "Elvis Presley, Graceland, and Celebrity Shrines," ponders the ways in which the star and his homestead share a similar southern persona of downhome simplicity and excess, as well as how they whitewash the region's racist history. While Presley was singing, Tennessee Williams was writing, and during the 1950s and 1960s many of his plays were adapted into a virtual subgenre of midcentury American film, allowing an array of actors, including Vivien Leigh, Marlon Brando, Paul Newman, Elizabeth Taylor, and Katharine Hepburn, to burnish their credentials as accomplished performers. The chapter "Great Actors, Southern Accents, and Tennessee Williams's Star Factory" illuminates the ways in which exaggerated tropes of the South, and particularly of southern accents, undermined these great actors' otherwise sterling performances. Notably, these stars' reputations suffered no harm, and were often enhanced, for hamming up their characters' southernness, demonstrating the easy utility of southern stereotypes in communicating to nonsouthern audiences. More than any other star considered in this volume, Andy Griffith faced the sting of typecasting throughout his career, and "Andy Griffith, *The Andy Griffith Show*, and the Paradox of Yokel Stereotypes" details his efforts to free himself of his southern persona. His starring role in *The Andy Griffith Show* cemented his celebrity through a folksy and friendly image of white southern masculinity while discounting the more troubling attributes of his southern schtick, both in his professional and private life.

The next chapter, "Tina Turner: Southern by Birth, Swiss by Choice," explores Turner's status as an expatriate—both of the South and of the United States altogether—tracking the ways in which she transcended her southern roots while never alienating audiences through a future-facing rhetoric of survivorhood. In key ways Turner aligned her abusive marriage to her first husband, Ike Turner, to her experiences growing up in the racist South while refusing to candidly disparage either the man or the region. Suturing over divisions between red states and blue states, country music megastar Dolly Parton, as explored in "Dolly Parton: The Hillbilly Queen of Crossover Self-Censorship," unites a divided nation through her unique merger of southern simplicity and cosmopolitan excess. As much as she is as universally adored as any celebrity could hope to be, Parton leaves herself oddly unknowable in the process, thus dispelling the fantasy of southern kindness and good neighborliness that the region promulgates. Not all southerners are recognized as such, and this tension is explored in the chapter, "Which Floridians Are Southerners? Tom Petty, Gloria Estefan, and the Vagaries of Pop-Star Southernness in the 1980s." Petty and Estefan, two Floridian pop singers who shone brightest in the 1980s and 1990s, exemplify the varying ways in which race and ethnicity influence the popular press's coverage of stars, as Estefan was rarely covered as a southerner while

Introduction

Petty's southernness played a key role in both his music and his performances. Three of America's most popular and influential book clubs are hosted by southern women, and the chapter, "On Southern Women's Book Clubs: Oprah Winfrey, Reese Witherspoon, Jenna Bush Hager, and the Performance of a Literary Star Persona," examines the ways in which these three celebrities inflect their personas through their passion for books and their embrace of bookishness. Southerners have long been derided for our purported lack of intelligence, and so the alignment of southern women with books and book clubs rebuts this dismissive stereotype. Winfrey and Witherspoon reframe both wider cultural codes and their unique star personas in these moves, particularly in their incorporation of books as a key facet of their media empires; Bush Hager, haunted by accusations of nepotism early in her career, expanded her professional identity as a journalist to include that of cultural arbiter.

The chapter "Ellen DeGeneres's Queer Voice of Southern (Un)Kindness" explores the ways in which this star attempted to balance between hospitality and hypocrisy, as she preached kindness on her talk show while treating her employees and others coldly. The South has long prided and publicized itself for its ostensible hospitality, and for many of its minority citizens, few reputations could appear more cruelly unwarranted. Myths of southern manners mask the savagery underneath the surface, and DeGeneres's rise and fall provide a striking illustration of these dynamics observable throughout southern culture as a whole. DeGeneres's fellow New Orleanian Tyler Perry serves as the subject of the following chapter: "Tyler Perry: Atlanta's Entrepreneur and Queer Auteur." Perry skyrocketed to fame in his many crossdressing performances as Madea, an irascible older woman with little patience but ultimately a generous heart; he then parlayed his acting success into a media empire, one that has reshaped Atlanta's city map through his shrewd entrepreneurship that dismantles longstanding anti-Black biases. In "Matthew McConaughey Crowns Himself Texas's Philosopher King" the analysis turns to this star's meteoric rise in the 1990s, his continued success in the 2000s, and his turn to more dramatic roles in the 2010s—the so-called "McConaissance"—and plumbs the ways in which Texan tropes define his appeal and its limitations. Throughout his career McConaughey has played up his southern charm and Texas-sized swagger, leaning into stereotypes of southern masculinity that many find troubling, or perhaps vexing, or perhaps simply vacuous.

The final two chapters—"Aziz Ansari: Comic Star of the Postsouthern South" and "Miley Cyrus's Queerly Authentic Southern Innocence"—examine two stars who have updated the look of the South in key ways: Ansari, by showcasing its increasing ethnic diversity, and Cyrus, by showcasing its increasing sexual diversity. South Carolinian Ansari, the child of first-generation immigrants from India, employs an outsider's approach to his southern childhood, recognizing the many challenges for nonwhite citizens of the U.S. South, which he then transmutes into comic fodder. Cyrus, the child star who skyrocketed to fame playing the eponymous role of *Hannah Montana* (2006–11) and who grew up before the nation's eyes, faced the challenge of bringing queer visibility to the U.S. South, openly sharing her pansexuality while navigating the region's conservative cultural traditions. As much as the South's cultural codes have long been cemented by binaries—Black and white, women and men, poor and rich, queer and heteronormative—Ansari and Cyrus highlight the possibility of a different future for a region often obsessed with looking back to a supposedly glorious past.

Each chapter of this book focuses on a star or a particular star cluster, but overlapping and interweaving themes extend across its pages. The South prides itself on its purported sense of southern hospitality and philanthropy, an issue most directly addressed in the chapter on Ellen DeGeneres but also relevant to those on Louis Armstrong, Elvis Presley, Dolly Parton, Tyler Perry, Matthew McConaughey, and Miley Cyrus. The status of Elvis Presley's Graceland as a premier tourist destination complements the reading of the singer's star persona, but the significance of tourism, tourist sites, and southern landscapes also figures prominently in the chapters on Louis Armstrong, Dolly Parton, Tyler Perry, and Tom Petty and Gloria Estefan. The South's lagging literacy rates are tangentially addressed in the chapters considering Oprah Winfrey's, Reese Witherspoon's, and Jenna Bush Hager's book clubs, as well as in Dolly Parton's and Matthew McConaughey's concern for children's education. Southern accents define the South in the wider U.S. imaginary, a theme addressed most directly in the chapter on the stars in cinematic adaptations of Tennessee Williams's plays but also in the examinations of Tom Petty, Ellen DeGeneres, and Aziz Ansari—and in this Introduction's opening discussion of Ava Gardner. Peculiar affinities also abound in the pages, such as the prevalence of Tennessean singers: Elvis Presley (after his relocation from Mississippi), Tina Turner and

Dolly Parton (born on opposite ends of the state but separated by only seven years), and Miley Cyrus (Parton's goddaughter). In the roughly chronological order of the Table of Contents from the early 1900s to the early 2000s, readers will see a shifting South but also persistent challenges, particularly in regard to race and racism, queerness and queerphobia, and other recalcitrant issues the region simultaneously faces and ignores.

Finally, *Southerners Acting Southern: On Celebrities and Their Star Personas in the Imagined South* concludes with a coda, "Southern Stargazing as the Universe Expands." As I was polishing the final draft of this book before sending it to Louisiana State University Press for publication, a meteor bolted across the skies of southern star studies: Beyoncé released her *Cowboy Carter* album on March 29, 2024. In that teetering seesaw between "stars born in the South" and "southern stars," I had misidentified—or prematurely identified—Beyoncé as belonging to the former but on this date she defiantly, proudly, and beautifully rewrote the codes of her own celebrity yet again by releasing a country music album. The Coda thus offers a space to meditate briefly on the many celebrities missing from these pages. No book such as this could possibly be considered "complete"—how would it be possible to include all stars born in the South who have inflected themselves and their careers with tropes of their southernness?—but the Coda allows an opportunity to consider not only the gauntlet thrown down by Beyoncé with *Cowboy Carter* but a variety of other stars who merit further study. In sum, *Southerners Acting Southern* could never make claims to covering the topic of southern stars, their star personas, and the geocultural myths of the South comprehensively. It is, instead, a collection of photographs of various stars and star clusters oscillating around issues of southern celebrity and southern tropes. It stands among the beginnings of a conversation but certainly not at its end, and I hope, not less valuable for its limitations.

1

LOUIS ARMSTRONG'S SMILE VERSUS NEW ORLEANS'S CONFEDERATE MONUMENTS

Some airport codes appear designed to perplex rather than to illuminate, and one must study a bit of local history to understand why ORD represents Chicago's O'Hare, or why MCO represents Orlando International, or why BNA represents Nashville—or why Louis Armstrong New Orleans International Airport is represented by MSY. Originally named the Moisant Stock Yards, where daredevil aviator John Moisant died in 1910, New Orleans's airport was renamed in honor of jazz legend Louis "Satchmo" Armstrong in 2001 to recognize the anniversary of this treasured hometown celebrity's 100th birthday.[1] In creating this bustling memorial traversed by thousands of travelers daily, New Orleans paid tribute to one of its most creative and widely beloved citizens, who was also one of its most tireless promoters. In one such paean to New Orleans, Armstrong extolled, "I could go on talking about my home town like mad because I love it. I always will. It has given me something to live for. Those millions of memories. Even with those hard times I'd be willing to live them all over again."[2] In a similar reverie, he affirmed, "Every time I close my eyes blowing that trumpet of mine—I look right in the heart of good old New Orleans. . . . It has given me something to live for."[3] For a city whose name conjures up the sounds and images of jazz and whose annual Jazz and Heritage Festival attracts music lovers from across the globe, Louis Armstrong New Orleans International Airport sounds an opening note of civic pride for an incomparable local talent and his lasting musical legacy.

The renaming of New Orleans's airport to honor Armstrong stands in striking contrast to the city's long history of racist memorials to the traitorous Confederate military and related white-supremacist institutions, which commemorated such figures as Robert E. Lee, Jefferson Davis, Pierre Gustave Toutant Beauregard, and the White League (a Reconstruction era racist/terrorist organization). In 2017 these statues were taken down in a necessary, if belated, recognition of their divisive message. As Mayor Mitch Landrieu summarized of these offensive relics, "To literally put the Confederacy on a pedestal in our most prominent places of honor is an inaccurate recitation of our full past, it is an affront to our present, and it is a bad prescription for our future."[4] Juxtaposing the symbolism of these contrasting memorials—Louis Armstrong New Orleans International Airport proudly proclaiming the city's jazz heritage and celebration of Black art, the Confederate statues powerfully demonstrating the lasting legacy of racism and white supremacy in Louisiana and beyond—illustrates the fraught dynamics of cultural mythmaking in the U.S. South, as well as the region's slow pace of change, as it also encourages a deeper accounting of Armstrong's southern star persona. To view Armstrong as a jazz icon recognizes his incredible achievements as a musician and actor while also acknowledging that his celebrity remained inextricably linked to issues of race and racism throughout his career and even decades after his death, particularly in the fraught issue of his beaming smile that some contemporaries interpreted as his refusal to directly condemn American racism. More so, Armstrong's celebrity persona is indelibly linked to his southern hometown's creation and maintenance of its own public image.

As his encomiums to New Orleans attest, Armstrong's life was shaped by his early years in New Orleans, which influenced both his career and star persona. As he recalled in his memoir, *Satchmo: My Life in New Orleans*, he was born and raised in "the crowded section of New Orleans known as Back o' Town,"[5] and throughout his life he frequently aligned his patriotism—another defining aspect of his public persona—with his birthday on the Fourth of July, although he was actually born a month later, on August 4, 1901. He began his musical career inauspiciously, singing with others in the streets, until a pivotal moment in his life. On New Year's Eve of 1912, he was arrested for participating in a New Orleans tradition both frighteningly dangerous and regrettably familiar: shooting a gun in the air. The presiding judge sentenced Armstrong to the Colored Waif's Home, where the institution's band director soon recruited him, for his musical aptitude could not be overlooked. Despite the harsh circumstances leading to his detention, Armstrong favorably reminisced over his time in the Colored Waif's Home, twenty years later expressing in a letter to its director, "I shall never forget the people who have done everything for me. . . . Am always proud to tell the world of the place [that] started me out as a first-class musician."[6] Upon his release, Armstrong pursued a variety of odd and ill-paid jobs such as selling coal, while advancing his musical interests by playing with a variety of local musicians and establishments, including those of Storyville, New Orleans's famed red-light district. Branching out from his hometown, Armstrong began playing on Mississippi riverboats. This exposure brought him wider recognition, and in 1922 Joseph "King" Oliver invited him to join his band in Chicago. Following this musical apprenticeship, Armstrong traveled to New York City in October 1924, as the Harlem Renaissance was flowering, to join the Fletcher Henderson Orchestra. He returned to Chicago the following year and formed Louis Armstrong and His Hot Five with Kid Ory (trombone), Johnny Dodds (clarinet), Johnny St. Cyr (banjo), and Lil Hardin (piano, and also his second wife).

Armstrong's fame skyrocketed throughout the 1920s and lasted for the ensuing decades of his life. Soon celebrated as "The World's Greatest Trumpet Player," he also gained recognition for his distinctive, gravelly voiced singing. Scores of singles and albums were released over the decades of his career, including such notable titles as *Satchmo at Pasadena* (1951), *Ella and Louis* (1956), and *The Real Ambassadors* (1962).[7] Subsequent incarnations of Armstrong's group included Louis Armstrong and the Stompers (with Earl Hines on piano), Louis Armstrong and His Hot Seven, and Louis Armstrong and His All Stars. Armstrong toured tirelessly both nationally and internationally, and his 1960s junkets under the aegis of the U.S. State Department earned him the epithet "Ambassador Satch." Beyond the immediate realm of jazz, Armstrong scored a No. 1 hit on the pop charts with his rendition of "Hello, Dolly!" (1964), for which he won the Grammy for Best Male Vocal Performance. Released in 1967, Armstrong's "What a Wonderful World" did not climb the U.S. pop charts in his lifetime but reached No. 1 in the United Kingdom and achieved such classic status that it hit the Top 40 in 1988, seventeen years after his death, when it was included on the soundtrack of the film *Good Morning, Vietnam* (1987). In another sign of his widespread popularity, Armstrong recorded the theme song, "We Have All the Time in the World," for the James Bond film *On Her Majesty's Secret Service* (1969). Armstrong died July 6, 1971.

This thumbnail biography points to some of the more pivotal moments of Armstrong's life and documents some of his more remarkable accomplishments, but it can only hint at the power and complexity of his southern star persona, which generated both his fans' deep affection and strong critiques from many contemporaries. Indeed, as much as his contributions to jazz history could hardly be overstated, several critics argued that his genial style, notably signified in his beaming smile, carried undertones of troublesome tropes derived from minstrelsy and Blackface traditions. As Michael Borshuk observes of his performance persona, Armstrong "tempered his innovative trumpet style with an affable onstage demeanor, in some ways a savvy revision of the Old Negro stereotype. Before a crowd Armstrong became Pops or Satchmo, a smiling, joking presence who dazzled audiences with downhome wit and folksy charm."[8] In an otherwise favorable article published in *Ebony*, Charles L. Sanders lamented that Armstrong "plays the role of a minstrel as if he were a white man in blackface," a performance style that Sanders linked directly to the South, further decrying Armstrong as "an Old New Orleans-type 'tailgate' entertainer through and through."[9] Many of his peers in jazz likewise criticized him for his onstage mannerisms, seeing in him a degraded image of a Black man attempting to please white audiences with a slightly modernized minstrel act, as well as for his reticence to forthrightly condemn American racism. As Dizzy Gillespie frankly avowed, "I criticized Louis for . . . his 'plantation image.' We didn't appreciate that about Louis Armstrong, and if anybody asked me about a certain public image of him, handkerchief over his head, grinning in the face of white racism, I never hesitated to say I didn't like it. I didn't want the white man to expect me to allow the same things Louis Armstrong did."[10] Sounding a similar note, Miles Davis bemoaned the ways in which the white power structures of the entertainment industry enforced rigidly demeaning expectations on Black performers: "Those talk shows would take a black man on television back then only if he grinned, became a clown, like Louis Armstrong did. I loved the way Louis played trumpet . . . but I hated the way he had to grin in order to get over with some tired white folks. . . . I just hated when I saw him doing that, because Louis . . . had a consciousness about black people."[11] The eponymous protagonist of Ralph Ellison's classic novel *Invisible Man* (1952), a searing indictment of U.S. society through the eyes of a Black man cognizant of his cultural invisibility, sees Armstrong as a kindred spirit: "Perhaps I like Louis Armstrong because he's made poetry out of being invisible. I think it must be because he's unaware he *is* invisible. And my own grasp of invisibility aids me to understand his music."[12] For Ellison, Armstrong camouflaged himself to the point of blankness, of virtual nothingness, in his desire to appease white audiences.

From viewing Armstrong's filmed concert appearances, it is apparent that he masterfully engaged with his audiences, moving from song to song with affable charm and impeccable musicianship, with his scatting style interjecting improvisatory flair to performances simultaneously under his deft control. Armstrong's charismatic smile and rich, deep laugh suggest his canny deployment of humor to win his audience's goodwill, and Frank Salamone proposes that Armstrong perceived the unique ability of "humor to subvert pompous platitudes regarding the established order" and thus incorporated humor as "an integral part of [his] persona."[13] Although more a part of his personality than of his public persona, Armstrong appreciated earthy and bawdy humor, as Laurence Bergreen documents: "He also reveled in his bowel movements. They were occasions for rejoicing, and he was not shy about sharing his enthusiasm for them with the world. His stationery, for instance, showed him sitting on a toilet, pants down around his ankles, grinning, glimpsed as if through a keyhole, with this legend underneath: 'SATCHMO SAYS: LEAVE IT ALL BEHIND YA!'"[14] Both in his performances and his private life, although to varying degrees, Armstrong reveled in the inherent humor of the human condition, but humor can be—although it need not be—viewed as antithetical to serious musicianship. That is to say, the comic aspects of Armstrong's onstage persona opened him to charges of mimicking minstrel traditions by engaging with audiences through both humor and music, rather than by prioritizing the music for which he was famed. His frequent performances of the song "Black and Blue" capture the contradictions of his comic persona. Its lyrics address the pernicious effects of racism, as Armstrong plaintively sings, "My only sin is in my skin / What did I do to be so black and blue?" One could certainly interpret these words as a pointed critique of American race relations, particularly when he sang them in East Germany in 1965, yet any critique is simultaneously undercut by his smiling as he sings.[15]

As these examples of his humor and his performances demonstrate, Armstrong faced the tense conundrum of responding to criticisms of his persona by refashioning it or by continuing in his preferred style, with the specter of southern racism hanging over either decision. It should also be recorded that, as much as Armstrong cultivated his unique persona, the aura of jazz in the popular imagination refused to see the complete complexity of many Black musicians and their preferred genres, as exemplified by Armstrong's appreciation for Guy Lombardo's music. The two men and their musical genres would appear at first glance as virtual opposites: the syncopated jazz stylings of a Black man versus the smoother, gentler harmonies of a white man. Yet Armstrong proclaimed his deep admiration for Lombardo's musical skills: "Lombardo! These people are keeping music alive—helping to fight them damn beboppers. You know, you got to have somebody to keep that music sounding good. Music doesn't mean a thing unless it *sounds* good." He also credited Lombardo's music for inspiring some of his own compositions.[16] Elijah Wald unpacks the racial politics of these assumptions: "Armstrong loved both heat and sweetness, and he always kept one foot in either camp, a practice not rare among the black jazz musicians of his day. The pressures on white and black musicians were very different, and a frequent complaint from that generation of black players is that they were stereotyped as hot bands, although they could play as smoothly and gently as the white bands."[17] By pigeonholing Armstrong as a jazz musician to the extent of overlooking other likely influences, fans and critics circumscribed the full range of his musical genius.

Certainly, Armstrong's genial performance style masked the deeper complexities of his music and his views of American culture. As with many musical storytellers, Armstrong encoded autobiographical experiences in his songs, thereby inviting his audiences to consider the alignment between his life and his lyrics, as well as their depiction of his hometown of New Orleans. For example, "Coal Cart Blues" recalls his childhood experiences carrying coal throughout the city's neighborhoods—"of course the cart was hot and / it almost kill me"—with these words encouraging listeners to consider the disjunction between his successful present and his impoverished past. Some lyrical subtexts would be apparent only to those cognizant of the seamier side of New Orleans's night life. For example, "Basin Street Blues" celebrates its eponymous thoroughfare as where "the elite always meet" and nostalgically paints the city as "the land of dreams / You'll never know how nice it seems"; the song refrains from mentioning that Basin Street was located in the city's notorious Storyville district, home to numerous brothels and speakeasys. Armstrong's "I Wish I Could Shimmy Like My Sister Kate" contains the lyrics "It's a shame how you're lyin' on her head" and "Get out of Katie's bed." Laurence Bergreen suggests that the song was likely inspired by the murder of Kate Townsend, a Storyville madam.[18] Other songs celebrating New Orleans, a smattering of which include "Back O' Town Blues," "Where the Blues Were Born in New Orleans," "Do You Know What It Means to Miss New Orleans," and "New Orleans Stomp," further linked the musician to his hometown.

Armstrong's place in world culture is ensured owing to his musical achievements, with his cinematic appearances further illuminating the contours of his celebrity persona. During his stay in Los Angeles in 1930, Armstrong was cast in Victor Halperin's film *Ex-Flame*, which inaugurated a string of roles, continuing nearly until his death, in which he played himself or thinly disguised versions of himself. Lamentably but not surprisingly, some of these films depict Armstrong with heavily racialized and racist tropes. In one of his first appearances as himself, in the Betty Boop cartoon "I'll Be Glad When You're Dead, You Rascal, You" (1932), Armstrong and his band first appear as themselves; they are then recast as cartoon cannibals menacing Betty and her companions Koko and Bimbo, as Armstrong sings the title song. These film appearances, often little more than cameo roles, cemented his persona for a wider public. Through his tours Armstrong could perform for hundreds and thousands of fans; through his films, he could perform for millions, including in such acclaimed titles as *Cabin in the Sky* (1943), *The Glenn Miller Story* (1954), *High Society* (1956), and *Hello, Dolly!* (1969). With the rare exceptions of such films as *Cabin in the Sky*, Hollywood films of this era primarily portrayed white actors as their leads, and so Armstrong shared the screen with such luminaries as Jimmy Stewart and June Allyson in *The Glenn Miller Story*, Grace Kelly, Bing Crosby, and Frank Sinatra in *High Society*, Danny Kaye in *The Five Pennies* (1959), and Barbra Streisand and Walter Matthau in *Hello, Dolly!* Further cementing the link between Armstrong and his birth city, films such as *New Orleans* (1947), remembered today as Billie Holiday's only notable cinematic appearance, and *Glory Alley* (1952), the title of which alludes to Bourbon Street, were set in New Orleans. *Cabin in the Sky*, a rare 1940s Hollywood production with an all-Black cast, featured Armstrong in a supporting role as The Trumpeter, who also serves as one of the devil Lucifer Jr.'s minions. Unsurprisingly, the film depicts its characters with numerous racial stereotypes, but the strong performances by such legends as Ethel Waters and Lena Horne transcend these limitations, resulting in the National Film Registry selecting it in 2020 as a work of cultural, historical, and aesthetic significance.

As Michael Meckna summarizes of Armstrong's cinematic roles, "in many of these films Armstrong . . . plays a pivotal role in helping the white star overcome musical and/or personal difficulties." He further states: "As so often was the case . . . Armstrong's performance adds musical color and atmosphere but has very little to do with the story line."[19] Meckna rightfully captures the limitations of Armstrong's appearances regarding a film's plot, yet the star's presence often contributed powerfully to its subthemes concerning civil rights. For example, in *The Glenn Miller Story* Miller and his wife attend one of Armstrong's shows in an integrated club as he leads an integrated band, and in *High Society* Armstrong plays himself but also bookends the film as a narrator figure. This musical adaptation of George Cukor's *The Philadelphia Story* (1940) includes as one of its showstopping numbers "Now You Has Jazz," with Armstrong sharing the stage with star Bing Crosby, but also featuring call-outs to each of Armstrong's musicians, including Barrett Deems, his white drummer. Integrated bands were forbidden in certain localities during this era—notably Louisiana—but *High Society* portrays integrated bands as a *fait accompli* rather than as a matter of cultural debate. This scene's advocacy of integration bears a pertinent correlation to the film's setting in Newport, Rhode Island, which inaugurated its jazz festival in 1954, to the dismay of several well-heeled locals. Armstrong's final film appearance in *Hello, Dolly!* captures the star power of his short performances, for certainly, it is a rather remarkable moment in film history, as two of the twentieth-century's greatest vocalists complement and contrast each other tonally. Barbra Streisand lightly scats in their duet, demonstrating his lasting influence on Broadway's vocal stylings. In this highly enjoyable film nominated for seven Academy Awards, their duet—a mere two minutes of screen time—stands out, with Armstrong bedecked in a tuxedo with red vest and red carnation and Streisand standing beside him in a glittering gold gown with golden plumes in her hair. His "You're looking swell, Dolly," to which she replies coyly, "Thank you, Louis," marks a noted advance from the racist caricaturizing of his earlier Betty Boop cartoon. (See figure 2.)

FIG. 2. In *Hello, Dolly!* (1969), his final film appearance, Louis Armstrong sings his solo No. 1 hit from 1964 as a duet with breakthrough Broadway diva Barbra Streisand, resulting in one of the most memorable musical screen pairings in film history.

Given his appearances in Hollywood movies for much of his career, Armstrong was keenly attuned to the fact that, at least in these productions, the majority of his audiences was white. If Armstrong's genial celebrity persona restricted his ability to speak candidly about race relations and racism in the United States, as his detractors alleged, he nonetheless acknowledged its pervasiveness on numerous occasions. In an illustrative passage from his memoir recalling his riverboat days, Armstrong acknowledged racism while concentrating more on his appreciation for white people:

There were often fights on board during those trips, and almost everyone working on the ship would try to stop them. But the members of the band never did. We were colored, and we knew what that meant. We were not allowed to mingle with the white guests under any circumstances. We were there to play good music for them, and that was all. However, everybody loved us and our music and treated us royally. I and some of the other musicians in the band were from the South and we understood, so we never had any hard feelings. I have always loved my white folks, and they have always proved that they loved me and my music. I have never had anything to be depressed about in that respect, only respect and appreciation. Many a time white folks have invited me and my boys to the finest meals at their homes, with the best liquor you would want to smack your chops on—liquor I could not afford to buy.[20]

Armstrong admits the prevalence of racism in this passage, evident in the telling phrase "we knew what that meant," but does not dwell on it, as he also mentions his southern upbringing to suggest that he "understood" the nation's racist strictures. Notably, he then professes his love for "white folks" and the reciprocal nature of their mutual affections, as well as the generosity of these wealthy, white benefactors. Recognizing the force of racism and the tactics necessary to deflect it indicate his nuanced understanding of its role in building his career, and he chafed against allegations that he was "'soft' on the race issue," taking particular umbrage that critics "accused me of being an Uncle Tom, of not being 'aggressive.'" To these allegations, Armstrong responded, "How can they say that? I've pioneered in breaking the color line in many Southern states (Georgia, Mississippi, Texas) with mixed bands—Negro and white."[21]

In examining Armstrong's life more closely, it is apparent that underneath his genial persona, he recognized and denounced American racism repeatedly. As much as Armstrong often presented himself as a native New Orleanian proud of his hometown roots, his memoir, *Satchmo: My Life in New Orleans*, documents his experiences in the Jim Crow South and his participation in the Great Migration, the exodus of roughly 6 million Black Americans between the years 1910 and 1970 from the South to the Northeast, Midwest, and West, in an effort both to escape the South's systemic racism and terrorist campaigns and to benefit from greater economic opportunities. In this work he shared his earliest memory of the Jim Crow South: "It was my first experience with Jim Crow. I was just five, and I had never ridden on a street car before. Since I was the first to get on, I walked right up to the front of the car without noticing the signs on the back of the seats on both sides, which read: FOR COLORED PASSENGERS ONLY."[22] Armstrong quickly learned the South's discriminatory codes, and his memoir details several more instances of systemic racism, notably in police harassment of Black people.

Immersed in the unique culture of New Orleans, Armstrong rarely criticized his hometown's mores directly, yet his memoir encodes his critique as he explains the reasons he left the South behind. Early in this work, Armstrong foregrounds his youthful adulation for trumpeter Joseph "King" Oliver (1881–1938) in a rhapsodic passage:

> The king of all the musicians was Joe Oliver, the finest trumpeter who ever played in New Orleans. . . . No one had the fire and the endurance Joe had. No one in jazz has created as much music as he has. Almost everything important in music today came from him. That is why they called him "King," and he deserved the title. Musicians from all over the world used to come to hear Joe Oliver when he was playing at the Lincoln Gardens in Chicago, and he never failed to thrill them. I was just a little punk kid when I first saw him, but his first words to me were nicer than everything that I've heard from any of the bigwigs in music.[23]

Within the annals of music history, Armstrong now stands above his youthful hero, and certainly many fans and music critics would apply Armstrong's descriptors of Oliver to Armstrong himself. Also in this passage, Armstrong subtly points out that in Oliver's journey from South to North, his hero transformed from "the finest trumpeter who ever played in New Orleans" to one who "play[ed] at the Lincoln Gardens in Chicago" and enjoyed the admiration of an audience composed of fans from across the globe. As well as emulating Oliver in his trumpet playing, Armstrong emulated his forebear in his northward journey, portraying himself as initially hesitant about leaving his southern roots. Describing his arrival in Chicago, he recalls his ambivalent reaction: "All the colored people . . . who had come up from New Orleans were getting into their cabs or relatives' cars. As they left they said good-bye and wished me good luck on my stay in Chicago. As I waved goodbye I thought to myself, 'Huh. I don't think I am going to like this old town.'"[24] Disoriented by his new surroundings, Armstrong is helped by a policeman to find his way to King Oliver's band. In contrast to the frequent harassment of Black people by the police in New Orleans, this policeman treats Armstrong respectfully; Armstrong remembers that the policeman "gave me a very pleasant smile" and then recognized him as "the young man who's to join King Oliver's band at the Lincoln Gardens."[25] Armstrong is gratified to learn of the greater respect accorded Black men in Chicago: "Then it struck me that he had just said *King* Oliver. In New Orleans it was just plain Joe Oliver." In this final paragraph of his memoir, Armstrong documents his triumph: "I had hit the big time. I was up North with the greats. I was playing with my idol, the king, Joe Oliver. My boyhood dream had come true at last."[26]

Satchmo: My Life in New Orleans could hardly be considered a screed against the racist injustices of the South, and originally published in 1954, Armstrong's memoir might well have been expected to address these matters more directly. His critique of the South is nonetheless apparent in his account of his northward migration. More so, following the 1954 U.S. Supreme Court decision in *Brown v. Board of Education of Topeka* that struck down "separate but equal" accommodations, the integration of Central High School in Little Rock, Arkansas, drew national attention due to the racist pushback of the white community, about which Armstrong stated, "It's getting almost so bad a colored man hasn't got any country."[27] Still, as much as Armstrong voiced his disgust with American racism, he was also deeply invested in presenting himself as a uniter, not a divider. He saw himself, in Jim Merod's words, as a "world ambassador for music and global fellow feeling," as evident in Armstrong's declaration at the 1958 Monterey Jazz Festival, "I represent the human race."[28] In the final analysis, the enigma of Armstrong and his persona emerges through his smile that served as a hallmark of his countless performances. Does this smile connote his comfort with racist tropes of minstrelsy and white appeasement, or does it connote his love for music and entertainment and the boundless joy he derived from his decades-long career? Certainly, his smile could indicate both of these possibilities simultaneously, or any measure along this spectrum. Whereas Gillespie harshly criticized Armstrong for his performance persona, he later reinterpreted the significance of his forebear's smile: "Later on I began to recognize what I had considered Pops's grinning in the face of racism as his absolute refusal to let anything, even anger about racism, steal the joy from his life and erase his fantastic smile."[29]

As much as Armstrong's smile conjures dual significations, so too do New Orleans's memorials to him suggest the duality of the city's efforts to fashion itself through its icons. Although Louis Armstrong New Orleans International Airport stands as the most prominent memorial to honor Armstrong and his legacy, it is by no means the first, and in a 1961 interview Armstrong pondered his conflicted status in New Orleans both as a local hero and as an artist prohibited from performing there. As he recalled, "A few years ago New Orleans gave me the keys to the city. And in 1959 Jefferson Parish, a neighborhood, dedicated a huge 'Louis Armstrong Playground.' But still I can't play in New Orleans, my hometown. There's a state law that doesn't allow mixing of Negro and white musicians. They want me to leave the two white boys in my band home. But I say, 'That wouldn't be my band.' So I don't go."[30] Honored with the city's key and an eponymous park yet prohibited from performing with his band, Armstrong recognized the limitations of civic honors to signify meaningful change.

Decades later, in the early days of the reckoning over New Orleans's racist monuments to the Confederacy, another jazz great and native New Orleanian, Wynton Marsalis, encouraged Mitch Landrieu to tackle the politically charged issue of removing the Confederate statues by appealing to Armstrong's memory. As Landrieu stated, "But [Marsalis] pricked my conscience and said, well, have you ever thought about it from my perspective, and I said no, and he said, well, you should, and he said, and did you know Louis Armstrong left here because of those monuments?"[31] While one should not take Marsalis's words too literally—as the above paragraphs demonstrate, Armstrong left New Orleans for multiple and converging reasons—his impassioned citation of Armstrong assisted a white man in realizing the necessity of reconsidering the cultural work of memorials. The Louis Armstrong New Orleans International Airport tells a particularly important truth about New Orleans's culture, celebrating a legendary figure whose artistic contributions cemented the city's place in jazz history, as it also reiterates the ugly irony that too many southern and American memorials commemorate those who erected countless obstacles for other citizens to live their lives unencumbered by prejudice and racial animosity. The enigma of Armstrong's smile testifies to the near impossibility of decoding a fixed meaning to his southern star persona, as well as the hope that he will indeed get the last laugh.

2

TRUMAN CAPOTE'S QUEER CELEBRITY AND THE DECADENTLY SENTIMENTAL SOUTH

In *Music for Chameleons*, his last major work published during his lifetime, Truman Capote famously declared, "I'm an alcoholic. I'm a drug addict. I'm homosexual. I'm a genius."[1] This statement from the twilight of the author's career reflects his determination to live his life openly, as it also reveals his canny understanding of how to employ his queer celebrity to maintain his presence in the public eye. These apparently shocking "confessions" were well known to anyone paying Capote the slightest attention over the previous decades, and so his pronouncement of his troubled genius served less as an expression of self-realization than as yet another illustration of his extraordinary ability to generate media coverage for himself. Surely, more than any other author of the twentieth century, Capote was recognized, if not lionized, as a celebrity, famous for being famous as much as he was revered as a remarkably talented writer. Moreover, he performed his celebrity queerly, living openly as a gay southerner in nonchalant defiance of mid-twentieth-century American mores. As Capote explained, in many ways, he enjoyed the role of the gay clown who minces to amuse his various audiences: "I'm this funny, sawed-off fellow with a high voice, and it's hard for people to accept me. But if I come in and say, 'I don't want to sit with the boys, I want to sit with the girls,' everybody giggles and everybody's more comfortable. I do that on purpose to make it easier for people to be around me because then *I'm* easier and the whole thing works better."[2] As a gay man employing a stereotypical persona, Capote benefited from his astute recognition that *acting* gay would allow him more comfortably to *be* gay.

Further to these points, Capote inflected his openly gay persona with strong southern tropes, particularly those of sentimentalism and decadence associated with southern gothic literary traditions. Estranged from the South owing to its homophobia, he nonetheless sentimentally upheld its charms in a string of short stories and other works; in complementary contrast, as he aged and found himself mired in alcoholism and drug addiction, he embodied the decadent tropes of southern literature that he had earlier penned in such works as *Other Voices, Other Rooms* (1948) and *A Tree of Night and Other Stories* (1949). As Jeff Solomon asserts, Capote's openness about his homosexuality defiantly rejected normative codes of mid-twentieth-century America: "Capote refuses certain silences and strategically performs his queer persona." Solomon adds that "such showmanship served not only as a support for Capote's career but also as one of the many acts of self-affirmation and articulation that, as the twentieth century progressed, would eventually force a greater freedom of expression and interpretation for homosexuals in literary as well as popular culture."[3] Capote's homosexuality, both his encoding of it in his fiction and his performance of it as a countercultural aspect of his literary persona, defines his southern star persona, in a performance of the self that also points toward the region's conflicting significations for queer people.

Born September 30, 1924, in New Orleans, Capote was heralded as a literary wunderkind in his early twenties. His short story "Miriam" won the 1945 O. Henry Award, an accomplishment for which Herschel Brickell dubbed him the "most remarkable new talent of the year."[4] Acclaim was soon followed by notoriety owing to the dust-jacket photograph of his first novel, *Other Voices, Other Rooms*—an image that launched his dual careers as an author and as a queer celebrity. (See figure 3.) In it Capote reclines languorously with pouty lips and come-hither eyes. Combined with the homoerotic themes of the novel, the photograph shocked readers of the time, for the author seemed quietly yet defiantly to be inviting them to join him in decadent pleasures. In a subsequent interview Capote described the photograph as "perfectly innocent," claiming elsewhere, "It was part of my complete naiveté. . . . There was nothing calculated about it at all."[5] He dismissed the public outcry: "When people read the book . . . and realized what the theme was, and coupled that with the picture, the whole thing took on a kind of *outré* peculiar quality that it was never meant to have had."⁶ Despite such proclamations of his guileless intentions, Capote puckishly revealed that he understood how the picture would be received: "I suppose some tiresome people thought I looked depraved—ready for man, woman, or fire hydrant."⁷ Quite simply, such protestations appear to be part of Capote's performance of innocence, for he also acknowledged that the scandalous photograph successfully marketed the book. John Malcolm Brinnin recalled Capote's defense of the picture—"It's sold a lot of copies, hasn't it? Been printed in every paper from here to Salt Lake City, hasn't it?"⁸—and it is likewise evident in the various professional and candid photographs taken of him throughout his life that he knew how to pose. In Richard Avedon's assessment, Capote "always thought of photography in the same way he thought of the press, as something to be used for the purposes of public relations. He was very inventive; he always had an idea for every session."⁹

With *Other Voices, Other Rooms* and its decadent setting of a decaying Mississippi mansion, Capote aligned himself with the traditions of southern gothic literature, and subsequent works strengthened his identity as a southern author,

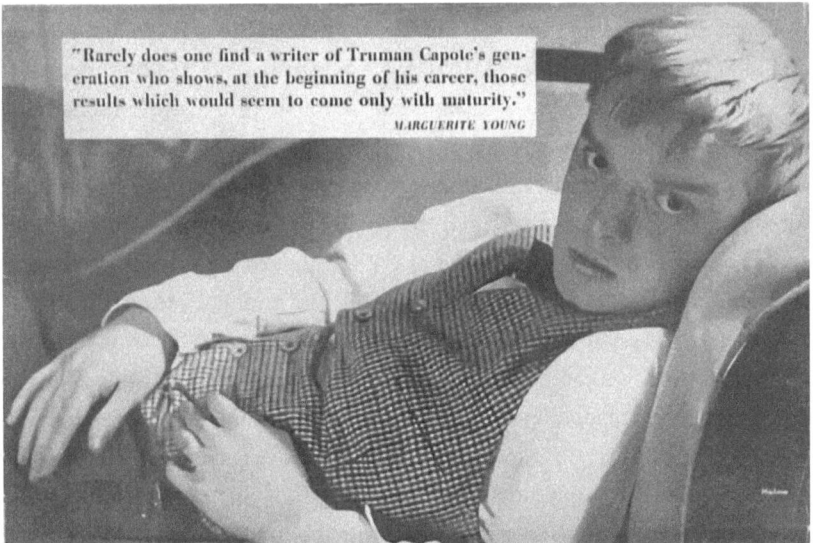

FIG. 3. In this author's photograph on the back cover of *Other Voices, Other Rooms*, Truman Capote seductively and unapologetically announces his homosexuality, all the while allowing for plausible deniability of his intentions to define his literary persona.

particularly *A Tree of Night and Other Stories* and *The Grass Harp* (1951). *Breakfast at Tiffany's* (1958) marked a turning point in his career away from the South for his major works, as the journey of its southern narrator to a life of Bohemian thrills in New York City could be seen as mirroring Capote's own trajectory. Yet as much as his later works, notably *In Cold Blood* (1965) and his unfinished novel *Answered Prayers* (1986), evince his intention to leave the South behind, it is noteworthy that he penned a string of sentimentally heartwarming southern holiday tales over the years, including "A Christmas Memory" (1956), "The Thanksgiving Visitor" (1968), and "One Christmas" (1984). Capote identified the autobiographical elements of "A Christmas Memory"—"That is the story of my childhood"[10]—with these words obscuring any sharp distinctions between his past, his present, and his presentation of himself to readers. From these contrasting works the South appears both decadent (rotting mansions, swampy landscapes, haunted characters) and wholesome (holiday celebrations, baking cakes, flying kites), and Capote availed himself of these contrasting traditions in forming his queer southern persona.

As evident through his many statements on the subject, Capote clearly understood the economic perks of stardom and the importance of celebrity personas. In discussing the careers of Clark Gable, Spencer Tracy, Bette Davis, and Joan Crawford, he observed, "They were real stars created by the studios for a very specific purpose who were continuously promoted."[11] Indeed, his definition of a movie star parallels (and predates) that of star theorist Richard Dyer: "Defined practically, a movie star is any performer who can account for a box-office profit regardless of the quality of the enterprise in which he appears."[12] In this blunt assessment of the economics underlying Hollywood stardom, in which he distills celebrity as irrelevant to a film's aesthetic success but crucial to its financial prospects, Capote also summarizes the conundrum of celebrity for his own career, for his celebrity often eclipsed his writing. Gossipy accounts quickly made Capote's life the stuff of legend, albeit a legend gilded with artifice, exaggeration, and posturing. Writing of the New Bohemians—his term for the early 1950s writers and gadabouts striking their way into the public eye—Charles Rolo summarized and questioned Capote's insouciant celebrity:

> It has been reported that on one of his trips across the Atlantic, Mr. Capote hired the bridal suite on the *Queen Mary*; that in Italy he was taken for

the President's son and, stepping into the role of good-will ambassador, did a power of damage to the Communist party; that after traveling through Spain, he landed in North Africa partially accoutered as a bullfighter (and so on in this vein). The legend contains one ounce of fact to every pound of fancy. And it must be said—without disrespect to Mr. Capote's talents as a myth maker—that not all of the fancy is pure Capote.[13]

Such coverage kept Capote a topic of gossip even when he was not publicizing his fiction, but, above all other concerns, the financial benefits of hype for selling books sparked Capote's fervent efforts at exposure.

Capote's assiduous attention to his star persona and its financial payoffs is also evident in his coffee-table book *Observations* (1959), a collaboration with Richard Avedon that combines Avedon's photographs of Hollywood stars with Capote's prose portraits of them. For this venture Capote explicitly advised Avedon on publicity for their venture, briefly observing that "Jack Paar sells books" and concluding sternly, after a litany of detailed instructions, "I know I don't have to emphasize how important these matters are, so buckle down."[14] On another occasion he explained the logistics and benefits of a marketing blitz: "My theory about publishing a book . . . is that everything—the reviews, the interviews, and everything else—has to happen within two weeks of publication. If it's scattered, it's not going to work. But if it all comes together simultaneously, you'll spin right up the list."[15] At the same time, Capote realized that serious artists should not be seen as hucksters of their craft, and he deplored publicity hounds in general ("The most pretentious thing is a person who hires a press agent to get his name in the papers") and Gore Vidal in particular ("Because Gore's books are number one or two on the best-seller list doesn't mean anything. That's because he spends half his life on TV").[16] In a 1963 letter to his friends Alvin and Marie Dewey, he criticized Harper Lee for promoting the film version of her novel *To Kill a Mockingbird* (1960): "our friend Nelle . . . is *so* involved in the publicity for her film (she owns a percentage, that's why; even so, I think it *very undignified* for any serious artist to allow themselves to be exploited in this fashion)."[17] Capote's hypocrisy is virtually palpable in these lines: the master publicist and self-promoter condemns his lifelong friend for engaging in the activities he himself pursues, and which he insists his collaborators likewise undertake.

Several of Capote's literary peers disdained his penchant for celebrity, attempting to discredit his authorial achievements by attacking his hucksterism. Brendan Gill, in his memoir of life at the *New Yorker,* recalled Capote avowing, "A boy must hustle his book," and concluded: "Capote promotes himself as other people promote lipstick or baby powder, with an endearing and profitable assiduity."[18] In a *Paris Review* interview in 1974, Gore Vidal scorned Capote for his attention to fame: "Every writer ought to have at least one thing that he does well and I'll take Truman's word that a gift for publicity is the most glittering star in his diadem."[19] To Vidal, Capote's literary achievements were merely "a public relations campaign masquerading as a career."[20] Mary McCarthy similarly sneered that Capote's "greatest contribution to literary innovation was to publicize the author first, the book second."[21] (Capote avenged himself on McCarthy in *Answered Prayers,* when his narrator P. B. Jones snipes, "Creative females are not often presentable. Look at Mary McCarthy!")[22] Even Capote's allies deplored his need for celebrity. His close friend Slim Keith declared in her autobiography, "Celebrity slowed him down and distracted him from his calling."[23] John Malcolm Brinnin sketched Capote's need for fame as almost an obsession: "More hungry for attention than anyone else, he's learned to bestow what he craves. For recipients, enchantment; for himself, a restless longing for a bigger audience." Brinnin also recalled that he once asked Capote, "How are you going to hide yourself in fame long enough to remind yourself who you are? As far as I can see, you've achieved a reputation at the cost of a career."[24] Capote responded to such charges with an appeal to the pecuniary advantages of his celebrity: "When the chips are down, what was it but my reputation that could parlay five figures into six?"[25] Tennessee Williams, among the few who appreciated Capote's talent in seeking publicity, complimented him as "a great self-publicist" due to his "theatrical personality."[26]

Undoubtedly the greatest social achievement of his life, and likely the apex of his fame, Capote's legendary Black and White Ball at the Plaza Hotel in New York on November 28, 1966, commemorated the successful publication of *In Cold Blood.* Capote selected Katharine Graham, matriarch of the publishing family behind the *Washington Post* and *Newsweek,* as the guest of honor, and as David Grafton wrote, "Truman's selection of the publishing magnate . . . was just one more example of his genius for publicity."[27] Truly, Capote orchestrated the media coverage of *In Cold Blood* and the Black and White Ball masterfully.

His sedulous attention to publicity led writers at the *New York Times* to marvel at and to lament his marketing chutzpah: William D. Smith referred to *In Cold Blood* as "one of the greatest promotional successes in publishing history," and Eliot Fremont-Smith railed against the "vast, self-generating promotional mill in which everyone—author, publisher, magazine editor, critic, bookseller and reader—is trapped."[28] As with his literary efforts, the cross-pollination between art and hyping art demanded Capote's detailed attention to his creation's public reception, and Leo Lerman equated the event's aesthetic pitch to that of Capote's literature: "The ball was one of his major works. As much a major work as some of his short stories."[29]

Beyond his high-profile lifestyle as an author, Capote kept himself and his queer southern celebrity in the public eye through numerous appearances on television talk and variety shows. The hosts of such programs appreciated Capote's appearances, as they often sparked publicity owing to Capote's brash performance of his queer celebrity, which mixed quick wit with trash talk about various stars. During an appearance on David Susskind's *Open End* in 1959 when he shared the stage with Dorothy Parker and Norman Mailer, Capote uttered his devastating assessment of Jack Kerouac's and other Beat writers' fiction: "What they do . . . isn't writing at all—*it's typing.*"[30] After Capote complimented E. M. Forster as the greatest living writer, Mailer interjected, "I must say, I find Mr. Capote here *far* the more exciting writer. He excites me far more," to which Capote, in reply, put his face in his hands and laughed.[31] As much as interviews allowed Capote to embrace the limelight, he could not fully control the ensuing discussions, as evident when Groucho Marx upstaged him in a 1971 episode of *The Dick Cavett Show*, to the extent that Cavett ironically queried, "Do you feel that Truman is dominating the conversation?"[32] In a moment of clarity, Capote proclaimed that writers should avoid alcohol to preserve their craft—"I don't think anyone can write when they're drinking"—but the conversation took a queer turn when Marx encouraged Capote to marry for the accompanying tax benefits: "Truman, have you ever thought of getting married and splitting the tax?" Capote, obviously nonplussed by Marx's apparent ignorance of his homosexuality, countered, "Well, you find someone for me to marry, and I'll consider it, okay?" Marx gamely replied, "I would marry you in a minute, if you would write another hit book like you did about Kansas. Will you consider this an engagement?" Marx's rhetorical ploy was brilliant, for in appearing to overlook

Capote's homosexuality, he prepared the audience for a final titillating line: "I can't give you what you're entitled to . . . ," a euphemistic but clear reference to sex, from which Cavett pivoted to a commercial break.

Johnny Carson, famed host of *The Tonight Show*, invited Capote to appear on his program many times, for Carson knew that Capote would be amusing, if at times rather cruel. Capote's feud with Jacqueline Susann, the sensationalist author of *Valley of the Dolls* (1966) and *The Love Machine* (1969), began on Carson's program when he said she looked like a "truck driver in drag."[33] She threatened to sue, but Capote responded acerbically, "She was told she had better drop that lawsuit because all they had to do is bring ten truck drivers into court and put them on the witness stand and you've lost your case."[34] On the episode of *The Tonight Show* airing November 27, 1973, Carson introduced Capote as a "writer and conversationalist of the first quality." When Capote entered the stage yo-yoing, Carson deadpanned: "Here I say one of the finest, distinguished writers, and you come out with a yo-yo." Their conversation ranged over a variety of topics, with Capote weighing in on censorship—"You cannot define pornography, and therefore you cannot censor it"—discussing his uncomfortable travels on the Orient Express, and detailing his recent appearance on the *Sonny and Cher Comedy Hour* (1971–74). He also commented on several celebrities, deriding the intelligence of John Gielgud (and of Laurence Olivier as well) and offering a scathing assessment of Marlon Brando: "you cannot get dumber than Marlon Brando . . . he's got great sensibility and no sense."[35] From his yo-yoing entrance to his insulting of various celebrities, Capote played his role of the queer gadabout to perfection—eccentric, candid to the point of rudeness, but always amusing.

The tables were turned on Capote—the taunter became the taunted—when, in 1974, he appeared as the guest of honor on *The Dean Martin Celebrity Roast* (1974–84). For this program Martin featured a Celebrity of the Week whom the various guest stars mocked good-naturedly, and the celebrities roasting Capote included Ted Knight, Audrey Meadows, Donald O'Connor, Rich Little, Joseph Wambaugh, Rocky Graziano, Jean Simmons, and Foster Brooks. Many of the jokes centered on Capote's sexuality, thus highlighting that any contemporary expectation that gay celebrities would remain closeted did not apply to him. Knight painted an ironic portrait of Capote as a heterosexual lothario, intoning, "Truman Capote is the biggest stud in Hollywood," and then suggesting with lascivious eyes, "Yes, as every leading lady in Hollywood knows, Truman Capote is not only a literary giant . . . ," trailing off to leave the audience surmising the size of Capote's genitals. In contrast, Audrey Meadows, channeling the persona of an editor of the *Saturday Review of Literature*, teased Capote about his gender identity: "He is living proof that in America, you can grow up to be anything that you want. And as a boy, Truman wanted to be Bette Davis." Joseph Wambaugh likewise needled Capote about his effeminacy: "I haven't heard such tributes to a man's background since I left the vice squad. . . . I respect Truman Capote. In my opinion, he's the greatest male literary figure since Jacqueline Susann." Ever the salesman, Capote accepted the ribbing in good spirits, and his final words to the audience revealed his pecuniary motives for appearing on the program: "If you people had any sense at all, you'd have turned your sets off long ago and started reading my new book, *The Dogs Bark*."[36]

Television appearances, both his interviews and his scripted performances, bestowed upon Capote the publicity he craved, but they came at a cost to his literary reputation. Capote's friend Peter Beard asserted that Capote's huckstering of himself detracted from his vision of himself as an artist: "He'd had a lot of very successful Johnny Carson shows, and he realized that the audience responded to him because it was the Johnny Carson show, not because of his writing."[37] For the author hoping to increase his readership, such moments revealed the paradox of his queer celebrity: fame kept him in the public eye, but often for reasons other than his literary talents. A gay man playing the bitchy queen and insulting other celebrities may have been amusing, but such performances did little to enhance the critical reception of Capote's literature; on the contrary, they contributed to the perception of him as fundamentally trivial.

Beyond these interviews and media appearances in which he subverted American norms by living as an openly gay southern man, Capote occasionally appeared in scripted programs, including the pilot episode of *The Sonny Comedy Revue* (1974), in a skit in which he played Herb Parns, a daredevil in a yellow jumpsuit and red plastic helmet in an obvious parody of Evel Knievel. Throughout the skit Capote hams up his southern roots for comic effect. "You know how it is with us ole southern boys," he drawls, as Sonny Bono, in the role of the interviewer Teddy, asks Parns why he undertakes his daredevil act of getting into a box packed with dynamite. Capote/Parns replies, "Aw shucks, Teddy, it's just that I—" as he then twitches and jerks in imitation of a crude redneck speech impediment, "I'm trying to commit suicide." The skit is not particularly funny, but it showcases Capote's "playing southern" to garner media attention, mocking his southern roots to signify his dismissal of the region. Also owing to his fame and wittily queer persona, Capote was cast in Robert Moore's murder-mystery farce *Murder by Death* (1976), written by Neil Simon. Playing alongside a truly all-star cast, Capote undertook the role of the mysterious Lionel Twain, a fan of detective fiction who summons parodic versions of famous sleuths to his estate to punish them for their outlandish plots and too-clever-by-far solutions. In Simon's hands, Agatha Christie's Hercule Poirot becomes Milo Perrier (James Coco); Jane Marple transforms into Jessica Marbles (Elsa Lanchester); Dashiell Hammett's Nick and Nora Charles metamorphose into Dick and Dora Charleston (David Niven and Maggie Smith); Hammett's Sam Spade becomes Sam Diamond (Peter Falk); and Earl Derr Biggers's Charlie Chan is reimagined as Sidney Wang (Peter Sellers). Although Capote claimed that "Neil Simon wrote [the role of Lionel Twain] for me,"[38] Simon refuted this assertion, insisting that the film's producer selected Capote because of the author's status as a celebrity: "Truman was the last person I would have thought of for the part of the mystery aficionado. On the other hand, Ray Stark, the producer, was always looking for publicity, perfectly willing to sacrifice the part and hire someone like Truman. . . . He was a great raconteur; we all know how funny he could be on his own, but he got stuck when he had lines to say."[39]

Capote's catty commentary on talk shows did not translate well into portraying a character on film, and his performance is indeed wooden, as he delivers his lines with mechanical venom. *Murder by Death* exploits Capote's queer celebrity, playing on lisping gay stereotypes even in the character's name, Lionel Twain, which puns on the children's toy Lionel Trains. When the detectives first meet Twain, he purrs, "Good evening, ladies and gentlemen. I'm your host, Lionel Twain." The shot captures a hand in an armchair pressing a button, which unleashes a burst of strobe lighting in various hues, accompanied by disorienting music that finally resolves in a harsh twang. Jessica Marbles exclaims, "Good God, what an entrance!" and Twain replies, with queer modesty, "Oh, a bit theatrical, Miss Marbles, but I do so love an illusion." Praising his performance in *Murder by Death*, Capote professed his acting skills with typical brio yet with tongue firmly in cheek: "The original intent may have been for me to parody myself, but that's not how it's going to work out. How am I as an actor?

Let's just say this, 'What Billie Holiday is to jazz, what Mae West is to tits . . . what Seconal is to sleeping pills, what King Kong is to penises, Truman Capote is to the great god Thespis!'"[40] Such exaggerated posturing could not shield Capote from harsh reviews, such as Vincent Canby's assessment: "Mr. Capote is possibly acting, but it looks more as if he's giving us an over-rehearsed impersonation of himself as people see him on unrehearsed TV talk shows."[41] Capote also self-deprecatingly proclaimed, "If they say I'm a lousy actor, who cares? Whoever said I was a good actor? That isn't the area where my vanity lies."[42] Capote also indicated that financial considerations influenced his decision to participate, claiming that he "did it for the moola—and to satisfy that clown side [of him] that's so exasperating."[43] Nonetheless, he was nominated for a 1977 Golden Globe for the male category of Best Acting Debut in a Motion Picture, losing to Arnold Schwarzenegger for *Stay Hungry* (1976).

Capote's southern queer celebrity in many ways served as a shield, but when the shield fell, his demons emerged to public view. As alcoholism and drug abuse took over his life throughout the 1970s until his death in 1984, he made public appearances when he was physically and mentally incapable of functioning, such as when he was removed from a speaking engagement at Towson State University after drunkenly declaring, "I'm going to read you something I like and if you don't like it, the hell with you."[44] A more widely viewed incident occurred on July 18, 1978, when he appeared on *The Stanley Siegel Show* (1975–80), a local New York City program. Obviously incapacitated during the interview, he sat with his head rolling, his mouth open, and his eyes staring off, as he grimaced and opened and closed his eyes, with perspiration visible on his face. "I haven't actually been to bed in forty-eight hours," he declared through slurred words as the interview began. When Siegel asked with concern, "When was the last time you've been to bed?" Capote managed a witty rejoinder: "With whom?" Capote also mused on the challenges of his life, "My life is so strange; it's not like anybody's." Siegel offered to stop the interview, but Capote insisted that they continue, despite his evident discomposure, as they discussed his problems with addiction. When Siegel confronted Capote about his addictions—"You have had a history of alcoholism"—Capote replied, "Alcoholism is the least of it." In a particularly poignant exchange, Siegel asked Capote, "What do you care about?" to which Capote blankly answered, "Well, that's a really good question. I'm beginning to wonder myself." When Siegel asked what would happen to him in the future, Capote candidly mumbled: "The obvious answer is that eventually I'll kill myself, without meaning to." After Siegel ended the interview, he called it "heartbreaking" and "one of the damnedest shows we've seen in a long time."[45] As Capote's editor Joseph Fox lamented, "over and over again at lunch during the last six years of his life . . . he was often almost incoherent because of drugs or alcohol or both."[46]

Yet throughout these years Capote also maintained the sentimentally southern aspects of his identity, as one who nostalgically yearned for the lost innocence of his youth. He frequently read his seasonal short stories to live audiences, who found themselves mesmerized by his recitations. Patricia Burstein documents of a reading of "A Christmas Memory": "The hall . . . falls silent. Capote begins reading 'A Christmas Memory,' a tender story from his childhood. The voice is nasal and simpering, the plump figure almost ludicrous, and yet he has captivated the young audience."[47] Also, a few years prior to his death, the cover of *People* magazine for January 26, 1981, announced, "Truman Capote debuts a new section, Going Home." In this ongoing feature, celebrities traveled to their hometowns to relive their youthful memories, and the article inaugurating the series carried the heading, "The famous author makes one of his periodic visits to the city of his birth, New Orleans, and finds sentiment and southern comfort."[48] In the article Capote affirms his affection for New Orleans—"I *love* this city"—and the author, Andrea Chambers, concludes the essay with the sentimental statement, "At last he seems to feel truly at home."[49] With media appearances such as these, Capote tempered the decadent edges of his queer southern persona, inviting readers and fans to view him as seamlessly united with his southern roots.

In light of Capote's reliance on the media to maintain his celebrity status, it is perhaps surprising that he often professed ambivalence concerning his fame: "It all depends on whether you think fame is an asset or a hindrance in an artistic career. I feel rather indifferent about the whole thing, but then, I've been in public life over twenty years now, and you become neutral about publicity," he proclaimed in a 1968 *Playboy* interview.[50] When *Mademoiselle*'s interviewers posed the question whether his public image was his creation, he denied, in a world-weary tone, that he controlled his celebrity: "Not exactly. There's a certain point where a celebrity image starts to be self-perpetuating. It's like a stone you sink in the sea where the shells and barnacles attach to it until you don't know the truth yourself."[51] His response achieves a surprising poignancy, as he confesses that he has lost himself in the miasma of his celebrity. With more insouciant flair, Capote also professed to David Frost (in a witticism often attributed to Dorothy Parker), "I don't care what anybody says about me as long as it isn't true."[52] Here his words reveal a core truth of celebrity culture: words spoken about a famous person are often more important than truths told, for chatter is more conducive to continued attention than silence. Summarizing his sense of his celebrity, Capote commented on himself in a *Rolling Stone* article by Jann Wenner: "I always attracted a lot of attention, because—well, really—there really isn't anybody else like me."[53] In this striking declaration of his uniqueness, one simultaneously arrogant and modest, Capote reveals he is cognizant of the limelight's benefits to his career. And truly this sword cut both ways, for as much as Capote's fame redounded to his benefit, it also detracted from his identity as an artist.

His queer southern celebrity and his close associations with Hollywood stars through friendships and filmmaking placed Capote in the public eye throughout his career. In assessing the potentially dire consequences of fame, Capote likened it to poison: "Somebody asked me about a year ago what am I famous for, and I said, 'I'm famous for being famous.' You know? That's one way people can be destroyed. I've always been famous for being famous; but at the same time, I was aware of it. So therefore it didn't affect me, and it wasn't the poisonous thing that it is. It's a subtle kind of poison, and people don't realize when it starts."[54] Capote pronounced himself impervious to fame's poison in this passage, as he also suggested that most people never feel its effects until it is too late to save themselves. It is difficult, when one considers Capote's downward spiral into drugs and addiction from the 1970s until his death, not to believe that he failed to perceive fame's subtle poison coursing through his veins. Capote's theme in *Answered Prayers*, that more tears are shed over answered prayers than unanswered ones, finds a striking echo in plaintive words he attributed to Elizabeth Taylor: "What do you suppose will become of us? I guess, when you find what you've always wanted, that's not where the beginning begins, that's where the end starts."[55] Capote pursued celebrity so relentlessly throughout his life to bring him prestige, fame, and wealth, but whether in or out of the South, whether painting it in gothic colors or sentimental tones, the queer persona he embodied as a writer, conversationalist, gossip, and publicity hound could not shield him from its toxic side-effects. Perhaps the least desired celebrity persona would be that of cautionary tale, yet, along with his status as one of the twentieth century's greatest southern writers and groundbreaking queer talents, Capote's sentimental decadence, in the final examination, cannot be divorced from its melancholy didacticism.

3

ELVIS PRESLEY, GRACELAND, AND CELEBRITY SHRINES

At the peak of its run after opening in 1979, the Liberace Museum of Las Vegas attracted 450,000 guests annually; it was shuttered in 2010.[1] Anne Murray sold over 55 million albums during her illustrious career, winning four Grammys and twenty-four Juno Awards along the way, but when visiting the Anne Murray Centre in Spring Hill, Nova Scotia, my husband and I constituted 50 percent of the patrons—even though it was June 20, 2022, her seventy-seventh birthday. The Ava Gardner Museum of Smithfield, North Carolina, only stayed afloat due to the assistance of federal funds during the 2020 Covid pandemic, when it lost approximately 75 percent of its already meager seven thousand annual guests.[2] In a final example of the ephemeral and quirky nature of celebrity museums, the Kentwood Museum of Kentwood, Louisiana, hosts two oddly juxtaposed permanent collections—the Kentwood Military Exhibit and the Britney Spears Exhibit—that celebrate the town's local heroes and its internationally renowned pop star.[3] On the whole, the mercurial and evanescent nature of pop-culture fame explains these curiosities. Notwithstanding the enormous success these and other such entertainers enjoyed at the height of their careers, as their initial fan base ages and eventually dies, and as succeeding generations fail to demonstrate the necessary enthusiasm to maintain their popularity, the shrines dedicated in their honor wither over the years.

Yet in stark contrast to these dead, dying, and ailing celebrity museums stands Graceland, located at 3764 Elvis Presley Boulevard in Memphis, Tennessee, a tourist destination for fans that, according to a virtual army of cultural commentators, also stands as a pilgrimage site for the truly devout among them. Presley's southern star persona aligns seamlessly with Graceland's "persona," thus creating a continuity between the star and his legacy that is simultaneously anchored in but transcends the South. Indeed, as James Davidson suggests, Graceland metonymically represents Presley himself: "In a very real sense, devotees have begun to see Elvis and Graceland as a unified whole."[4] To view Graceland as a site of southern pilgrimage is thus to take seriously the prospect that, when celebrity intersects with hagiography, the sanctity of the land overwrites—or at least attempts to overwrite—the South's more troubling mythologies. As Presley rocketed to international fame by incorporating Black rhythm-and-blues traditions and dance styles into his performances, so too does Graceland overwrite its roots in the architecture of plantations—now widely demythologized and referred to as forced labor camps—to create a palatable view of troubling racial politics. The South defines key aspects of Presley's and Graceland's joint appeal, as long as the more appealing tropes of white southernness shine forth and thereby overshadow the mostly unacknowledged tropes of racial appropriation, marginalization, and discrimination.

PRESLEY'S SOUTHERN STAR PERSONA

"The King of Rock & Roll": Elvis Presley's star persona is captured in this epithet, and even a brief overview of his career overwhelms with the astonishing list of accomplishments that merit it. He burst onto the national scene, in Jon Landau's words, as an "adolescent high-energy rocker straight out of the Delta," scoring his first major hit soon after turning twenty-one years old.[5] "Heartbreak Hotel" reached No. 1 on the Billboard charts in March 1956 and reigned there for eight weeks; incredibly, Presley hit No. 1 three more times that year with "I Want You, I Need You, I Love You," "Don't Be Cruel," and "Love Me Tender." Over two decades later, he notched his final No. 1 hit with "Suspicious Minds" in 1969 and scored an astounding 114 Top 40 hits over the course of his career—forty of which hit the Top 10, and eighteen of which hit No. 1. Overlapping with and complementing his singing career, there were thirty-one films in which Presley starred, from *Love Me Tender* (1956) to *Change of Habit* (1969), in which Mary Tyler Moore plays a nun facing the vexing conundrum of choosing

FIG. 4. As Mary Tyler Moore's Sister Michelle sits in the pews, Elvis Presley, in the role of Dr. John Carpenter, performs for the faithful (with Jesus on the crucifix behind him).

between Presley and Jesus. (Ultimately, she cannot choose, and the film thus appears to pose the query, who could? See figure 4.) Presley's television appearances, beginning with Jackie Gleason's variety program *Stage Show* (1954–56) in 1956 and including as well *The Milton Berle Show* (1948–56), *The Steve Allen Show* (1956–60), and *The Ed Sullivan Show* (1948–71), quickly became the stuff of legend, with adults gasping at his hip-shaking performances that seemingly mesmerized their children. Presley was nominated for fourteen Grammy awards and won three: Best Sacred Performance for "How Great Thou Art" (1967); Best Inspirational Performance for the gospel album *He Touched Me* (1972); and Best Inspirational Performance for the live concert version of "How Great Thou Art" (1974). He also received a Grammy Lifetime Achievement Award in 1971. The accolades continued after his death in 1977: induction into the Rock & Roll Hall of Fame, the Award of Merit from the American Music Awards, the W. C. Handy Award from the Blues Foundation, among a treasure trove more.

Presley's southern roots played an indelible role in the creation and reception of his celebrity persona, for these touches of his character rooted an otherwise excessive figure as homegrown, humble, and charitable. His modest childhood in Tupelo, Mississippi, bespoke a youth of meager means but boundless aspirations, and he frequently stressed the rags-to-riches arc of his life. For instance, once when accepting a humanitarian award, Presley presented himself as humbled and awed by his success: "When I was a child, ladies and gentleman, I was a dreamer. I read comic books, and I was the hero of the comic book. I saw movies, and I was the hero in the movie. So every dream I ever dreamed has come true a hundred times."[6] As his career skyrocketed, Presley was drafted into the U.S. Army; stationed in West Germany, where he met his future wife, Priscilla Ann Beaulieu, he served from 1958 to 1960. Presley's military experiences emphasized not only his patriotism but also, by living alongside the other enlistees, he evinced his willingness to deprive himself of the excesses of superstardom, which similarly tempered the glamour of his performance persona. "I'm going into that service and do the best I can. If they want me to sing for the boys, I'll sing. If they want me to march—anything they want me to do is all right,"[7] he was quoted as saying. His words registered not merely his recognition of the basic facts of army life—everyone in the army must do precisely what their commanding officer dictates—but his ready embrace of service for his country. In this manner Presley bridged the gaps between his audience and himself, demonstrating the real possibility that he would not just perform before them but live among them. In another example of Presley bridging cultural divides, despite the cultural brouhaha surrounding his television appearances, particularly on *The Ed Sullivan Show,* Sullivan introduced Presley as "a real decent, fine boy" and added that he had "never had a pleasanter experience on our show with a big name than we've had with you. You're thoroughly all right."[8] Both excessive and everyman, Presley embodied the contradictions of his performance persona as both a small-town southern boy and a big-city American entertainer.

While the legions of cheering teenage girls might indicate that Presley's fan base skewed predominantly to women, men also found Presley a compelling and attractive star. As William Henderson, author of *Stark Raving Elvis*, explains: "Elvis appeals equally to men and women—although perhaps women tend to show more of an overt response to that appeal. Men see him as a buddy, the guy who plays sports with them . . . a take charge guy, a standup guy who served his country, who's not afraid of a fight, and so on. Women see him first as drop-dead sexy.... He's not afraid to be pretty, he's not afraid to be sensitive, ... he's idealistic, he's an honorable lover, he's a protector, he's good to his mother and so on."[9] Transcending the gender divide in his fandom, Presley registered as highly desirable to many women yet simultaneously as likeable to many men (and surely he conversely registered as highly desirable to many gay men and as likeable to many gay women, among myriad other constructions of desire and iconicity). Moreover, whether Presley's fans found him sexually attractive or not, his fluctuating weight—the "skinny Elvis" of his youth versus the "fat Elvis" of his later years—underscored his everyman allure.

Presley's spirituality, rooted in southern evangelical traditions, expanded his appeal for countless followers, and this aspect of his star persona is most evident in his many recordings of gospel music. His first album of sacred music, *His Hand in Mine* (1960), reached No. 13 on the Billboard charts, which indicated that his fans embraced this aspect of his character, that the devoutness expressed in his gospel music balanced out the excess of his rock-and-roll persona. As the epithet "The King of Rock-and-Roll" defines Presley's character as a whole, it also became implicated with Christlike significance when shortened to "The King," creating an overlap between him and Jesus as "The King of Kings." A virtually ineffable aspect of Presley's mythos arises in the Christological significance accorded him by many fans and in the various moments when he assumed a Christlike stance to them. For instance, his father, Vernon quoted his son as once stating, "You see their wants. I look beyond their wants and can see their needs."[10] It matters little whether Presley actually spoke these words or if his father simply attributed them to him, for Presley's fandom, as has been extensively documented, is drenched with religious significance. And certainly, Presley was internationally recognized for his charitable endeavors and widespread generosity. Biographer Charles Ponce de Leon documents the man's extravagant generosity: "Always one to share his wealth, Elvis ... became impetuously generous toward his family, friends, and business acquaintances—sometimes even perfect strangers."[11] Elvis himself famously declared, "Money's meant to be spread around. The more happiness it helps create, the more it's worth. It's worthless as old paper if it just lies in a bank and grows there without having been used to help anybody."[12] One might quibble that Presley did not follow the Christian maxim that one should perform one's generosity quietly, but as a man of both eye-popping wealth and astounding charity, he ingratiated himself to his fans through his acts of kindness that could only be possible through the accumulation of a great fortune.

Furthering these Christian themes in Presley's persona, Christine King outlines his appeal with evocatively religious overtones: "His cult bears symbols evocative enough to encompass critic and fan alike: hero, martyr, and saint. [Fans] attest to how Elvis makes them feel; how he 'lifts their spirits' and makes them young and whole."[13] In another passage, she hypothesizes that Presley's death at a relatively young age elevated the significance attributed to him: "Elvis is the modern equivalent of the corn king, a primitive sacrificial figure who catches the world's imagination, is raised to a position of wealth and fame for a brief period before being ritually destroyed, sealed as a martyr, and taking our suffering with him."[14] Several volumes document the religiosity of Presley's fans, including Gregory Reece's *Elvis Religion: Cult of the King*, John Strasbaugh's *E: Reflections on the Birth of the Elvis Faith*, and Erika Doss's *Elvis Culture: Fans, Faith, and Culture*. While it is easy to dismiss the fervor of his followers, Elvis's star persona encouraged such a response through his steady attention to gospel music and charitable endeavors.

When Presley died of cardiac arrest resulting from excessive drug use on August 16, 1977, no less a figure than President Jimmy Carter eulogized him for the nation: "Elvis Presley's death deprives our country of a part of itself. He was unique, irreplaceable. . . . He burst upon the scene with an impact that was unprecedented and will probably never be equaled. His music and his personality, fusing the styles of white country and black rhythm & blues, permanently changed the face of American popular culture. His following was immense. And he was a symbol to people the world over of the vitality, rebelliousness, and good humor of this country."[15] In Carter's words, Presley represents the United States of America in its entirety—he is a beloved icon, one whose loss has left the lives of his many fans emptier than they were the day before. It is also worth considering the ways in which the South functions metonymically as the nation in Carter's words, for "fusing the styles of white country and black rhythm & blues" could likely only have happened in the South. Moreover, the descriptors of "vitality, rebelliousness, and good humor," while certainly not limited to southerners, capture the region's ethos within the national imaginary.

Carter's phrase "His following was immense" carries undertones of religiosity, even messianism, thus acknowledging and accentuating the religious undertones of Presley's fandom.

Notable as well in Carter's eulogy is the celebration of Presley's "rebelliousness," a word laden with meaning in light of the U.S. South's rebellious history to defend the horrors of slavery and racism. Other cultural critics have joined Carter in celebrating Presley's rebelliousness. For example, Charles Reagan Wilson rhetorically ponders, "What was the nature of Presley's rebellion?," and answers thusly: "In short, he crossed the South's racial boundaries and tapped into black cultural creativity, combined it with his own, and performed his rebellion to appreciative audiences, especially young ones."[16] "Rebelliousness" thus appears to serve virtually as a code word in discussions of Presley's career, one that condenses his appropriation of Black culture into an act of rebellion, although appropriation is virtually the opposite of rebellion. As is well known, Presley's hit "Hound Dog" was first recorded by Big Mama Thornton, who took it to No. 1 on Billboard's Rhythm & Blues chart several years before Presley released his version.[17] Sam Phillips, the founder of Sun Records and Sun Studio, where Presley recorded his first singles, recognized the inherent marketability of a white man singing Black songs and reportedly declared, "If I could find a white man who had the Negro sound and the Negro feel, I could make a billion dollars!"[18] In critical race theory, whiteness is framed as a virtually invisible feature of white people, who benefit from being seen as a culturally unmarked norm. Presley's whiteness simultaneously encodes an invisible Blackness, framed as rebelliousness, even though such an invisible formation of Blackness remained unavailable to Black people. The visibility and invisibility of race ties into the long history of white artists finding inspiration from Black art and Black artists, as the white artists then incorporate these stylings into their performances and personas. Paul C. Taylor dubs this trend the "Elvis effect" to acknowledge Presley's trailblazing role in such appropriations:

> Black people participate almost exclusively in a cultural practice, mostly untouched by the interest, interference, or acclaim of the white community. A white person finds his or her way into the practice, becomes proficient, and is "discovered" by the white community. The community embraces the

practice, but only in the person of the white "pioneer" who introduced it
... all the while oblivious to the fact that the true pioneers are probably still
toiling in obscurity and poverty, and that the black community has probably
moved on to something else that has yet to be "discovered."[19]

Ironically, artists indulging in the "Elvis effect" might indeed be characterized as and present themselves as rebels, but they are rebelling against the codes of white culture through their embrace of Black ones. This is not to suggest that the rebellious aspect of Presley's persona exclusively represents the usurpation of Black art for ultimately venal purposes, and many Black entertainers, such as Chuck D. of Public Enemy, have praised Presley for the authenticity of his sound: "Elvis had to come up through the streets of Memphis and turn out black crowds before he became famous. It was like he cheated to get there. He was a bad-ass white boy."[20] The irony here is more subtle, but yet more barbed, when set within the history of the U.S. South. Surely many Black people would have preferred Presley to rebel against white culture by rebelling against its racism rather than by rebelling against the 1950s pop sounds of crooners such as Pat Boone and Andy Williams.

GRACELAND'S SOUTHERN "PERSONA"

Presley purchased Graceland on March 26, 1957, and, on June 7, 1982, approximately five years after his death, his ex-wife, Priscilla, and daughter, Lisa Marie, opened it to the public. "Graceland is the ultimate tribute to this very special man,"[21] they wrote in a dedicatory letter published in *Elvis Presley's Graceland: The Official Guidebook,* thereby establishing it not merely as a place to celebrate his accomplishments but to memorialize his loss. Jack Soden, executive director of Elvis Presley Enterprises, affirmed of Graceland's listing on the National Register of Historic Places: "We've said from the beginning we wanted the presentation of Graceland to be one of historical significance. That a guy who changed the world lived here."[22] The historical significance accorded to Graceland, however, registers not merely as the home of a singer who changed the course of pop-music history but of a man who changed the wider world surrounding him. Again, grandiosity combines with humility, as Presley is simply "a guy," or even in Priscilla and Lisa Marie's words a "very special man," yet one who "changed the world," not merely the more limited reach of mid-twentieth-century popular culture.

As much as Presley and Graceland are faultlessly merged to present a unified image of the star and his environs, it is notable that this represents a shift in the house's cultural meaning because it previously represented a barrier separating him from his fans, as Bob Greene records: "When Elvis was alive, the cardinal rule was that his fans and the press could attend his concerts, buy his records, go to his movies—but that Graceland was reserved solely for his family and friends. To everyone else it was totally off limits."[23] Indeed, as Priscilla Presley recalls, "When Elvis had friends and family visit Graceland, he would have them stay at a hotel down the street."[24] Following his death, however, Graceland was reenvisioned as a site of community between the deceased star and his fans, one where they could not merely walk among the physical trappings of his earthly existence but also contemplate the deeper meanings of his stardom and their fandom. To extend the analogy of Presley's military service, the opening of Graceland assured fans that they could enter Presley's home on an equal footing with him, in an invitation impossible to extend during his lifetime.

With the fence that once separated Presley from his fans now open, key aspects of Graceland's "persona" are designed to match Presley's. For instance, *Elvis Presley's Graceland: The Official Guidebook* emphasizes the everyman aspects of this otherwise outsized residence, likening it to the home of every guest who passes through its doors: "Visiting Elvis Presley's Graceland in Memphis, Tennessee, is not just another famous house or museum tour. Graceland is and always will be Elvis Presley's family home, a place full of the same joys, laughter, sorrow and tears experienced in your home."[25] As Presley portrayed himself as an American dreamer who achieved his childhood ambitions, *Elvis Presley's Graceland* sounds a similar note, "But most importantly, it still represents, just as it did for Elvis, a part of the American Dream."[26] Robert Kiely posits that much of Graceland's emotional power arises owing to its location in Memphis, calling it an "eminently powerful and magnetic site" because it functions as Presley's "larger than lifesize facemask," one that provides "brick and mortar 'proof' that, despite fame and fortune," Presley was himself an "orthodox home-body" who chose Memphis as the "home of his heart, and [his] final resting place."[27] Quite simply, Presley never left the South, as so many other southern stars do, and so Graceland roots his persona as eternally southern. Todd Morgan, writing for Presley's estate, stresses "there's just something in the air, a presence, a warmth, an indefinable feeling that makes even the most casual visitor feel as though he were dropping in on an old friend."[28]

With Presley's persona encoding various aspects of southern spirituality to the star, so too has Graceland been imbued with spiritual undertones. Presley did not name Graceland—the previous owners of the property, Ruth Brown Moore and Thomas Moore, named it in honor of Mrs. Moore's great-aunt—and so no overt religious denotations were originally encoded in its name. The name nonetheless connotes a range of spiritual meanings, in hints of salvific grace, in wisps of a pilgrimage of atonement, in allusions to heaven and eternal life. In his song "Mansion over the Hilltop," included on the *His Hand in Mine* gospel album, Presley sings, "I've got a mansion just over the hilltop, / In that bright land where we'll never grow old"; these lyrics aptly link the earthly and spiritual homes merged in the name Graceland. Further enhancing these religious subtexts, Graceland is not merely a destination, as many cultural commentators have observed, but a site of pilgrimage. Presley's fans are often referred to as "devout," and one fan stated of its spiritual aura, "His spirit is you can feel it! Graceland could be the heart of the world . . . because love is generated so much."[29] Soon after Graceland opened to the public, its status as a pilgrimage site was well established, as evident in the words of the lyric speaker of Paul Simon's "Graceland," who speaks of his journey as a pilgrimage, noting the "poor boys and pilgrims" with whom he is traveling. The song concludes with the salvifically hopeful line, "We all will be received in Graceland." James Davidson distinguishes between Graceland's "transient pilgrims" and its "immigrant pilgrims," between those who come to visit and those who relocate to Memphis to stay forever more near their idol.[30] With tongue in cheek, Karal Ann Marling comments on Presley's status as a secular saint. She first proposes that, although not all Graceland tourists "believe that Elvis died for their sins and just might rise again during the 8 am tour on a Sunday morning," it is nonetheless "unfortunate that Protestantism doesn't have official saints to bridge the gap between the here and the hereafter. You could do worse than good St. Elvis."[31] As Marling additionally notes, the proprietors of Graceland have adopted the medieval practice of selling artifacts attached to this "saint's" life: "Even the relics were for sale. Slivers of wood from the trees around the house were embedded in the cases of pricey grandfather clocks like pieces of the True Cross."[32] Similar to the medieval practice of hawking relics of dubious value, so richly travestied in Geoffrey Chaucer's portrayal of the Pardoner selling a grain-multiplying mitten and a miraculous sheep's shoulder bone in his *Canterbury Tales*, Graceland profits off those faithful to the memory of its deceased owner and hoping to bring a token of his greatness home with them.

Presley was known for his exuberant costuming, and Graceland reflects his excessive style that often spills over into tackiness. As with virtually every aesthetic question, tackiness lies in the eyes of the beholder, and not everyone would agree, for example, that the mirrored staircase leading to the basement, the approximately four hundred yards of pleated cotton fabric hanging in the pool room, and even the existence of the "Jungle Room," with its interior custom-built stone waterfall feature, would qualify as tacky. Indeed, the eighty-foot-long Hall of Gold that houses Presley's gold and platinum albums makes for a rather gaudy display; at the same time, it simply reflects the vast extent of his professional accomplishments. Interpreting the stylistic mishmash of the man and his estate, Charles Reagan Wilson opines, "The King of southern tacky is surely Elvis. Born into a poor Mississippi family, Presley developed an aesthetic of bright colors, opulence, and sensuality that has much in common with the fantasies of other poor, rural, white southerners. . . . Graceland seems to some visitors a nightmare of the garish, but it is filled with touches of vitality and good humor."[33] *Elvis Presley's Graceland: The Official Guidebook* attempts to mediate between Presley's tackiness and Graceland's, noting that Presley's 1970s jumpsuits "became more and more elaborate, soon adding metal and rhinestone studding, and matching capes and studded leather belts to the look. . . . The designs seem dated now, but at that time they were supercool."[34] (Alas, the fleeting nature of the supercool!) Despite those who sneer at tackiness, it is essentially a humanizing and equalizing feature of a home: virtually everyone can afford tacky, far fewer can afford sophistication, and so when those who can afford sophistication opt instead for tacky, they reassert their allegiance to the so-called "everyday people." In this manner tackiness illuminates a key aspect of Presley's and Graceland's joint appeal.

Most importantly, Graceland transcends the limitations of most celebrity museums by literally incorporating Presley into its grounds, for he is buried in its Meditation Garden. According to *Graceland: The Living Legacy of Elvis Presley*, "The Meditation Garden was inspired by Elvis's fascination with various

Eastern religions and philosophies in the Sixties.... It was never intended as a place of burial."[35] In 1978 Vernon Presley oversaw the reinterment of Elvis's and his mother Gladys's bodies to Graceland from a local cemetery, Forest Hill, and so the Meditation Garden now houses their remains, along with those of Vernon and of Presley's paternal grandmother Minnie Mae Presley. A bronze tablet also commemorates Presley's stillborn twin brother, Jesse Garon Presley. More recently, Elvis's daughter Lisa Marie, who died in 2023, and his grandson Benjamin Presley Keogh, who died in 2020, have been entombed there. The inclusion of this small family cemetery transmutes the erstwhile home of a deceased celebrity into the sanctified ground of his burial place, thereby necessitating that visitors modulate their tone and mood. It is socially acceptable to chuckle at the tackiness of the Jungle Room, but much less so to chortle while passing the man's grave. As one passes from the interior to the exterior, Graceland demands a mood shift, one as spiritually significant as the fact that the same man sang "Hound Dog" and "How Great Thou Art" with equal fervor.

Finally, as Presley's performances and persona benefited immeasurably from his appropriations of Black music and culture that were then widely perceived as his own invention, so too does Graceland simultaneously allude to and occlude the history of southern racial relations. As Marling explains, "Graceland was a timely and evocative copy of the historic architecture of the Middle South," suggesting that it was likely inspired by "Clanlo, a surviving Memphis plantation house of the 1850s fronted by a four-column portico of exceedingly slender proportions and Corinthian capitals bearing flattened acanthus leaves." She describes this as "a kind of antebellum Memphis style."[36] Owners of southern plantations are increasingly grappling with the ethical challenge of maintaining their commercial viability without whitewashing their histories, even as many others simply overlook their troubling past and reframe them as entertainment venues that offer romanticized, *Gone with the Wind*–inspired visions of antebellum life, or repurpose them as wedding and convention venues. Other voices now rightly question the desirability of reframing forced labor sites as scenes of mirth and merriment. Amy Potter and her colleagues document the troubling erasures persistent in such presentations of southern life: "Southern plantation museums ... are fraught with contradictions. At these heritage tourism sites, tour guides, visitors, curators, and owners struggle, to varying extents, to reconcile the coerced labor, torture, rape, and daily acts of terror—large and small—inflicted on millions of people of African descent on antebellum plantations that are now home to museums' pretty landscapes and 'cute,' revenue-generating gift shoppes and restaurants."[37] And so just as Presley was inspired by Black music, Graceland's architecture was inspired by overlooking Black suffering, by focusing on the symmetry and aesthetics of its architectural heritage rather than by considering what such architecture might convey. Away from Graceland tourists can find the deeper historical truths of southern race relations at the National Civil Rights Museum at the Lorraine Motel, as well as much smaller museums celebrating Black singers: the West Tennessee Delta Heritage Center and Tina Turner Museum (121 Sunny Hill Cove, Brownsville, Tennessee) and Al Green's Full Gospel Tabernacle Church (7867 Hale Road, Memphis, Tennessee).

On the whole, Presley's persona lives on through Graceland's, the one enhancing the other in a cycle that shows little sign of abating. Excessive and modest, unrestrained and wholly relatable, Presley lives on, as evident in the longstanding rumors that he never died but simply absconded himself away to once again live a simple life free of the demands of stardom. One of the more notorious rumors of Presley's life centered on the question of whether, one night at home in Graceland and outraged or merely greatly annoyed by the evening's entertainment offerings, he shot his television set. His father Vernon confirmed the rumor's truth, stating "the story that Elvis shot at the TV set is true. But he was in his own home, and shot out his own TV set and when he'd done it he could afford to buy a new one."[38] In many ways this incident serves as an apt metaphor for Presley's southern star persona as a whole: outrageous yet relatable, excessive yet somehow warranted. (Who hasn't wanted to shoot their television on occasion?) Yet it also trivializes an act of violence through a somewhat winking humor, in an act in which southern excesses yet again are tacitly dismissed with southern excuses, in which the King somehow rises above it all.

4

GREAT ACTORS, SOUTHERN ACCENTS, AND TENNESSEE WILLIAMS'S STAR FACTORY

In polishing a key aspect of their celebrity personas, and virtually irrespective of the many other facets of their unique personalities and idiosyncratic styles, most actors crave critical accolades to confirm that their performances are not merely passable but good, even great. Stars repeatedly recognized by the Academy Awards clinch their positions as the top talents of the entertainment industry, as evident in the legendary careers of Katharine Hepburn (twelve nominations, four Oscars), Jack Nicholson (twelve nominations, three Oscars), and Ingrid Bergman (seven nominations, three Oscars). In a slight wrinkle to this dynamic, strikingly attractive stars must negotiate the ever-present possibility that their talents might be dismissed owing to their looks, and stars once dismissed as lightweights who found their careers rejuvenated following acknowledgment by the Academy include Marisa Tomei, Kim Basinger, and Brendan Fraser. Further along these lines, comic actors face the likelihood of being dismissed as "merely funny" and thus as incapable of tackling meaty dramatic roles, even though comedians such as Bill Murray, Eddie Murphy, and Melissa McCarthy have time and again proved these critics incorrect, with the Academy's nods attesting to their wide-ranging skills. Finally, precisely because all people act to some degree in their private and professional lives, the actor's art is subject to denigration for its very ubiquity. Dramatic awards, and particularly Academy Awards, can only enhance an actor's star persona, elevating them higher into the ranks of the celebrity stratosphere.

For actors seeking to burnish their artistic reputations in the 1950s and 1960s, few avenues to rave reviews were as close to certain as starring in an adaptation of one of Tennessee Williams's magnolia-drenched dramas. Hollywood studios filmed a steady stream of Williams's plays from 1950 to 1968, most notably Irving Rapper's *The Glass Menagerie* (1950), Elia Kazan's *A Streetcar Named Desire* (1951), Daniel Mann's *The Rose Tattoo* (1955), Kazan's *Baby Doll* (1956), Richard Brooks's *Cat on a Hot Tin Roof* (1958), Joseph L. Mankiewicz's *Suddenly, Last Summer* (1959), Sidney Lumet's *The Fugitive Kind* (1960), Peter Glenville's *Summer and Smoke* (1961), José Quintero's *The Roman Spring of Mrs. Stone* (1961), Brooks's *Sweet Bird of Youth* (1962), George Roy Hill's *Period of Adjustment* (1962), John Huston's *The Night of the Iguana* (1964), and Joseph Losey's *Boom!* (1968). Indeed, one could consider adaptations of Williams's plays virtually a subgenre of mid-twentieth-century American cinema, such that reviewers came to these works with preconceived notions of what they would encounter, evident in Stanley Kauffmann's dismissive opinion, expressed in a contemporary review, of Williams's "trade-mark of sweaty sexuality wrapped in perfumed poesy."[1] Despite such snipes, and given their status as high-culture artifacts of serious drama, Williams's vehicles afforded stars the opportunity to hone this essential aspect of their celebrity personas, whether they were commencing their careers or were already well established—and despite the many lapses in their performances predicated upon longstanding southern stereotypes.

Of these many films, only *The Glass Menagerie*, *The Fugitive Kind*, and *Boom!* failed to earn any Academy Award nominations. In contrast, *A Streetcar Named Desire* was nominated for twelve Oscars and won four. To date no film has swept the acting categories, but *Streetcar* has tied for the closest, with Vivien Leigh, Karl Malden, and Kim Hunter respectively winning Best Actress, Best Supporting Actor, and Best Supporting Actress.[2] Many film critics remain chagrined that Marlon Brando lost the Best Actor Award to Humphrey Bogart, who was viewed as the sentimental choice, for *The African Queen* (1951). *The Rose Tattoo* was nominated for eight Oscars and won three, including Anna Magnani's selection as Best Actress and Marisa Pavan's nomination for Best Supporting Actress. *Baby Doll* merited four nods, including Carroll Baker for Best Actress and Mildred Dunnock for Best Supporting Actress. Earning six nominations altogether, *Cat on a Hot Tin Roof* featured noteworthy performances by Paul Newman and Elizabeth Taylor, who were honored as candidates for Best Actor and Best Actress.

Despite its lurid themes of cannibalism and incestuous desire, *Suddenly, Last Summer* earned three nominations, including two pitting Elizabeth Taylor and Katharine Hepburn against each other for the prize of Best Actress (although both lost to Simone Signoret for *Room at the Top*). Geraldine Page garnered back-to-back Best Actress nominations for *Summer and Smoke* and *Sweet Bird of Youth*. For the former film, which garnered a total of four nominations, Una Merkel merited a nod for Best Supporting Actress; for the latter film, Ed Begley won Best Supporting Actor, and Shirley Knight was considered for Best Supporting Actress. *The Roman Spring of Mrs. Stone*'s sole nomination recognized Lotte Lenya for Best Supporting Actress. *Period of Adjustment* was likewise nominated for only one award, whereas *The Night of the Iguana* was nominated for four, including Grayson Hall as Best Supporting Actress for her scene-stealing turns while cast alongside such luminaries as Ava Gardner, Deborah Kerr, and Richard Burton; the film won for Best Costume Design.

Critics might quibble over the particular significance of some of these nominations—indeed, throughout its history the Academy Awards has been known for honoring dubious performances and overlooking extraordinary ones—but on the whole, these many awards and nominations testify to the cultural prestige attached to Williams's plays and the accompanying assumption that their cinematic adaptations would likely capture that mercurial, evanescent, and often indefinable essence of a quality production. Williams stands tall in Hollywood history, along with such figures as Billy Wilder, Greta Gerwig, and the Coen Brothers, for his extraordinary ability to fashion characters so compelling that the actors playing them were invaluably assisted in creating memorable performances. Given the southern settings of many of Williams's works, these stars, most of whom were not southerners themselves, relied on stereotypes of southern accents to transform themselves into Williams's characters, no matter how exaggerated, cornpone, or otherwise dissonant they then sounded; conversely, others simply ignored the demands of southern speech and spoke as themselves. Many of Williams's plays hinge on their southern settings—*A Streetcar Named Desire* could not be seamlessly transported to New York City or Seattle without losing much of its dramatic power—and while the southernness of his characters is similarly essential and evident in much of the dialogue, for many critics of this era it was curiously irrelevant in considering whether the actors delivered a praiseworthy performance. And so as much as the critical consensus lauded these actors and bedecked them with accolades and honors, a small counter-contingent decried their inability to play southerners convincingly (as the ensuing analysis will discuss). In effect, the patina of Williams's celebrity compensated for the many flaws in their performances, which indicates that the perpetuation of southern stereotypes can at times be viewed as inherently artistic. The easy stereotypes of the South enhanced the artistic reputation of a range of actors in the 1950s and 1960s now generally recognized among the greatest of their generation—including Vivien Leigh, Marlon Brando, Elizabeth Taylor, Paul Newman, and Katharine Hepburn—no matter their (in)ability to sound recognizably southern.

The *Atlas of North American English* documents the southern accent as pervasive in Virginia, North Carolina, South Carolina, Georgia, Alabama, Mississippi, Tennessee, Kentucky, Arkansas, and Louisiana, and also prevalent in southern West Virginia, northern Florida, and much of Texas.[3] As a whole, southern accents are characterized by a distinct drawl that results from lengthening vowels, sometimes into diphthongs; the inverted stresses of common words (evident in "guitar" and "police"); and the often undistinguished "i"s and "e"s such that "pen" and "pin" are pronounced as homophones. Southern accents are not uniform, of course. Variations occur throughout the region, such as the distinct locutions of Atlanta and Savannah, Georgia, and of Charleston, South Carolina, as well as the addition of Cajun and New Orleans accents in Louisiana. It should also be noted that race factors into the presentation and reception of southern accents, particularly in the complex interrelationship of white southern accents and African American Vernacular English. (Because Williams's plays primarily focus on white characters, the characteristics of Black southern accents do not play a part in the following discussion, as only white actors could avail themselves of the career benefits of Williams's vehicles during this era.) As sociolinguists have long documented, people stereotype others based on their language pronunciation,[4] and prevailing stereotypes have long linked northern accents to intelligence, in contrast to southern accents, which are associated both with kindness and with stupidity. As Katherine Kinzler and Jasmine DeJesus document, stereotypes connecting southern accents with low intelligence are learned from a very young age: "The finding that even school-aged children in both the Northern and Southern US endorse linguistic stereotypes and think of Southern speech as being 'less smart' suggests that accent-based social bias is early-forming and consequential."[5]

Williams's plays are not responsible for these dynamics, nor would I claim that either his characters or his storylines perpetuate them. Yet with these sociolinguistic factors in mind, I must confess that, while the cinematic adaptations of Tennessee Williams's plays stand as some of my favorite films, particularly *A Streetcar Named Desire*, *Baby Doll*, *Cat on a Hot Tin Roof*, and *Suddenly, Last Summer*, I have long found the performances of the lead characters strangely askew and verbally off-kilter, as various stars attempted to sound southern or simply ignored southern accents altogether, and ended up sounding like what a nonsoutherner thinks southerners sound like rather than how we actually do. On a certain level, such an elocutionary mishmash is to be expected, for Hollywood studios and their stars long overlooked the need to pronounce dialects correctly. The history of dialect pronunciation in Western film exceeds the scope of this chapter, but, on the whole, the industry did not overly concern itself with dialects for much of the twentieth century. Drama professor Edith Skinner published her *Speak with Distinction* in 1942, and this influential book encouraged actors to talk in a regularized and largely artificial form of "Standard American English." Many film historians view Meryl Streep's Academy Award–winning performance in *Sophie's Choice* (1982), in which she speaks fluent Polish, as a turning point in Hollywood's concern for the proper pronunciation of accents, dialects, and languages—in contrast to such racist caricatures of the past as Mickey Rooney's performance as an Asian-American man in *Breakfast at Tiffany's* (1961), or such curiosities as Charlton Heston's performance as a Mexican drug-enforcement officer in *Touch of Evil* (1958) speaking with a Middle American accent.[6] Casting agents began to see that accurately reproduced dialects, those that would immediately convey to the audience the authenticity of the performance, could assist actors in creating memorable characters. I first watched these adaptations of Williams's plays in the 1980s and 1990s and then continuing to the present day, and thus viewed them with different expectations than their original audiences. To put it bluntly, the South sounds funny in many of these films, which thus undercuts the strength of the actors' performances, as the following discussions of Leigh, Brando, Newman,

Taylor, and Hepburn, along with a potpourri of critical potshots directed toward their costars, demonstrate.

Twelve years after her indelible and Oscar-winning performance as southern spitfire Scarlett O'Hara in *Gone with the Wind* (1939), British actress Vivien Leigh scored another triumph playing Williams's aging southern belle Blanche Dubois in *A Streetcar Named Desire*. A trailblazer among her peers, Leigh studied southern accents for her film roles, annotating her scripts to enhance the delivery of her lines.[7] Among her many rave reviews, however, a few critics suggested that her performance was exaggerated and ultimately off-kilter, such as John McCarten's assessment that she "wrings a lot of pathos out of her role as the bedraggled magnolia."[8] Writing for *The Nation*, Manny Farber similarly opined, "Miss Leigh interjects a bitter-sweet fragrance and acrobatic excitement into the role, but the effects are freakish, too ambitious and endless."[9] The *Time* reviewer specifically focused on Leigh's delivery of her dialogue: "Vivien Leigh seems overshadowed by the skilled actors around her. Among her handicaps: a somewhat watered-down characterization, and most of the movie's talkiest passages."[10]

Indeed, Blanche does talk quite volubly, but rarely in a southern accent. Her most famous lines—such as "I want to kiss you just once, softly and sweetly on your mouth" and "I have always depended on the kindness of strangers"—are delivered in an artistically effective lilt but without sounding particularly southern. Such a statement might seem counterintuitive, as few phrases convey southernness in the popular imaginary more immediately than "I have always depended on the kindness of strangers," but the words, in effect, have become unmoored from Leigh's delivery of them, as imitators simply supply—and often campily oversupply—their missing accent. On a more positive note, Leigh occasionally intones Blanche's southern accent correctly. For example, when she states, "Deliberate cruelty is not forgivable. It is the one unforgivable thing in my opinion and the one thing of which I have never, never been guilty," she stresses the first syllable of "opinion" rather than the second, which follows the southern linguistic pattern of accenting first syllables of certain words. Williams later said of Leigh's performance in *The Roman Spring of Mrs. Stone*, "I . . . watched the grace and tragic style of Vivien Leigh. I think that film is a poem. It was the last important work of both Miss Leigh and of the director,

José Quintero, a man who is as dear to my heart as Miss Leigh is."[11] Notably, however, the character of Mrs. Stone is not a southern woman (even though several reviewers linked her to Blanche Dubois and to Amanda Wingfield of *The Glass Menagerie*), and so Leigh did not need to concern herself with the complexities of a southern dialect in this role.[12] (Also in *The Roman Spring of Mrs. Stone*, Warren Beatty's portrayal of the Roman gigolo Paolo di Leo is characterized by a hammy Italian accent, providing further evidence of Hollywood's disregard for effective performances of dialect.)

Continuing with the critical response to *A Streetcar Named Desire*, several reviewers pondered Brando's curious delivery of his lines as Stanley Kowalski. When Brando surged into international fame in the early 1950s, he was "alternately looked upon as a genius and a screwball," in the words of Grady Johnson,[13] and much of his curiously conflicted reputation arose owing to his singular style of speech. In his *New Republic* review of *A Streetcar Named Desire*, Robert Hatch stated of Brando, "If he speaks as though language had just been discovered, it is clear that he was the discoverer,"[14] and in an otherwise positive review, Al Hine concedes "the fact that much of [Brando's] dialogue sounds as if he were saying 'woodge, woodge, woodge,' for once is no barrier."[15] (But how could "woodge, woodge, woodge" not be a barrier to comprehension?) Manny Farber viewed Brando's Kowalski as wildly exaggerated and thus as inherently uncredible: "Marlon Brando . . . has upped the voltage of every eccentricity by several thousand watts. . . . The addition of a lush physicality and a show-off's flamboyance to the character of Stanley makes him seem like a muscular version of a petulant, crazily egotistical homosexual."[16] Listening to the film and its critics, it is apparent that Brando sounds more like Brando than like a New Orleanian of Polish descent. One might rightly rebut that Williams does not divulge Kowalski's entire backstory, and it is within the realm of reasonable conjecture to posit that he is perhaps a second-generation Polish American who recently relocated to New Orleans and thus not one raised with its accents. If so, the play's New Orleans setting then becomes curiously unmoored from the characters who live there and the words that they speak. Linguistically, Stanley Kowalski would be expected to speak with New Orleans's "Yat" accent, which is prevalent among its lower- and middle-class white citizens. The word "Yat" is a shortened form of the greeting "Where y'at?," and this accent resembles stereotypical Brooklynese, in which "the" and "there" are pronounced as "de" and "dere," along with other rounding and lowering pronunciations. Brando delivers his dialogue with a coarse brutishness reflective of Kowalski's character, but without a corresponding accent, whether broadly southern or specifically "Yat," to convey his regional identity.

Following *A Streetcar Named Desire*, Brando was nominated for the Best Actor Academy Award four more times in the 1950s, for *Viva Zapata!* (1952), *Julius Caesar* (1953), and *Sayonara* (1958), and for his winning performance in *On the Waterfront* (1954). Brando then returned to the Williams corpus in *The Fugitive Kind*, but again his attempts at a southern accent resulted in a verbally disjointed performance. Williams himself praised Brando's acting skills—"Of the male performers, Marlon Brando is outstanding. I think he is probably the greatest living actor"[17]—while also criticizing Brando's "offbeat timing and slurred pronunciation" for undermining the potential of *The Fugitive Kind*.[18] Pete Martin characterized Brando's voice as "the coarse rumble he'd used in *A Streetcar Named Desire*," mentioning as well "the rocks-in-the-mouth mumble he'd invented for his part in the stage version of *A Streetcar Named Desire*."[19] The *Time* reviewer lauded his overall performance, declaring that "Brando gives an uncannily affecting performance, and what affects the audience is not his acting—he passionately refuses to act—but his own luminous, personal intensity," while also noting the limitations of his vocal performance: "too many scenes bog down in Brando's synthetic Southern drawl."[20] John McCarten condemned *The Fugitive Kind* as "corn-pone melodrama" and took particular aim at Brando for "prefer[ring] mumbling to normal articulation."[21] In a final example of critical exhaustion with Brando's attempts to speak with a southern accent, the *McCall's* reviewer lamented, "Mr. Brando underplays his part to such an extent that his words are often indistinguishable."[22]

Through the strange alchemy of his star persona, Brando suffered no serious consequences to his professional reputation as an extraordinarily talented actor for his "southern" mumblings, precisely because they connect to one of the more intriguing aspects of his celebrity persona: his simultaneous acknowledgment as both a Great Actor and a Great Pretender. Over the course of his career, numerous critics complained that Brando did not act beyond incarnating yet another recognizable version of himself, as evident in an assessment published in *Time*: "Brando plays the same character he always plays, the only character who seems to interest him: Marlon Brando. A childish thing indeed."[23] When interviewing Brando, John Nugent alerted him to the criticism that "he kept doing Stanley Kowalski, of *A Streetcar Named Desire,* all over again," to which the star replied: "Inevitably in an actor there is a marked individual manner. . . . I don't suppose I'm good enough to be free of that."[24] Brando memorably turned the tables on any debate about his talent by deriding the actor's art: "Acting is a bum's life. . . . You get paid for doing nothing and it means nothing. Acting is fundamentally a childish thing to pursue."[25] Profiting handsomely from a career in acting while dismissing its significance, Brando undercut any assumption that he would hope to be considered a great actor while positioning himself, and often his politics, at the heart of any discussion of him, as famously occurred when he refused his second Best Actor Award for *The Godfather* (1972) to protest the mistreatment and misrepresentation of Native Americans in contemporary entertainment. As Dwight MacDonald summarized, "Mr. Brando has always aspired to something Deeper and More Significant, he has always fancied himself as like an intellectual,"[26] but as his forays into southern settings demonstrated, Brando never needed to concern himself with the finer points of southern speech patterns to accomplish this goal.

Similar to *A Streetcar Named Desire, Cat on a Hot Tin Roof* was greeted by a discordant dynamic of rave reviews clashing with those noting that the performances failed to capture the complexities of southern tonality. Their words akin to the overwhelming praise that showered Leigh and Brando, most critics agreed that Newman and Taylor excelled in their performances, as evident in the *Newsweek* review: "Newman's cynical young man is a standout portrayal. Elizabeth Taylor, who never has been known as a dramatic star of particularly commanding stature, is more than satisfactory as Maggie the Cat, the first role she has been given which is not bigger-than-life."[27] At the same time, the film's southernness rang hollow for many, including Hollis Alpert, who wrote, "One can complain, too, that the movie does not seem sufficiently 'Southern.' . . . The South one does not see at all."[28] The *Time* reviewer stated that Williams's productions are "filled not with actors in a drama, but with dancers in a psychiatric striptease,"[29] which points to the actors' failures to fully inhabit their roles. With the South somewhat absent from the film's southern setting, *Cat on a Hot Tin Roof* evinces the potential emptiness of the omnipresent southern signifiers in Williams's cinematic corpus.

Paul Newman's star was rapidly rising in the mid-1950s, and his Academy Award nomination for Best Actor in *Cat on a Hot Tin Roof*—the first of ten nominations over his career, including his winning performance for *The Color of Money* (1986)—clinched his status as a talented up-and-comer. Williams himself praised Newman's performance: "Paul Newman is also terribly good. He works up to a part slowly, but when he finally gets to it he's marvelous."[30] Among the naysayers, Hollis Alpert opined, "Paul Newman is adequate as Brick, even though the character is now virtually a static one,"[31] and John McCarten derided his acting as the "I'm-all-shook-up-but-won't-show-it-if-I-can-help-it style of Marlon Brando."[32] A brief article in *Vogue* knocked Newman as the "king of the Ornamental Lug School of acting" and added, "Even off stage, Mr. Newman continues that famous Tennessee Williams' actor voice that almost everyone can mimic: the difficulty is not to keep talking that way after the performance."[33] These words highlight Newman's performance of an exaggerated and cornpone southern accent, one that is easy to imitate precisely because of its exaggerations. Prior to *Cat on a Hot Tin Roof*, Newman had played the southern role of accused barn-burner Ben Quick in Martin Ritt's *The Long, Hot Summer* (1958), which was based on William Faulkner's stories, and he would return to southern settings and southern roles in *Hud* (1963, set in Texas) and *Cool Hand Luke* (1967, set in Florida). Viewing Newman's career holistically, what is most notable about his performance as a southern man in *Cat on a Hot Tin Roof* is that he sounds remarkably similar to his role as Ben Quick in *The Long, Hot Summer*, despite the social chasm between these two characters that would likely be registered in their accents. Social class inflects southern accents in myriad ways, and quite simply, many rich southerners sound quite different from most poor southerners. On the whole, southern accents are often disparaged as the speech of "hillbillies" and "rednecks," which fosters a blanket understanding of southern speech that overlooks the ways in which its tonalities are modulated among various social circles and classes, and one that Newman overlooked in his otherwise compelling performances.

In the mid-1950s Elizabeth Taylor was transitioning from her childhood and teen successes in *National Velvet* (1944) and *Father of the Bride* (1950) to more dramatic roles. In the year prior to *Cat on a Hot Tin Roof* she scored her first Academy Award nomination for *Raintree County* (1957), a *Gone with the Wind*–

inspired drama in which she plays southern belle Susanna Drake Shawnessy. Altogether she was honored with three consecutive Best Actress nominations for playing southern women, with *Suddenly, Last Summer* completing this trifecta. (She then won her first Oscar the following year, for *BUtterfield 8*.) Many critics evaluated her performance in *Cat on a Hot Tin Roof* by tracing her evolution as an actor, such as in Stanley Kauffmann's assessment: "The lovely Miss Taylor lacks the inner fire from which all else grows . . . but she is a diligent pupil and . . . has worked so hard that she gives a certain surface to her performance."[34] The reviewer for *Look* affirmed, "Elizabeth Taylor gives the best performance of her career as Maggie the Cat in MGM's *Cat on a Hot Tin Roof*."[35]

In the following year, Taylor returned to the Williams canon in *Suddenly, Last Summer*, in which she plays the role of Catherine Holly, a young woman threatened with a lobotomy by her imperious aunt determined to bury the sexual secrets behind her son Sebastian's gruesome demise. Similar to Newman's limited perception of the complexities of southern speech, what is most notable about Taylor's performance in *Suddenly, Last Summer* is that she sounds very much the same as she does in *Cat on a Hot Tin Roof*, despite the distinct settings of the films: the former in New Orleans, the latter in the Mississippi Delta. These accents diverge notably, particularly because New Orleans accents represent a wider amalgamation of linguistic cultures. Founded by the French in 1718, the city imported speakers of various languages over the next centuries. Due to its status as a port city in an antebellum slave state, a number of these immigrants were enslaved people speaking a variety of African languages, and the nineteenth century witnessed a large influx of German, Irish, and Italian immigrants. Again, it is important to stress that many reviews of Taylor's performance glowed, but the *Time* reviewer lamented that "Taylor's inability to reproduce a recognizable emotion becomes almost an advantage in a role that contains no recognizable emotions."[36] Williams ruefully remarked, "As for Liz's performance in *Suddenly, Last Summer*, if it did nothing else, it demonstrated her ability to rise above miscasting."[37] On another occasion, he similarly stated, "But while Elizabeth Taylor was very good as Maggie in *Cat on a Hot Tin Roof*, she simply wasn't right as Catherine Holly in *Suddenly, Last Summer*."[38] The bizarre role of Catherine Holly—both a damsel in distress threatened with a lobotomy and the alluring romantic interest of Montgomery Clift's Dr. Cukrowicz—would challenge any actress to credibly deliver such lines as "There's only one 'little operation' they perform here! It's on the brain! It's called a lobotomy! ... In cases of hopeless lunacy—he bores holes into the skull and operates on the brain!," but a New Orleans accent would have at least grounded the performance in its southern setting.

Katharine Hepburn stood as an established star in the 1950s, having won her first Best Actress Oscar for *Morning Glory* (1931) and notching six more nominations before *Suddenly, Last Summer* for *Alice Adams* (1935), *The Philadelphia Story* (1940), *Woman of the Year* (1942), *The African Queen* (1951), *Summertime* (1955), and *The Rainmaker* (1956). Hepburn viewed the role of the domineering, morally corrupt Mrs. Venable askance, declaring, "Tennessee Williams, now—he uses words brilliantly, brilliantly. But whose time is he writing about? Not mine, certainly. Williams gives us the middle-aged woman's answer to sex—she can go ahead and sleep with her son."[39] Williams realized her discontent with the role, stating "I don't think Hepburn was happy with the part of the poet's mother in the screen version of *Suddenly, Last Summer*,"[40] although, on another occasion, he applauded her performance, "At first, I wasn't sure about Katharine Hepburn as Violet Venable. I thought she was quite too young to play such an older woman, as I visualized the part. . . . But I admitted that casting Miss Hepburn might be daring, and it took me a while to get accustomed to the idea. Now, of course, I know she was brilliant."[41] Williams's praise notwithstanding, many critics found themselves flummoxed by his outré story and her off-key performance, evident in Peter Cowie's assessment: "In *Suddenly, Last Summer* [Hepburn] is in a part that is, even by Tennessee Williams' standards, repulsive," and adding that "on the screen Joseph Mankiewicz' microscopic direction and the weight of three world stars makes it sprawl."[42] Bosley Crowther similarly sniped: "Katharine Hepburn plays the arch and airy dowager with what looks like a stork's nest on her head and such bony and bumptious posturing that she acts a Mary Petty caricature."[43] On the issue of her vocal performance, Hepburn's Mrs. Venable sounds like the many other characters that she played before and after this role, with her rich, New England, patrician inflection creating an memorable effect while sounding strikingly unlike a doyenne of New Orleans's rarefied elite. The *Newsweek* review proposed that Hepburn "manages to overlay her cultured voice effectively with touches of the stuttering 'method' style of acting,"[44] but any method acting does not extend to a successful presentation of a New Orleans accent. Mrs. Venable's blatant attempts to seduce young Dr. Cukrowicz—with such lines as "Am I only wearing one earring? Have I forgotten my lip rouge?" and "I must say, you're much handsomer than your photograph in the paper without that awful paraphernalia you doctors wear"—allow Hepburn to create a character both sympathetic in her lost youth and monstrous in her efforts to permanently quiet Catherine Holly, but the strength of the performance is at least partially undone by vocally removing the character from the South.

One of the odder lapses in both Hepburn's and Taylor's performances in *Suddenly, Last Summer* arises in the fact that they play southern women who primarily speak with southern accents when insulting or imitating other southerners, thus oddly undermining the coherency of their portrayals. In her simmering distaste for her nephew, George, Mrs. Venable archly states, "I said take the clothes, George. Don't flaunt them in my face." She then shifts into a cornpone dialect and continues, "Why don't you both kindly let yourselves out?" and then returns to her normal timbre: "Get the rest of the clothes another time." Similarly, Catherine impersonates Sebastian's southern accent while speaking to Dr. Cukrowicz: "Mr. Venable was a good man, but dull to the point of genius," she states, and then continues in her usual tone, "That was Sebastian you just heard talking." Notably, Mrs. Venable uses her exaggerated southern accent to insult despised George, whereas Catherine mimics esteemed Sebastian; these southern accents, then, are not so much markers of the characters' geographic identities but of these actors' reliance on exaggerated and stereotypical tropes. Camp often emerges in failed performances, and Hepburn's and Taylor's unsteady play with dialect imbues *Suddenly, Last Summer* with an ironic distance between the actors and their characters. (See figure 5.)

Along with the various criticisms and dialectal difficulties experienced by Leigh, Brando, Newman, Taylor, and Hepburn, their costars similarly slipped in their linguistic portrayals of southerners. John McCarten commented on the surprising vocal effects of Judith Anderson in *Cat on a Hot Tin Roof*, who earlier enjoyed a Best Supporting Actress nomination for her towering performance as Mrs. Danvers in Alfred Hitchcock's *Rebecca* (1941): "Big Mama . . . alternates between broad you-all dialect and a clipped English accent."[45] Concerning *The Fugitive Kind*, Hollis Alpert noted, "Miss Magnani, unfortunately, has trouble articulating, an understandable difficulty since she is not only working with a language not her own, but with a variation of the language that would

FIG. 5. In a highly charged emotional scene, Elizabeth Taylor's Catherine Holly attempts to force Katharine Hepburn's Violet Venable to confront the truth of her dissipated son Sebastian's life and untimely death. Taylor's and Hepburn's nominations for Academy Awards surely overlooked their meager attempts at southern accents.

trouble native-born actresses."[46] Assessing *Summer and Smoke*, Brendan Gill wrote ironically, "Laurence Harvey, as the virile young man, has worked up a Southern accent that is no better than it should be."[47] As Brando's Kowalski in *A Streetcar Named Desire* should likely speak with a "Yat" accent, the same point holds for Karl Malden's performance as Mitch. It is also noteworthy that some critics transcribed the actors' dialogue into a cornpone southern dialect in their reviews. In an evaluation of *Baby Doll*, the *Time* reviewer quoted several of Carroll Baker's lines and transcribed them into a southern dialect notably more exaggerated than her delivery of them: "Ah'm not athaletic," "Oooo . . . Ah feel so weak," "Yew c'd curl up." He suggested as well "that the language of Tennessee Williams, no less than his subject matter, often seems to have been borrowed from one of the more carelessly written pornographic pulps."[48] The *Newsweek* reviewer quoted some of Geraldine Page's dialogue in *Summer and Smoke*—"Ah am just reprimanding you—castigating you verbally, as it were," "Ah'm beginning to feel like a water lily in a Chinese lagoon"—and then archly commented, "The character who speaks these lines may feel like a water lily, but, as conceived by Williams and played by Geraldine Page, she behaves more like a stand of marsh grass."⁴⁹ Both the actors and the critics could only speak in a southern accent of excess and hyperbole, one rarely heard in the South itself but circulated throughout the wider United States as a shorthand for the region's ignorance and backward ways.

As Leigh's, Brando's, Newman's, Taylor's, and Hepburn's performances demonstrate, southern accents challenge actors to incarnate recognizably southern characters, and this dynamic can be viewed within the persistent issue of the way the South is portrayed in the wider U.S. culture. Critics of these films often praised or bemoaned the ways in which a given film reproduced or reenvisioned how the South should be depicted, such as in John McCarten's review of *Baby Doll*: "Mr. Kazan's decision to make the picture in the cotton belt has paid off beautifully in photography that really conveys the look of a section lost in ignorance, poverty, and despair."⁵⁰ Or consider Hollis Alpert's review of *The Fugitive Kind*, in which he proposed that the South had been slandered by Williams's narratives: "The deep South, as any faithful movie-goer knows, has had a tough enough time already in other Tennessee Williams movies," suggesting further that the citizens of the South should "commission a movie based on the biograph[y] of Tennessee Williams . . . and at least attempt to gain some mild form of revenge."⁵¹ Any type of vengeance, even when suggested lightheartedly as in this instance, takes matters a bit too far, as forgiveness so often forges a brighter path, and forgiveness appears the better path in this instance, too, as southerners can take light umbrage at the dialectal mishaps unleashed on the movie screens in the 1950s and 1960s, and marvel as well at how these stars shone all the brighter for their flawed performances.

Tennessee Williams's plays, a veritable star factory of talent, highlight the complex ways in which myths of the South so often matter more than its truths, and the rewards so readily available to those who need not bother to refute them in their star-making performances. Perhaps not too terribly surprising, and despite the greater attention paid to dialects in much of the entertainment industry, southern accents still sound stilted and fake, imagined and exaggerated in many otherwise high-quality productions. Scout Brobst, analyzing the southern speech of such stars as Daniel Craig, Margaret Qualley, Harris Dickinson, Daisy Edgar-Jones, and more, elegiacally laments, "But if accents are what come with being from a place, then it is no small loss to let them slip into something unrecognizable. What are we supposed to hear through the distortion?

The Southern pantomime feeds and sustains itself, bringing to bear a linguistic tradition all its own. It doesn't reflect real heritage or culture; through it, there is no way for us to access the world as it has ever been lived."[52] Whether in the cinematic adaptations of Tennessee Williams's films in the 1950s and 1960s or in the blockbusters of today, Hollywood evinces little concern for capturing the South's unique vocality, and perhaps also for capturing any deeper truths of the region as well.

ANDY GRIFFITH, *THE ANDY GRIFFITH SHOW*, AND THE PARADOX OF YOKEL STEREOTYPES

When Andy Griffith burst into stardom in the mid-1950s, the popular press did not hesitate to label him a hillbilly, bumpkin, or yokel—often in their headlines. "Hillbilly's a Hit," trumpeted a review of Griffith's Broadway debut; the article concluded, "Yokel boy makes good."[1] In a lexical coincidence—or perhaps an instance of punning plagiarism?—Lawrence Elliott titled his profile of the actor "Andy Griffith: Yokel Boy Makes Good" and referred to him as a "barefoot boy from out yonder."[2] "Bumpkin to Big Timer," announced *Newsweek* magazine, in a story about Griffith's breakout appearances on *The Ed Sullivan Show*.[3] As Duane Carr comments on southern stereotypes in literature, "urbanites frequently view all people from southern rural areas and small towns as generally inferior types and the subject more of jokes than of serious consideration,"[4] an observation that extends as well to the general reception afforded many southerners in 1950s and 1960s popular culture. For some midcentury American critics, Griffith's southern roots defined his appeal while also allowing them the pleasure of disparaging southern people. This tension would define both Griffith's career and the legacy of his most successful program, *The Andy Griffith Show* (1960–68), as he both profited from and railed against prevailing southern stereotypes. Concurrently, Griffith's genial southern star and his eponymous program overshadowed his own violent temper and whitewashed southern racial violence, offering Americans of the era a wholesome view of the South that clashed directly with the images displayed on daily news programs. Thus, the paradox of the yokel stereotype: it limits perceptions of white rural southerners, whether into gentle characters or exaggerated caricatures, while also liberating them of the region's uglier underbelly long complicit with violence and racism.[5]

Born June 1, 1926, in Mount Airy, North Carolina—the inspiration for Mayberry, the folksy setting of *The Andy Griffith Show*—Griffith opted for a career in the entertainment industry following his graduation from the University of North Carolina at Chapel Hill in 1949. He initially worked as a music and drama teacher at the local high school of the Goldsboro region but skyrocketed to fame in the early 1950s for his comedy monologues, most notably "What It Was, Was Football." This performance features Griffith playing a country rube who stumbles into a college town on game day but then cannot decipher the strange events unfolding on the football field. Mistaking referees for convicts and locker rooms for outhouses and otherwise misinterpreting the game's many perplexing elements, Griffith's character states in wonder: "It was that both bunches full of them men wanted this funny-lookin' lil punkin to play with. They did, friends, and I know that they couldn't a eat it because they kicked it the whole evenin' an' it never bust." With his folky direct address to "friends" and his slow and amiable drawl, with the final g's of gerunds and participles almost uniformly dropped, Griffith created a memorable character, one based in southern yokel stereotypes but one that, in the strange alchemy of humor, invites audiences more to laugh *with* the speaker at football's oddness than to laugh *at* him for his bumbling backwoods ways. "What It Was, Was Football" sold so well in North Carolina that national record companies took notice, and as he continued garnering attention, some critics professed themselves baffled by his appeal. A reviewer in *Time* commented on the upward trajectory of Griffith's celebrity and ruefully surmised, "Probably nothing can be done about it."[6]

In many ways, "What It Was, Was Football" captures the crux of Griffith's southern star persona and the steady refusal of many critics to acknowledge any difference between the actor and his roles during these foundational moments of his career. The subjects and titles of his other monologues—including "Swan Lake" and "Romeo and Juliet"—indicate Griffith's knowledge of various masterworks of Western culture, which serves as an essential ingredient of any effort to parody or satirize them. That is to say, Griffith the creator was sufficiently versed in ballet terms for Griffith the performer to mispronounce and mischaracterize them in "Swan Lake," and in "Romeo and Juliet," his character says of

Romeo's speech, "It wasn't about bein' or not bein'; it was about doin' or not doin'"—a pithily comic encapsulation of the inner turmoils roiling and motivating Hamlet and Romeo. Another of his comedy monologues, "Make Yourself Comfortable," tells the tale of a vamp pursuing a young man so innocent that he does not understand the very nature of the pursuit, and this record stands as one of the rare comedy hits to crack the Top 40 chart, reaching No. 26 in 1955. Despite the fact that he graduated from one of the United States' finest educational institutions—UNC Chapel Hill—many of his critics simply collapsed the performer into his roles, no matter how far afield he later strayed from them.

Following these early successes, Griffith bolstered his nascent career by playing the role of Private Will Stockdale in *No Time for Sergeants* in multiple formats: on television in the anthology series *The United States Steel Hour* (1953–63); on Broadway at the Alvin Theatre, for which he earned a Tony nomination; and in Mervyn LeRoy's 1958 film. As Griffith realized of his make-or-break audition for *No Time for Sergeants,* "Here was this hillbilly and all . . . and I figured that if I couldn't play the part, well then, maybe I'd better try me another business. I mean, I was getting pretty well fed up with night clubs by that time, I'll guaran-damn-tee you!"[7] Griffith's incarnation of Will Stockdale charmed audiences and critics, as evident in Leo Lerman's glowing review of his Broadway performance: "Not a female in the house doesn't sit up pert and radiate, 'Isn't he a love!' and twenty-nine-year-old Mr. Griffith from Mount Airy, North Carolina, making his Broadway stage debut, does what comes naturally—to him. He innocently radiates right back at the girls. What ensues is about the most wholesome, cornstalk-chewing affair being blatantly carried on in any public place today. Result: Andy Griffith is America's Sweetheart, 1956. He's strictly an All-American charmer—South-to-Southwest variety, and with loads of laughs."[8] Some of Lerman's geographical markers appear oddly misplaced—corn is more associated with the Midwest than the South, it is unclear how Griffith would register as southwestern—but the overarching thrust of his review, evident in such words as "innocently," "wholesome," and "Sweetheart," testifies to the actor's affable appeal when playing up his southern roots for laughs.

The many southern stereotypes on display in *No Time for Sergeants* contributed to the typecasting that Griffith faced throughout the remainder of his career, but amid his many turns as Will Stockdale yet prior to LeRoy's film, he played the role of Lonesome Rhodes, a demagogic entertainer who rises from an

Arkansas jail to a New York penthouse in Elia Kazan's *A Face in the Crowd* (1957). This character allowed him to simultaneously play southern but against type and so, to some degree, might have liberated him from the threat of typecasting. As Budd Schulberg, the film's screenwriter and author of its source story, "Your Arkansas Traveler," commented on his initial hesitation over casting Griffith: "Griffith could give us the hillbilly stuff all right, but what about the power madness that dominates the whole second half of the picture? Andy seemed pretty one-dimensional with his quaint backwoods expressions and wide-eyed innocence. But we sensed another sort of talent underneath—an untapped strength, a wolf-in-sheep's clothing kind of thing."[9] To assist Griffith in delivering such a memorable performance, Kazan relied on tactics common to Method actors yet tainted with antisouthern prejudices, reportedly telling the star, "I may have to use extraordinary means to make you do this. I may have to get out of line. I don't know any other way of getting an extraordinary performance out of an actor."[10] Kazan, in effect, modified Method acting into the "Jack Daniels Method," plying Griffith with whiskey to lubricate his performance.[11] Also, as Gilbert Millstein documented in a contemporary article in the *New York Times Magazine*, "Thereafter Kazan would come up to Griffith on the set and whisper 'white trash' at him."[12] In various interviews Griffith recalled the sting of this epithet when it was directed at him as an eleven-year-old child,[13] and he also explained that in Mount Airy, he lived on "the wrong part of town, and 'white trash' means rejection to me."[14] Tormenting an actor with bigoted epithets does not appear to be a strikingly nuanced way of encouraging a noteworthy performance, and it seems likely that Griffith would have successfully portrayed Lonesome Rhodes without such hectoring, but in any event, reviews of the film praised his performance. The critic for *Life* exclaimed, "From the moment he first appears, uncurling from a drunken sleep on the floor of an Arkansas jail, it is clear that Andy Griffith is a powerful film personality. . . . He proves his versatility by acting a wily, guitar-playing bum"; the review ended with the observation that Griffith gives a "commanding performance."[15] John McCarten declared in his *New Yorker* review that "Mr. Griffith proves himself to be a man of vast abilities,"[16] and Arthur Knight, writing for *Saturday Review*, stated approvingly, "As Rhodes, Andy Griffith creates from the start a figure of demoniacal intensity, of frightening lapses from rough amiability to sullen rage, a man consumed at the same time by a tremendous egotism and profound self-doubts."[17]

It is intriguing to ponder the trajectory of Griffith's career had he filmed *A Face in the Crowd* after completing his run in *No Time for Sergeants* with LeRoy's film. If *A Face in the Crowd* proved that Griffith's acting abilities extended beyond the genial antics of Will Stockdale in *No Time for Sergeants*, LeRoy's adaptation of the latter story constricted his star persona back to the limited sphere of the rural southerner. It must be acknowledged that even Griffith acknowledged the limits of his talent—"Look, I know darn well there's some things I can't do, now or ever. I ain't no Shakespearean actor, that's for day-yum sure. But this Lonesome, he got to me. I thought I understood him. I thought I could *be* him"[18]—but any possibility that *A Face in the Crowd* would encourage directors and casting agents to recalibrate their perception of his star persona was likely undone by his return to the role of Will Stockdale. For the most part a genially farcical comedy, *No Time for Sergeants* relies on many hoary stereotypes of the southern hayseed. The opening shots of the film establish the poverty and squalor in which Stockdale resides with his old and old-timey father, as encapsulated in the line, "He's used to sleeping with the hogs." Stockdale's fellow enlistees in the army find themselves repeatedly amused or simply befuddled by his ignorance, for he does not understand the meaning of the word *latrine* or know how to read an eye chart, among other such instances exhibiting his isolation in the rural South, and thus his jaw-dropping ignorance. (See figure 6.) He is dismissed as a "plowboy" and often says in wide-eyed wonder, "Golly," stretching this two-syllable word into five or six. Learning of his father's proclivity for moonshine, some of his army friends put kerosene in his drink, and a knockabout bar fight ensues. Notwithstanding such tired southern tropes, the film's reviewers praised Griffith's performance, assessed by John McCarten as "outstanding," by Earle Walbridge as "superb," and by Philip T. Hartung as "first-rate."[19] In many ways, Marshall Scott's review for *Cosmopolitan* summarized the film's general reception: "Without Griffith to bring Will Stockdale to larger-than-life-size, the whole thing would probably collapse like an underbeaten soufflé. With the lad on hand, it is possibly the funniest Army picture to appear in the dozen or more years since the end of World War II."[20]

However much Lonesome Rhodes might have liberated Griffith to play against type, his next major role, as Sheriff Andy Taylor in *The Andy Griffith Show*, cemented his preeminent persona as a genial southerner for the remainder of his career. This program spun off from Griffith's guest-starring appear-

FIG. 6. Andy Griffith portrays Private Will Stockdale in Mervyn LeRoy's *No Time for Sergeants*. In this image he stands in a spotless latrine that amazes his superiors, with his facial expression capturing the bewildered confusion that often defines this yokel character.

ance on Danny Thomas's *The Danny Thomas Show* (1953–65), also known as *Make Room for Daddy*, in the "Danny Meets Andy Griffith" episode (season 7, episode 20). The storyline depicts Andy Taylor arresting Thomas's Danny Williams for running a stop sign; Williams disparages Taylor as a "hayseed," calls Mayberry "hickville," and upbraids Taylor, "Go buy yourself a comb, and rake the hayseed out of your hair." In the standard narrative arc of so many television sitcoms, Danny realizes the error of his ways and soon apologizes for being a "city slicker . . . who had Andy all wrong." At its foundation, this episode depends entirely on southern yokel stereotypes—first their expectation and then their transcendence—and this narrative structure anchored many ensuing episodes of *The Andy Griffith Show*.

Following Griffith's guest appearance, Thomas sensed the comic appeal of a sitcom set in the fictional town of Mayberry, and, as one of the producers of *The Andy Griffith Show*, fostered its transition into a stand-alone program. "Andy is just a normal hillbilly,"[21] he pronounced of his star, thus distinguishing Griffith from the abnormal hillbillies ostensibly located throughout the South. In any event, *The Andy Griffith Show* debuted October 3, 1960, running for eight seasons and consistently ranking in the Top Ten. As Griffith explained, the show's original premise involved him recreating his success with his earlier comedy monologues: "I was supposed to tell funny stories about people in Mayberry."[22] This comic formula, so successful for "What It Was, Was Football," would likely have proved static on television. Don Knotts, who costarred with Griffith in the Broadway and film versions of *No Time for Sergeants*, suggested the addition of a key cast member, Sheriff Andy Taylor's right-hand man, ever-bumbling-and-fumbling Deputy Barney Fife. As Griffith recalled, "Actually, I didn't know I was going to be the straightman when my show started. I was supposed to tell funny stories about people in town. That would have lasted two weeks. But after the pilot was shown, Don [Knotts] called and said, 'Don't you need a deputy?' By the second episode, I recognized that Don should be the comic and I should play the straightman."[23] Knotts's role as Barney Fife fortified the program's comic premise, with Andy Taylor the calm and likeable protagonist amiably responding to the humorous shenanigans surrounding him. This premise expanded to a range of secondary characters, as Griffith further elaborated: "But in the second episode, I knew Don [Knotts] should be funny and I should play straight for him. That made the show, because I was then able to play straight for all the other comedic characters—Floyd the barber, Otis the town drunk, even Aunt Bee and Opie."[24]

To this day, *The Andy Griffith Show* is remembered for its nostalgic and gently comic perspective on southern life. The storylines of many episodes feature gentle and readily resolved conflicts, such as Opie playing a practical joke on his father, or Andy fretting over a miscommunication, or Barney hoping to triumph over any criminal unlucky enough to cross his comic path. In one episode, Barney worries that the state police will laugh because their jail is empty. "They're going to think this is just a hick town where nothing ever happens," but Andy soothes his agitated deputy: "Well, now, you've got to admit, that's about the size of it" ("Manhunt"). Several plots feature the townsfolk outsmarting outsiders, whether the state police or traveling musicians or any other sophisticates who might wander across Mayberry's borders, but these issues are readily resolved. When an out-of-town prisoner calls Andy a "hick troublemaker," his son Opie impetuously kicks him for the antisouthern insult ("The Guitar Player"). It does not require much more narrative struggle to resolve the plot.

As Griffith stated simply of his program, "The central theme was love,"[25] and David Bushman, a curator of The Paley Center for Media, praised its wholesome themes: "Mayberry embodied a childhood view of the world, where morality was unambiguous and people were kind."[26] Robert Thompson, professor of popular culture at Syracuse University, extolled Griffith's generosity in his performances—"Andy let Sheriff Taylor become the pillar of normalcy and sanity, and let the jokes go to Barney. That's hard for a star to do"—and commented on his admiration for the actor's character: "If I had to give a warmth award . . . I can't think who in the history of television would exceed Sheriff Andy Taylor."[27] In a retrospective summary of Griffith's career, Wayne Curtis noted the star's ability to win his audience's favor: "[Griffith] had a way of cocking his head upward before delivering any line that had a slightly ironic edge, just to let you know we were all in this together. Andy gathers us in the comfortable middle."[28] For many viewers of *The Andy Griffith Show*, the program and its star infused standard storylines of the sitcom format with a warmth and good-natured humor found to be lacking in other network fare, both among its contemporaries and successors.

Notable as well, *The Andy Griffith Show* mostly treated its characters as characters, not caricatures, and depicted southern life respectfully, if comically, in a stark shift from prevailing television portrayals of wacky southern yokels. During the initial broadcasting of *The Andy Griffith Show*, it competed for viewers against several other southern-themed sitcoms, including *The Real McCoys* (1957–63), *The Beverly Hillbillies* (1962–71), *Petticoat Junction* (1963–70), and *Green Acres* (1965–71).[29] For the most part, *The Andy Griffith Show* portrays southerners with sympathy and respect, in contrast to these other southern sitcoms that depicted the region as mostly inhabited by rubes and yahoos. To some degree this is likely an effect of the fact that, more so than most southern sitcoms of this era, *The Andy Griffith Show* featured southern actors, not actors playing southern, notably in the lead roles of Andy Griffith's Andy Taylor and Don Knotts's Barney Fife. Born in Morgantown, West Virginia, and a graduate of West Virginia University, Knotts commented on his roots: "All of my family in West Virginia were rural people."[30] At the very least, these stars contributed a level of (comic) authenticity to their performances, and as Knotts recalled,

Griffith frequently suggested edits to the show's writers, encouraging them to create more realistic, if nonetheless humorous, dialogue: "Andy was a great one for calling the writers when they had written something that didn't ring true. He would say, 'I have an uncle in North Carolina who's just like this guy and he wouldn't say that.' 'Well, what would he say?' He'd tell them and they'd write it down."[31] In their supporting roles as Goober and Gomer Pyle, George Lindsey and Jim Nabors employed a cornpone southern dialect, yet as much as this exaggerated diction leans into regressive stereotypes, the two men, separated in age by only two years, grew up in the nearby towns of Fairfield and Sylacauga, Alabama, and impart a whiff of authenticity into otherwise heavily stereotyped roles.[32] Although not a native southerner, Manhattanite Frances Bavier, who played Aunt Bee, relocated to the South soon after completing her tenure with *The Andy Griffith Show*, choosing Siler City, North Carolina, as her new home. This is not to suggest that *The Andy Griffith Show* completely avoided southern stereotypes, but, as evident in the words of Jyles J. Coggins, former mayor of Raleigh, it hit closer to the mark than its rivals: "Although I believe the shows are somewhat exaggerated in reflecting the naiveté and hickishness of small-town Southern people . . . the basic qualities of goodness of the people and genuine concern for one another and the community are still true to North Carolina."[33]

Despite the fact that Griffith reigned as one of Hollywood's most popular actors for the eight-year run of *The Andy Griffith Show* and lived in California during this time, the popular press continued to treat him as a southern rube, thus shackling him with a persona that would prove extremely limiting once his program concluded. For example, Chester Morrison's article in *Look* included a captioned photograph of Griffith with his gun and dog that reads: "He likes huntin' too, and if you can take his word for it, his dawg is one of the best retrievers anybody ever saw."[34] Another article of this era, Donald Freeman's profile of the star in *The Saturday Evening Post*, gyrated between mocking Griffith as a hillbilly and simultaneously acknowledging his sophistication: "Griffith, at 37, reshaped by show business and Southern California, seems to belie [the label of hillbilly]. He knows now what room service is. He has learned to yell '*Ole!*' with the bullfight crowd in Mexico. He enjoys concerts and opera and talks knowledgeably of music, from Mozart to Monk. He tips well. He can read a wine list. He has developed a taste for fettuccini and enchiladas."[35] The litany of southern stereotypes Griffith has now apparently transcended—an ignorance of such basic amenities as room service, an inability to speak a single word of another language, a refusal to tip servers, and a distaste for drinking wine (it goes unsaid, but surely in contrast to an assumed preference for moonshine)—testifies to the widespread and unquestioned prevalence of antisouthern prejudice. Surely the entertainer who could parody Tchaikovsky's *Swan Lake* and Shakespeare's *Romeo and Juliet* had long been aware of Mozart's compositions, but Freeman appeared unable to divorce the star from his roles.

One of the savvier aspects of Griffith's star persona arises in the fact that he would at times accentuate his southern mannerisms and at other times downplay them, depending on which audiences, from producers to audiences at home, were before him. Certainly, Griffith's associates believed he emphasized his southern qualities to disarm his interlocutors, a viewpoint expressed by Sheldon Leonard, one of the producers of *The Andy Griffith Show*: "Andy still tries to get you to underrate him as a rube, with this impression of excessive simplicity. He'll be happier when he accepts the natural changes in himself as inevitable."[36] Jim Fritzell, one of the program's script writers, similarly affirmed: "Like so many country people, Andy doesn't want to outgrow his past. He'd like to remain earthy, but his education and his awareness of the world keep sneaking in."[37] Comments along these lines presume a sharp break between the South and the rest of the United States, such that its natal denizens are inherently conflicted by their loyalties to their past and their increasing sophistication beyond its borders.

As much as *The Andy Griffith Show* represents the apex of his career, it also left Griffith typecast as Andy Taylor. He recalled that Hollywood executives attributed "my success to some nonsense that I was only playing myself,"[38] and he further stated: "People out here in California thought Andy Taylor was who I was. So I had to prove I was an actor."[39] In a particularly gruesome visualization of his desire to escape typecasting, Griffith dreamed that he murdered Don Knotts, beating him to death with his fists: "It was so vivid.... His head was just swinging there. I had people get rid of his body. Then I woke up, wet all over.... I'm sure part of the dream was an expression of my self-doubt at that time. But the biggest message was quite simple: I was trying to kill the image of Sheriff Taylor and everything connected with it. I had to kill it, you see, or I wasn't going to get work—which would have *truly* killed me."[40] Griffith's dream of murdering Don Knotts speaks to his desperate attempts to reframe his southern star persona, which industry executives consistently denied him. He recalled asking his manager, "Say, you think I oughta lose my southern accent?," to which his manager replied, "Sure . . . if you want to try another line of work."[41]

Throughout the 1970s and early 1980s, Griffith attempted to recalibrate his star persona through new roles, and although he remained in the public eye and occasionally drew strong reviews, his career appeared to be heading slowly downward. His 1971 sitcom, *The New Andy Griffith Show*, which echoed the basic premise of *The Andy Griffith Show*, flopped. He played a range of other roles, including guest-starring turns in *The Mod Squad* (1968–73), *Hawaii Five-O* (1968–80), and *The Doris Day Show* (1968–73), as well as several, mostly forgettable, TV movies, such as *Winter Kill* (1974) and *The Girl in the Empty Grave* (1977). In these latter productions he played sheriffs, suggesting the lingering influence of Sheriff Andy Taylor even in noncomic roles. Throughout this period, Griffith felt hampered by his southern persona: "What I was doing didn't mesh with their image of me, and they weren't going to let me out of the box."[42]

After fighting against southern typecasting for the approximately twenty years since the conclusion of *The Andy Griffith Show*, Griffith accepted the lead role in *Matlock* (1986–95), playing a cantankerous and thrifty defense attorney in Atlanta, who, in the tradition of Perry Mason, exonerates his clients by solving the crimes of which they are accused. In a teasing nod to Griffith's past starring role as Andy Taylor, the series' first episode, "The Judge," features Matlock identifying Dick Van Dyke's character as the killer, thus putting leading stars of eponymous 1960s sitcoms in direct competition in a fictional courtroom. Griffith appreciated his new character, saying, "I happen to love the character. He's a very bright, cagey guy. He's very vain and cheap. I always loved Jack Benny. And I do little takes of Jack Benny as Matlock."[43] Once again, Griffith comfortably inhabited a southern character, and as television executive Fred Silverman observed: "The appeal of *Matlock* isn't in any tricks but in Andy's skill in creating such a memorable character. He has that thing, which you almost can't define, that likability that audiences go for on television year after year."[44] After so many years trying to escape southern typecasting, Griffith again succumbed to its allure and financial remuneration. *Matlock* ran for nine seasons, on NBC from 1986 to 1992 and then on ABC from 1992 to 1995, again keeping Griffith in the public eye as a genial embodiment of easygoing, if also eagle-eyed in his crime solving, southern charm.

Andy Griffith, The Andy Griffith Show, and Yokel Stereotypes

As much as Griffith's career testifies to the challenges of overcoming southern stereotypes, so too does the legacy of *The Andy Griffith Show*, for it remained an outlier in depicting the South in a manner relatively free of stereotypes for the decades from the 1950s to the 1990s. In contrast, many films and television programs portrayed the good-natured shenanigans of backwoods southerners clashing with law enforcement, such as *Smokey and the Bandit* (1977, along with its sequels in 1980 and 1983), starring Burt Reynolds (a Michiganer), and television programs such as *The Dukes of Hazzard* (1979–85), starring John Schneider (a New Yorker) and Tom Wopat (a Wisconsinite). To some degree, *The Golden Girls* (1985–92), set in Miami, heralded a new vision of the southern sitcom, even if only one of its four lead characters—Rue McClanahan's Blanche Devereaux—was herself a southerner. Linda Bloodworth-Thomason, originally from Poplar Bluff, Missouri, created two of the more successful southern comedies of the late twentieth century—*Designing Women* (1986–93) and *Evening Shade* (1990–94)—further advancing television's portrayal of southern people away from the hick stereotypes of decades past. Among the four lead actors of *Designing Women*, Dixie Carter (McLemoreville, Tennessee), Delta Burke (Orlando, Florida), and Annie Potts (Nashville, Tennessee) were native southerners, again illustrating that one of the more effective strategies for tempering stereotypes is to cast actors who recognize, and can thus eschew, their exaggerations.

Notwithstanding the genial southern persona he presented for so much of his career, Griffith acknowledged the wide divergence between Sheriff Andy Taylor and himself, most notably in admitting his emotional detachment and even violent tendencies. Perhaps surprisingly, his candor on these issues did not notably detract from his widespread appeal. Concerning his reticence to show emotion, Griffith once stated, "It's the way we mountain people are. . . . My own grandpappy never showed big emotion but once in his life. Lying on his deathbed, he suddenly got up and kissed my grandma gently on the cheek—he'd never been seen before even to touch her! Then he took to his bed and died. One emotional act in his whole life, but no one ever forgot it."[45] Indeed, Griffith wished he could emulate Andy Taylor's laidback manner instead of unleashing his anger: "I wish I could be like Andy Taylor. He's nicer than I am—more outgoing and easygoing. I get awful mad awful easy."[46] During the filming of *A Face in the Crowd*, he hinted strongly that he abused his wife: "I did a lot of things to Barbara [his wife] . . . mostly with silence."[47] In another interview he expounded further: "I guess I sort of became this character during shooting. That's how it is with me: I can't just play-act a part; I have to *be* it. And more'n once I'd come home still all wound up in the story and give Barbara a little dose of Lonesome Rhodes. And I'll clue you in. That was tough on Barbara because he ain't a very decent guy to have around the house."[48] In an article published during the run of *The Andy Griffith Show*, Donald Freeman reported that the actor's explosive temper was well known in the industry—"Griffith does harbor one of the most ferocious tempers extant, his low boiling point—along with his otherwise gracious manners—being parcel to the tradition of the hot-blooded Southerner."[49] Fans of *The Andy Griffith Show* likely noticed that in a few episodes he wore an arm cast owing to a "fishing accident"; in reality, the broken bones resulted when he punched a door.

In another instance of a southern star embodying troubling aspects of southern culture—in this instance, its violent underbelly—Griffith and *The Andy Griffith Show* comforted Americans with a wholesome depiction of the South, even though the networks' news programs documented the brutal force of racism and white southerners' intransigent resistance to integration. As Sara Eskridge acknowledges of the purported pleasures of "rube-tube" programming in the 1960s, "For southerners, shows like *The Real McCoys* and *The Beverly Hillbillies* provided a positive portrayal of southern people in contrast to the near-constant images of southern violence shown on the news. For the rest of the country, rural comedies had an anesthetic effect that was based partly on their ability to invoke nostalgia as well as their ability to conveniently ignore or gloss over troubling aspects of the present."[50] In observing the cloaked aggression hidden by Griffith's southern star persona and the anti-Black violence prevalent in the South throughout the 1960s and beyond, I am not attempting to draw a parallel in their scope, or even in their intentionality, but simply in their baring of a simple truth behind personas and other cultural fantasies, both those of individual stars and of entire geographic regions: best face forward with sunny smiles turned up, and the unsavory, even violent and hateful, elements cloaked far from view.

6

TINA TURNER
Southern by Birth, Swiss by Choice

With her 1964 song "Mississippi Goddam," Nina Simone told the South precisely what she thought of its long history of racism and her horror over its persistent dehumanization of Black people. Following a stunningly brutal string of racist violence, including the killings of Emmett Till and Medgar Evers in Mississippi and the 16th Street Baptist Church bombing in Alabama that killed four children, Simone sang in angry reply, "Alabama's got me so upset, / Tennessee's made me lose my rest, / And everybody knows about Mississippi *goddam*." Simone believed her candor about southern racism torpedoed her recording career, and she later left the United States altogether, living as an expatriate in such lands as Barbados, Liberia, England, the Netherlands, and France. Looking back at her experiences, she mused, "I wouldn't change being a part of the civil rights movement . . . but some of the songs that I sang . . . hurt my career"; concerning her status as an expat, she stated simply, "I left this country because I didn't like this country. I didn't like what it was doing to my people and I left."[1] As this brief example attests, those who tell the truth about southern racism, particularly Black entertainers, are often penalized for their honesty. For all its purported liberalism, the entertainment industry frequently marginalizes stars who speak openly about racism, sexism, and other forms of discrimination, fearful of generating a backlash from any racist, sexist, or otherwise discriminatory patrons. And so as much as authenticity stands as a hallmark of so many star personas, authenticity coupled with candor can threaten a star's livelihood.

Similar to Simone in her status as an expat, Tina Turner also left the South far behind, but she suffered no penalties to her star persona, despite the real potential that fans might take umbrage at her rejection of the South in particular and of the United States as a whole. Born in neighboring southern states and separated by only six years in age—Simone was born in 1933 in Tryon, North Carolina, and Tina in 1939 in Nutbush, Tennessee—the two encountered the racism of the South during their formative years and their professional careers.[2] The trajectory of Tina's career, both as an individual and as a singer, involves her early identification as a southern star but then her muted transcendence of the South and increasing embrace of European cultures. In many ways, this trajectory overlaps with Tina's singing partnership with Ike Turner. Ike is often credited as recording the first rock-and-roll song, "Rocket 88" (1951), and the pair met when Tina joined Ike and his band for a set one evening at a St. Louis–area nightclub. They married in 1962, and their Ike and Tina Turner Revue scored a number of hits in the 1960s and 1970s. Following years of spousal abuse, Tina divorced Ike in 1978. After several years attempting to restart her career, Tina phenomenally succeeded with her multiplatinum *Private Dancer* album (1984), for which she won three Grammy awards and which buoyed her to superstar status. Moving forward from this pivotal year, she released a string of successful records and headlined sold-out tours for the ensuing decades until her retirement. Notably, Tina's 1980s comeback coincided with her divulging of her abusive marriage to Ike, and in many ways she codes the abuses of the South as reflective of the abuse meted out by her former husband. Tina survived, and thus transcended, both an abusive husband and a racist region, and by consistently employing a forward-looking rhetoric, she maintained her appeal by determinedly moving beyond her painful past.

For fans encountering Tina in the 1960s and early 1970s, her southernness stood out as a strong part of her performance persona, owing to the simple fact that several of her hits were either autobiographical or otherwise southern in their settings. Considering the songs associated with her, Tina affirmed in her autobiography *My Love Story* (2018), "How did I pick my songs? It didn't have to be a song I could relate to in terms of experience. In fact, I never liked autobiographical songs because I'd done enough of those, and I sometimes got tired of singing the blues. I had to like the lyrics, but the melody was also very important to me because that's what motivates me to get into the delivery. I like songs that can go both ways and appeal to the young and the old."³ As these words suggest, Tina segued from her early autobiographical songs—the ones that she had "done enough of"—to ones that related to her experiences more generally. Of course, Tina did not always pick her songs, especially during her years with the Ike and Tina Turner Revue, but they nonetheless evince strong connections to her life story. Ike and Tina scored three Top 40 hits in 1960 and 1961: "A Fool in Love" (No. 27), "It's Gonna Work Out Fine" (No. 14), and "Poor Fool" (No. 38). "A Fool in Love" and "Poor Fool" tell standard stories of unrequited love and are mostly memorable for Tina's paradoxically soaring yet earthy vocals, but in "It's Gonna Work Out Fine," she sings directly to Ike and alludes to their 1962 marriage. "Ike, I went to see the preacher man," she intones, to which he replies, "The preacher man, you must be losin' your mind"; she soon continues, "I started making wedding plans." In this lyrical example of art imitating life, Tina and Ike established themselves as a couple for new fans, asking them to consider their songs as a reflection of their lives together.

While not directly relevant to her southern star persona but of deep significance to the ways in which racism influenced her career, in 1966 Tina recorded "River Deep—Mountain High" with producer Phil Spector, famed for his "Wall of Sound" formula. Now recognized as a classic, the record flopped in the United States, as Tina documented: "That record just never found a home. It was too black for the pop stations, and too pop for the black stations. Nobody gave it a chance."⁴ The song nonetheless flourished in Europe, hitting No. 3 on the charts in the United Kingdom, No. 1 in Spain, and No. 9 in the Netherlands. Most importantly, impressed by Tina's vocal dynamism and her infectious performance style, the Rolling Stones invited Ike and Tina to perform as their opening act. The positive European reception of "River Deep—Mountain High" foreshadowed Tina's eventual decision to become an expat, as it signaled the wider possibilities available to Black artists there.

As further evidence of the ways in which racism shaped Tina's career during this era, contemporary reviews, even positive ones, were often racially coded. Such bias is evident in Ernest Dunbar's comparison of Tina to an animal: "She springs out onstage like a lioness in heat, mini-skirt cut to just below her womanhood"; he later commented that she was "twisting like a rutting mink" in her performance.⁵ A *Newsweek* article in 1969 described Ike and Tina's show as a "sexual-revival meeting . . . [that] is the soul brother's answer to Radio City

Music Hall" and commented as well on "the Mississippi Ike who flavors his speech with words like 'onliest' and 'gunmens.'"[6] For the cover of their 1968 *Outta Season* album, Tina and Ike responded to such racism and further established their southern roots by parodying the South's blackface minstrel shows. The image depicts them in whiteface, smiling and eating watermelons, in a defiant, if comic, retort to rampant bigotry.

In the early 1970s, Tina and Ike scored three more Top 40 hits: "I Want to Take You Higher" (No 34), their cover of Creedence Clearwater Revival's "Proud Mary" (No. 4), and "Nutbush City Limits" (No. 22). The latter two are set in the South, and reflecting on their interpretation of "Proud Mary," Tina enthused, "We made that song our own. . . . I loved the Creedence version, but I like ours better after we got it down, with the talking and all. I thought it was more rock 'n' roll."[7] The autobiographical and southern aspects of her persona are also captured in "Nutbush City Limits," which Tina described as "the hit song I'd written about my hometown. The words 'A church house, gin house,' came naturally to me—these were my childhood memories set to music."[8] In their concerts Tina and Ike frequently performed the Rolling Stones' 1969 No. 1 hit "Honky Tonk Woman"—another song set in the South, telling the tale of "a gin-soaked barroom queen in Memphis." Tina commented on the racial back-and-forth between the song's creators and her interpretation of it as "Honky Tonk Women": "I like the blues influence in Mick [Jagger]'s music. . . . He takes old, old black songs and makes them over, and I take them from him and make them sound the way they might have originally sounded."[9] More so, in changing this lyric singer's voice from male to female, Tina identifies herself as one of these "honky tonk women," and as Maureen Mahon explicates, wholly reformulates the song's sexual politics: "In just over three minutes, Turner's version of 'Honky Tonk Women' creates a sexy and self-possessed character who can keep up with the guys when it comes to sexual appetite and introduces a singer who can more than keep up with the rock guys when it comes to music-making."[10]

In a mostly overlooked episode of her biography, during the ambiguous period when her marriage to Ike was crumbling but before their divorce was finalized and before she firmly rebranded herself as a solo artist, Tina recorded a country album, *Tina Turns the Country On!*, in 1974. The album sold poorly but earned her a Grammy nomination for Best Female R&B Performance, and it was certainly no shame to lose to Aretha Franklin for "Ain't Nothing Like the Real Thing." This album includes covers of Hank Snow's "I'm Movin' On," Dolly Parton's "There'll Always Be Music," and Kris Kristofferson's "Help Me Make It through the Night," among others, and showcases her vocal talents in a genre that has long marginalized Black voices. In her study of Black talents in country music, Francesca Royster states of *Tina Turns the Country On!*, "Tina has the chance to . . . reengage traditional country modes of lyricism and nostalgia and the yearning for freedom in an extended and public way, something that has been difficult for other Black women to accomplish as either fans or performers."[11] Had this album been a greater success, Tina would likely have leaned more heavily into country music, potentially accentuating the southern aspects of her star persona in groundbreaking ways and even shifting the history of Nashville itself.

As these collective fragments framed Tina as a southern entertainer during the early years of her career, her divorce from Ike signaled a sea change in her public persona, one who shed the troubles of her past, birthed a new self, and rarely looked back. She now represented herself as a survivor moving forward with her life, as one who had endured abuse that would have incapacitated others but instead demonstrated her impossible fortitude. "She is nothing if not a survivor,"[12] wrote Nancy Collins for *Rolling Stone*, and sounding a similar note while commenting on the *Private Dancer* album, Brian D. Johnson posited that she had "form[ed] a fresh image for [herself] as a wise survivor of the sexual wars."[13] Despite her mistreatment at Ike's hands, Tina refused the label of victim, thus further embodying a virtually preternatural strength: "Someone tells me I was a victim, I become *angry!* . . . I was *not* a victim. . . . If you tell my story to somebody who knows nothing about Tina Turner, they would label me a victim. But I was in control of everything I was doing."[14] Also, she explained the ways in which various circumstances, notably familial and financial ones, left her few options: "It's easy to say I should've [left Ike]. But look at my situation then: I already had one child, and I [had given birth to] another by him. Singing with Ike was how I made my living. And I was living better than I ever had in my life? . . . I was hurt and I was scared, but I couldn't think about going back. I had to keep going forward."[15] In so many instances, progress for Tina entailed pushing forward to a life free from Ike and the South rather than dwelling on any mistreatment she endured.

In addition to the many interviews in which Tina presented this new side of her star persona, several of the songs of the *Private Dancer* album heralded her refashioned identity. As Kurt Loder, the coauthor of Tina's (auto)biography *I, Tina* (1986), observed: "while no encompassing theme had been intended, several of the titles—'I Might Have Been Queen,' 'What's Love Got to Do with It,' 'Show Some Respect'—had the appearance of referring to Tina's life story."[16] (Certainly, "Better Be Good to Me" could be added to Loder's list.) As part of this fresh image, southern references are notably absent from the album—even from "I Might Have Been Queen," written by Jeanette Obstoj and arguably the most biographical song on the album. As Loder documented, "Obstoj listened as Tina narrated her life story, from the cotton-field years back in Nut Bush through Ike and the Revue—the whole saga of pain and oppression, right up to the present."[17] Such lyrics as, "And I might have been queen / I remember the girl in the fields with no name / She had a love / Oh, but the rivers won't stop for me," hint at Tina's past, but the fields are not identified as cotton fields; the river is not named the Mississippi.

A similar pattern can be discerned on Tina's follow-up album, *Break Every Rule* (1986), for she explicitly identified its autobiographical elements as indicative of her post-Ike transformation: "Every track is about the last ten years since my days with Ike, describing what I feel and how I think. It's my life on vinyl."[18] The eponymous track doubles as an achingly touching love song and a strong statement of feminist possibility, and the ironically yet aptly titled "Overnight Sensation" aligns with her phenomenal career renaissance. "Mark Knopfler summed it up perfectly when he wrote the song 'Overnight Sensation' for me,"[19] Tina stated. The song "What You Get Is What You See" riffs on the title of Tina and Ike's 1971 album, *What You Hear Is What You Get*, a live recording of a Carnegie Hall performance. If this song in any way responds to her time with Ike, it pointedly includes the lyric, "And if you wanna love a woman like me / It takes a man to do it / If what you get is what you see / Then I don't want your kind of love." This overview of *Private Dancer* and *Break Every Rule* is not intended to suggest that a clean division can be made between Tina's recordings with Ike and her solo efforts, as she continued performing such crowd-pleasing numbers as "Proud Mary" and "Nutbush City Limits" in concerts throughout the rest of her career. Still, even though she did not drop these southern hits from her set list, nor did she expand their ranks.

While her recording career was rebounding to hitherto unknown heights, Tina starred in *Mad Max: Beyond Thunderdome* (1985) as Aunty Entity, a woman who, having survived an apocalypse, seizes the opportunity to reinvent herself as the ruler of Bartertown, as she explains to the eponymous protagonist played by Mel Gibson: "This nobody had a chance to be somebody." (See figure 7.) This disclosure from Aunty Entity aligns the character with Tina's life story—not that I would refer to her as a "nobody" but in the sense of her meteoric rise from her modest southern roots—and even though Aunty Entity serves as Mad Max's chief antagonist in the film, she remains sympathetic and likeable in the villain's role. Indeed, in a departure from the plot of so many adventure films, she is not killed at the film's conclusion, instead chuckling to Max, "Well, ain't we a pair, raggedy man? Goodbye, soldier." Perhaps surprisingly, Tina rejected the role of Celie in Steven Spielberg's *The Color Purple* (1985): "The part's too old—she's been with every man in town and this man brings her into his house with his wife. No, I know this already from my past."[20] In another account, she criticized this film as a depressing vision of Black life: "Black people can do better than that. I've lived that life with my husband. I've lived down south in the cotton fields. I don't want to do anything I've done."[21] This woman who toiled in cotton fields as a child would never return to them, even to collaborate with Hollywood's hottest director, as she also distanced herself from the film's southern setting. Further along these lines, Tina sought movie roles that would strengthen her persona as a strong, independent woman, as she declared: "They give me drug-bust parts, female police officers. I'm not interested in busting drugs. . . . I don't want to be a part of that. I want to do the period type of stuff that Schwarzenegger did with *Conan*. More *Mad Max*, energetic warrior-woman stuff."[22] In one interview she proposed that she and Cher should have played the title roles of the feminist classic *Thelma and Louise* (1991).[23] Except for music videos and rare short appearances, such as her role as The Mayor in Arnold Schwarzenegger's *Last Action Hero* (1993), Tina eschewed acting for singing owing to the dearth of strong roles for Black women.

Another key aspect of Tina's rejuvenated star persona in the 1980s celebrated her sexiness, a noteworthy achievement for a woman in her forties working in the youth-obsessed milieu of pop music. In a significant shift, she was no longer subjected to the animalistic commentary of certain 1960s critics

FIG. 7. Tina Turner's status as a survivor of southern racism and spousal abuse aligned her with the character of Aunty Entity, who, having survived the terrors of an apocalypse, rose from modest roots to a position of wealth and power.

and was instead celebrated for her apparently eternal beauty, particularly her incredible legs. Joan Gelman recorded of Tina's publicity events, "The paparazzi go wild. They want legs,"[24] and later commented on the exercise regimen that maintained the star's physique: "doing 20 numbers a night is enough to keep the most admired legs in the world rock solid."[25] Notably, her legs drew the admiring eyes of royalty, as Elizabeth Sporkin reported, "Even Prince Charles commented. 'I say,' he told Tina, 'you have the most marvelous legs I've ever seen.'"[26] Not surprisingly, Tina landed an endorsement deal with Hanes hosiery. In the words of John Martin, programming director of the Much Music rock video network: "Her success corresponds with a new way of looking at sexy, self-assured women. She's doing it on her own and she's a heroine because of that."[27] To all her fans amazed by her indefatigable display of beauty and stamina in her forties, Tina confidently stressed her fortitude and future-oriented outlook with one of her favorite lines from her contemporary concert tours, "They ask me when am I going to slow down, and I tell them I'm just getting started."[28]

Tina clearly discerned the importance of her star persona for endearing herself to her fans, while also acknowledging the disjunction between her persona and her personality. As much as her post-Ike image stressed her enduring strength—and thus highlighted her authenticity as a woman who had survived unfathomable suffering—she simultaneously acknowledged that, if her fans assumed a seamless unity between her performing and her private self, her performing self was, in fact, authentically inauthentic. In numerous interviews she admitted that "excitement is what I project onstage. That *is* the exciting things going on in my life. But offstage, you'd probably think I was boring, because I don't live that life I'm projecting. I have a presence about me that prompts people to yell across the street to get my attention, but when they approach me, they quiet themselves."[29] As she explained further, "Onstage I'm Tina Turner. But offstage I love elegance. Onstage, I don't want to be elegant. I like being raw. I mean, I want everything in place, and I want to look good, but the personality presented onstage is about being naughty and having power. That doesn't go with being elegant."[30] Most troubling for Tina was any assumption that the sexually charged image she presented in her performances represented her personal view of sexuality: "It's not something I've been proud of—having sexuality as an image—because mine usually gets associated with raunchy. . . . And it's based solely on what people see when I'm onstage. Even I have thought, *God, look at the picture*. What else can you think when you can look up from the audience and see someone's crotch?"[31] In an extended statement concerning her self-image, she defined herself as a lady, seemingly resigned to the fact that many of her fans might not perceive this deeper aspect of her personality: "I patterned myself from classy ladies. I take as much from them as I can, but I take it naturally, because I'm not going to be a phony about it. I'm not going to walk around in Chanel suits or Gucci suits—that's a little bit too much, because that's not my nature. But watching my manners, caring about not being overdressed at the wrong time—it matters how I carry myself—that's what I'm concerned about as far as being a lady. Nobody would ever think that Tina Turner is a lady. I am."[32]

As these statements evince, Tina carefully constructed her public persona throughout her career, and thus they hint that she long curated her presentation of herself as a native southerner. Certainly, she frequently commented on the South, and for the most part, she succinctly yet nostalgically recalled her southern upbringing, as told in her autobiographies *I, Tina* and *My Love Story*, as well as in various interviews over the course of her career, portraying herself as a contented child despite the familial contretemps that occasionally flared. "I enjoyed growing up in Nutbush, a don't-blink-or-you'll-miss-it little town on Highway 19 in Tennessee,"[33] she stated, and she depicted herself as enamored by the southern countryside: "Listen, roaming the pastures of Tennessee, it was green and beautiful. You could never find me; I was always out there."[34] At the same time that she adopted a generally optimistic framing of her childhood, she employed cotton fields as a synecdoche for any distaste she felt for the South, speaking candidly about the backbreaking labor expected of the region's Black people: "I wouldn't change a thing [about my childhood] except that I hated working in the cotton fields. No, thank you, I could live without that,"[35] she averred, as she also mentioned the ways in which this grinding work fueled her dreams: "As a kid, I wanted to get away from working in the cotton fields of Tennessee. I dreamed of going to Hollywood, although I had no idea where that was."[36] Growing up in the South prior to the U.S. Supreme Court's *Brown vs. Board of Education* decision of 1954, Tina attended segregated schools and registered the injustice of such discrimination by again focusing on cotton-field labors: "But Carver [High School] was all black; the white kids went across town to Haywood High. And we had a split season because of the cotton. We picked it with our hands, didn't have the machines yet, and the children had to help."[37] As these examples demonstrate, many of Tina's critiques of the South are somewhat muted, yet others strike a surprisingly piquant note, such as her final thoughts regarding Tennessee upon moving to St. Louis at a mere sixteen years old: "I felt I had outlived Tennessee. There was nothing there for me anymore."[38]

    This is not to suggest that Tina ignored southern racism in accounts of her life, but that she mostly mentions its brutal force in passing and then proceeds to another topic—that is to say, she looked forward to her life beyond the South rather than dwelling on past travails, in a manner similar to her reluctance to discuss her violent marriage to Ike in detail. In one of her more candid moments, she asserted of life in the South, "The whites had a fear instilled in the blacks so they could control them and keep them respectful."[39] In describing her travels with the Ike and Tina Turner Revue, she cited several racist incidents, such as the following: "During the 1960s, it was very hard for us to travel in the Deep South because we were likely to run into dangerous racial situations. I can't tell you how many times I witnessed *this* conversation," as she then explained the necessity of bribing policemen who harassed them over bogus offenses.[40] Tina and the other members of the Revue knew to present themselves as inconspicuously as possible, a challenge that became even more difficult when traveling with a white woman: "When Rhonda [Graam, the band's road manager] started working for us in 1964, we had to be extra careful on Southern roads because the sight of a white woman traveling with a black band was guaranteed to attract attention and hostility."[41] Occasionally hints of her distrust of southern states and white southerners creep into accounts of her past, such as in her recollection of the fateful night when she fled from Ike: "I had 36 cents and a Mobil credit card in my pocket, my face was battered, and my clothes were filthy and stained with blood. And I was black. In Dallas. It occurred to me that, under the circumstances, any sensible innkeeper would probably turn me away."[42] In another retelling of this moment, she said of this hotel manager who allowed her a room without payment: "And out of the goodness of that man's heart—I mean, this was *Texas*, you know?—he said, 'All right.'"[43] The phrases "In Dallas" and "this was *Texas*" convey her incredulousness that kindness to Black people would be extended in this southern redoubt of troubled race relations. Also, in a telling passage, Tina acknowledged southern racism but then simply moved forward: "Then we'd be traveling through Alabama or someplace, and getting run off the road by pickups full of honkies with rifles. I mean, I saw everything down there."[44] She admits that she "saw everything down there"—a troubling statement of the perniciousness and prevalence of violent white supremacy—but then continues her narrative to other matters.

Notably, some of the more troubling racist events recorded in *I, Tina* are narrated by her coauthor Kurt Loder. For example, Loder recounts the agonizing death of Ike's father after white men kicked holes in his stomach, the local hospital refused him treatment, and he died slowly over the subsequent three years.[45] Loder also mentions the horrifying moment when the mother of Ike's business manager "witnessed a black man being castrated in the street back in Shreveport, Louisiana."[46] On the whole, Tina acknowledges southern racism but does not dwell on it, rhetorically pushing forward to more triumphant aspects of her life story.

In contrast to her style of recalling incidents of southern racism with succinct candor, Tina rapturously described her first visions of life beyond the South and anticipated her eventual status as an expat: "For a girl coming from Nutbush and St. Louis, it was like being transported to another world. I felt an immediate connection with the city [London] and its people, like love at first sight. Then, *even* then, I didn't want to go back to America. I wanted to stay! I felt the same way when I saw France and Germany for the first time. Somehow, these faraway places seemed like home."[47] As early as 1987 she announced her plans to leave the United States, as reported in *Jet* magazine: "The singer . . . said . . . she's looking forward to the move across the Atlantic. 'This is where I feel I belong.'"[48] "Europe offers me security. It is a place where I have found more success, more appreciation, and that makes me feel comfortable," she mentioned on another occasion.[49] As part of her forward-looking rhetoric, and in her move from the rural South to Switzerland, from an abusive marriage with Ike to a happy marriage with her long-time partner Erwin Bach, and from her faltering stardom in the late 1970s and early 1980s to international superstardom for the remainder of her life, there is, as Brian D. Johnson declares, "a storybook quality to Turner's life."[50] Indeed, in her later years, Tina looked back on her career as somewhat of a fairy tale, particularly in describing her marriage to Bach: "I'd already tried my luck with American men, so I decided to look into the European variety. . . . They're so sensitive to women. I'm not putting down American men, but European men have a different attitude when it comes to women."[51] Comparing her wedding with Ike to her wedding with Bach, Tina declared, "Well, if that wedding was a nightmare, the day I became Mrs. Erwin Bach was going to be a dream. No, a fairy tale, complete with a princess, a prince, and a castle!"[52] She soon added about her wedding dress, "When I tried it on, I had a real Cinderella moment."[53] Part of Tina's fairy tale necessitated her final break with the United States and her pursuit of Swiss citizenship: "I also made a commitment to our life together in Switzerland by applying for citizenship. I don't want to give the wrong impression about my decision to give up my American passport. A lot of thought went into it. I will never surrender the part of me that was born in America, or that feels 'American.' But my life changed when I fell in love with Erwin and started living in Europe. With every passing year, I had fewer and fewer reasons to go back to America."[54] In a nostalgic view, Tina aligned her birth state with her new homeland, discerning their geographical similarities: "Switzerland is not Tennessee, but I'm always reminded of the landscapes I enjoyed when I was growing up, especially when I see the farms and meadows in the Swiss countryside."[55] Appreciative of her past but now living halfway around the world from it, Tina, both herself and as represented through her star persona, appears to have fully transcended her southern roots.

Similar to her forward-looking rhetoric in her autobiographies, Tina mostly refrained from addressing Ike following the dissolution of their marriage, preferring to discuss her accomplishments and career trajectory rather than looking back to her painful past. Yet in a few intriguing passages, she explicitly linked Ike to the South itself, connecting her abusive husband to its mores. "Despite his reputation for being an outlaw, Ike had a personality that people liked. He was fun. Kind of Southern,"[56] she stated in her autobiography *My Love Story*. Also, in a moment of compassion, she blamed the South for Ike's abuse: "He had a lot of anger as a Black man growing up in Mississippi."[57] Surviving an abusive husband like Ike could be considered metaphorically akin to surviving the South's racism, but Tina was determined to see herself, and to be seen by others, as a survivor, even to the extent of appreciating Ike's role in her life: "I can't even say my relationship with Ike was a bad one, because I took from that. I took from everything. And I won."[58] The "everything" that Tina alludes to would apparently also refer to her southern upbringing and the sting of the region's racism. And while this chapter has focused on Tina as an entertainer, she adopted a similar rhetorical strategy in discussing her spiritual evolution from the Baptist Church, a prevalent faith of Southerners, to Buddhism: "I went from Baptist prayers to Buddhism—different words at a time when I needed different words—but I was always spiritual."[59] Always moving forward, rarely looking back for more than a lingering glance, progressing from an abusive husband to a doting one, from the Baptist Church to Buddhism, from Nutbush, Tennessee, to Zurich, Switzerland, Tina polished her star persona by allowing her southern roots to wither, slowly but determinedly, until they were literally half a world apart.

DOLLY PARTON
The Hillbilly Queen of Crossover Self-Censorship

"I'm proud of being from the South. At least rednecks and hillbillies are interesting," affirmed Dolly Parton in her autobiography *Dolly: My Life and Other Unfinished Business* (1994), in a full-throated, if ironic, defense of her regional roots in eastern Tennessee.[1] In another such statement of regional pride, she proclaimed, "But I'm proud of my hillbilly, white trash background. To me that keeps you humble; that keeps you good. And it doesn't matter how hard you try to outrun it—if that's who you are, that's who you are. It'll show up once in a while."[2] With her winsome stream of hillbilly humility, and from the early moments of her career to the present, Parton has navigated a steady stream of paradoxes—overtly sexy yet endearingly wholesome, glamorously glitzy yet heartachingly sincere, unabashedly southern yet wholeheartedly all-American—all the while both dissolving and fortifying any perceived borders between her show business persona and her inner self. Along the way she has notched an extraordinary range of achievements and accolades: written over three thousand songs; sold over 100 million records; scored twenty-five No. 1 country singles; won eleven Grammy Awards (with over fifty total nominations); earned nominations for Oscar, Emmy, and Tony Awards; been honored with a Country Music Association Lifetime Achievement Award and the designation as a Kennedy Center Honoree. From her country music roots in the 1960s to her crossover to mainstream pop in the 1970s, from the onset of her film career and the opening of her Dollywood theme park in the 1980s to her established status as an American icon in the 1990s, and then continuing throughout the ensuing decades, Parton has carefully designed her southern star persona such that she transcends longstanding cultural divisions by maintaining yet another paradox of her persona—inscrutable candor. She speaks with a spunky forthrightness while also clouding any controversial views she might hold, particularly in regard to religion, feminism, and politics.

For so many stars, authenticity serves as the bedrock, virtually unassailable foundation of their personas, and as Graham Hoppe summarizes of this dynamic for Parton, "What Dolly Parton understands is that the 'hillbilly' aspects of her upbringing, her origin story, endear her to people who share that background and create an unmistakable air of authenticity for those who don't."[3] But as authenticity anchors the personas of many stars, Parton, in complementary contrast, simultaneously presents herself as wholly inauthentic, as a genuine fake, for few stars so candidly admit that their personas are facades designed to enhance their appeal, that they recognize the necessity and benefits of playing characters representing themselves to their fans. As she bluntly stated of her self-presentation, "The thing that's always worked for me is the fact that I look so totally artificial, but am so totally real,"[4] as she has also recognized the necessity of separating her persona from her personal identity: "I'm careful never to get caught up in the Dolly image . . . because if you start believing the public persona *is* you, you get frustrated and mixed up."[5] On a fundamental level, Parton designed her persona as a ploy to pique the audience's attention and to seize the public spotlight: "The glare and the glitter is a gimmick—fun for the audience, fun for me, something we can share together. . . . If people think I'm a dumb blonde because of the way I look, then they're dumber than they think I am."[6] Sounding a similar note, she stated, "I've got my work to do and I *like* to look good, but I don't try to keep an image other than just this gimmick appearance that I have."[7] Parton's ready and self-deprecating wit further enhances her appeal, and she has repeatedly summarized the duality of her star persona by noting the high costs of her dazzlingly artificial appearance: "*As I always say, 'It costs a lot to make a person look this cheap.'*"[8] Moreover, Parton, who defines "star quality" as "a combination of personal charisma and intense sex appeal,"[9] recognized that talent alone would never guarantee her—or anyone else—success in the entertainment industry: "If you have talent, people are gonna overlook it . . . unless you've got somethin' to get attention."[10] As Judith Mahoney Pasternak summarized of Parton's celebrity, "Much of her popularity is due to her talents—including her gift for projecting a persona of such immense appeal. Dolly's uncanny mix of candor and coyness has intrigued audiences and critics alike from the start of her career."[11] Notably as well, part of this intrigue emerges from the intersection of frankness and self-censorship, for when speaking on potentially controversial topics, Parton, employing her cagily excessive persona, evades stating any personal opinion she might hold, thus denying fans access to her authentic self while preserving her appeal across various spectrums, both southern and national. Following a brief overview of her career in its building of the authenticity of her southern star persona, this chapter turns to Parton's steadfast refusal to speak candidly about religion, feminism, and politics, thus to better gauge the ways in which her external authenticity creates the paradoxical need for self-censorship.

A longtime Tennessee joke proposes that the state has so many Baptist and Pentecostal churches because they keep splitting into new sects when any argument among parishioners erupts, and it is worth pondering the influence of such conditions on Parton as a young child. Born January 19, 1946, she found herself, the fourth of her parents' twelve children, in a household without electricity tucked in the foothills of the Great Smoky Mountains, a subrange of the Appalachians. Throughout her career Parton has candidly detailed the poverty the family endured, such as in an interview with Connie Berman: "Sometimes I'd see Daddy work until his hands would bleed and bust open. Sometimes Mama would be lyin' there sick and we couldn't afford a doctor. We didn't have nothin' material at all. But we had a lot of each other and that's what counts."[12] Several of Parton's songs detail memories from her youth, including "Coat of Many Colors" (a heartwarming tale of her mother's love), "My Tennessee Mountain Home" (an evocative celebration of Tennessee's idyllic landscape), "I Remember" (a recollection of her parents), and even "Dr. Robert F. Thomas" (an ode to the doctor who delivered her). Perhaps her characterization of her southern upbringing is best summarized in the song "In the Good Old Days (When Times Were Bad)," in which she cherishes the memories of her childhood but sings as well, "No amount of money could pay me / To go back and live through it again."[13] Parton graduated from Sevier County High School in 1964 and immediately moved to Nashville, married Carl Dean in 1966, and enjoyed early success with such songs as "Dumb Blonde," "Something Fishy," and "Just

Because I'm a Woman." With her Smoky Mountain roots showing so clearly in her songs, Parton could enact an authenticity predicated on her modest background. No matter how big a star she became, she would never forget her past.

Parton's big break came in 1967 when Porter Wagoner selected her to replace his retiring "girl singer," Norma Jean Beasler, for his highly successful *The Porter Wagoner Show* (1960–81). They scored an early smash with their first album together, *Just between You and Me,* which won the 1968 Country Music Award for best duet. In short succession the duo recorded a series of songs regarded as classics of this era: "Daddy Was an Old Time Preacher Man," "Please Don't Stop Loving Me," "Put It Off until Tomorrow," "The Pain of Loving You," and many more. Concurrent with her years with Wagoner, Parton scored a number of solo hits, including "Joshua," "Jolene," "Coat of Many Colors," and her cover of "Mule Skinner Blues." Parton's signature look, notably her wigs and sequined dresses, was modeled on what she termed "a loose woman, the ones who throw it around a bit,"[14] and she further explained, "I always liked the looks of our hookers back home. Their big hairdos and makeup made them look *more*. When people say that less is more, I say *more* is more."[15] Pamela Wilson notes of the trajectory of Parton's career that she "was one of the first female country musicians whose career developed in front of the television cameras,"[16] and her good looks and sexy outfits contributed to the buzz generated around her and her performances. Despite the benefits of her flashy appearance, Parton could still identify herself as a musician from and of the rural South throughout her career, such as in the following self-description that stresses her interior authenticity and the benefits of her gimmicky appearance: "I am at heart a simple country woman. . . . I think it's because my persona is oversized and flashy. That makes me a kind of a fish out of water in normal surroundings, but when I am surrounded by things that are just as flashy, I become a fish in water and tend to get lost in the shuffle."[17]

In the defining moment of her career, Parton ended her partnership with Wagoner to pursue a solo career and to broaden her appeal beyond her country music fans—despite the real possibility that her fan base might reject her transitioning to a more pop-based sound. In other words, she might lose the authenticity at the core of her southern star persona by embracing a musical style less connected to the South. Parton memorialized this moment with two songs offering strikingly opposed viewpoints of the same events, evidencing the potential for her songs to express a duality similar to that of her persona. "I Will Always Love You" testifies to her enduring appreciation to Wagoner for the opportunities he granted her, whereas "Light of the Clear Blue Morning" looks forward to a future freed from the shackles of their tempestuous relationship. With typical bravado, Parton asserted her ability to maintain her identity while expanding it: "I'm not leaving country; I'm taking it with me."[18] Her 1977 single "Here You Come Again" trumpeted her crossover appeal, as it became her first million-selling record while hitting No. 1 on the country charts and No. 3 on the pop charts. Blistering reviews of her albums of the late 1970s and early 1980s document music critics' distaste for this new sound, evident in Tom Carson's assessment of her 1978 album *Heartbreaker*: "the quality of her music has gone dramatically down while her fame vaults toward the tinsel regions of instant media celebrity. . . . Parton doesn't act like a sellout as much as she acts like she's had a lobotomy."[19] In his appraisal of her 1979 album *Great Balls of Fire*, Neal Coppage similarly sniped, "If she'd let more of her real self, whoever that is, into her work, we'd no doubt have an album connected with feeling and ideas deep enough to be satisfying."[20] Both reviewers tacitly allude to a perceived conflict between Parton's shifting persona and their expectations for her music—Carson's suggestion that she is a "sellout," Coppage's pining to hear again "her real self"—predicated on the unstated assumptions of country music's genuineness and pop music's fakeness, and not discerning the ways in which her capacious persona incorporates both. At this pivotal moment, Parton's authenticity sparked heated debate among her fans and music critics.

As her fame blossomed with this new crossover sound, Parton began her film career with the blockbuster hit *9 to 5* (1980), costarring with Jane Fonda and Lily Tomlin as administrative assistants trapped in a soulless corporation working under their boss, Mr. Hart (Dabney Coleman), who is repeatedly characterized as a "sexist, egotistical, lying, hypocritical bigot." Notably, Fonda advocated casting Parton in the role of Doralee Rhodes precisely because of her southern roots, as Parton recalled: "[Jane Fonda] is a smart businesswoman and was very up-front about the fact that she thought I would help the film do well in the South."[21] Fonda commented on Parton's star persona: "We developed a character based on who she is and what she seems like. . . . Her persona is so strong, you get somebody mucking about with that and making her self-conscious, and it could be negative."[22] Notably, Doralee Rhodes aspires to success as a country-western singer, and in one of the character's memorable lines she threatens Mr. Hart, "I got a gun in my purse and, up to now, I've been forgiving and forgetting. If you ever say another word about me or make another indecent proposal, I'm gonna get that gun and change you from a rooster to a hen with one shot!" (See figure 8.) Like her fictional counterpart, Parton is known for carrying a gun with her, and such cross-pollinations between the actor and her role have bolstered her star appeal.

Parton's breakout success in *9 to 5* launched a string of movies—*The Best Little Whorehouse in Texas* (1982), *Rhinestone* (1984), *A Smoky Mountain Christmas* (1986), and *Steel Magnolias* (1989)—all of which allowed her to play variations on the theme of her Dolly persona and thus to cement her crossover status with a newly confirmed sense of authenticity. In another indication that she and other country musicians in the 1980s recognized both the challenges and the financial payoffs of enhancing their crossover appeal, she collaborated frequently with Kenny Rogers, another country crossover artist. Their 1983 single "Islands in the Stream" hit No. 1 on the pop charts, and they joined forces again for a

FIG. 8. In her battle with her boss, Mr. Hart, Doralee Rhodes tries to quell her mounting frustration, only to then hogtie him to a chair. Jane Fonda believed casting Dolly Parton in the role would boost the film's profits in southern states, despite any conflict between the region's conservatism and the film's strong feminist message.

Christmas album, *Once upon a Christmas* (1984), that also spawned a television special. In another sign that Parton could successfully juggle the various aspects of her persona that might appear in conflict with one another, she cemented her reputation as one of the greatest country singers of her era with the 1987 release of her *Trio* album with Emmylou Harris and Linda Ronstadt, which was (justly and instantly) heralded as a classic. Branching beyond singing and acting, in 1986 Parton rebranded the theme park Silver Dollar City in Pigeon Forge, Tennessee, as Dollywood, thereby announcing herself as an entrepreneur as well. In this move she encoded another level to her persona and to the myths of the South, as Graham Hoppe describes it as "not just Dolly Parton's imagined South made real . . . [but] the reification of myriad southern imaginaries."[23]

Moving from the 1990s to the present, and with her celebrity so strongly established, Parton has sustained her lasting appeal through a range of high-profile projects. As she assessed her role in the film *Straight Talk* (1992), her biggest Hollywood production of the decade, "We Dollyized it as much as we possibly could. . . . I drug up every old country saying I'd ever heard."[24] Yet as much as Parton had established her crossover superstar status in the years since "Here You Come Again," she, in effect, crossed back over to a primarily country music sound in the late 1990s and early 2000s, releasing a string of bluegrass and country albums that reestablished her *bona fides* as a country musician, with *The Grass Is Blue* winning the 2001 Grammy for Best Bluegrass Album. As she ironically mused of her career trajectory, "Well, the tits and the hair and the personality helped build the whole Dolly deal, but it was my music that brought me out of the Smokies. I had to get rich in order to afford to sing like I was poor again."[25] In the ensuing years Parton has pursued an astounding, almost frenzied, number of projects, including releasing albums and films, producing television shows, pursuing philanthropic endeavors (notably her Dollywood Foundation and her Imagination Library, which sends free books to children), touring the world, and even publishing a novel (*Run, Rose, Run*, cowritten with James Patterson, in 2022).

Given these impressive accomplishments and her continued hold on the public's attention for seven decades, Parton's status as one of the biggest and most beloved southern, national, and international stars stands unquestioned. Indeed, as the United States finds itself mired in increasing partisanship—red states versus blue states, rural versus urban, Republicans versus Democrats—

Parton has lifted herself above the fray, and she is now heralded as a unifying force for a divided nation. In an affirmative assessment of Parton's celebrity, Lindsay Zoladz's *New York Times* article marvels, "Is There Anything We Can All Agree On? Yes: Dolly Parton," and *People* magazine similarly lauds her as "The Music Icon Who Brings the Country Together."[26] Linda Ronstadt, her friend and longtime collaborator, called her a "Southern magnolia blossom that floats on the breeze,"[27] in an apt metaphor of how the singer rises above all cultural frays, particularly those concerning religion, feminism, and politics.

Aligned with the duality of glitzy authenticity in her persona, Parton signals her religious faith in nearly secular (but not agnostic) terms, in which she expresses a firm commitment to God while refraining from revealing any denominational affiliation or recognizable theology. Among the United States, the southern states, frequently referred to as the Bible Belt, are populated with the most religious citizens, with Alabama, Mississippi, and Tennessee leading the nation, followed by Louisiana, Arkansas, and South Carolina.[28] Many southerners, whether natives or newcomers, report that one of the first questions posed to them upon moving to a new town concerns which church they plan to join, and the denizens of many small communities readily recognize the fault lines that must be negotiated among various faith traditions. To wit, identifying as a Baptist may not ensure one's ready inclusion in a new community featuring a range of subdenominations, including Southern Baptists, Free Will Baptists, and Primitive Baptists, among others. Given her awareness of the sometimes-fractious relationships between neighboring churches in eastern Tennessee, and recognizing the possibility that religious affiliations can increase discord and rancor rather than comity and fellowship, Parton bleaches religion of doctrinal issues in favor of an ecumenical spirituality available to all. As Pasternak notes, "although she speaks freely of a close relationship with God, she has never specified what religious denomination she was born into or follows."[29]

Of course, one need not adhere to a particular denomination to experience spirituality, and Parton expresses in her autobiography the importance of her spiritual life: "I felt a need for God and always wanted to have a relationship with him, but I was the ultimate nightmare for a fundamentalist Christian out to save souls. I was a kid with her own opinions."[30] Her sense of spirituality intersects with a gentle gospel of self-improvement, for she sees people's personal relationships with God as their path to more enriching lives: "Whatever will make you your better self and allow you to serve God better, to fulfill your mission, that is your salvation."[31] Parton describes her songwriting as an opportunity to communicate with God, explaining that she composes by entering her "God space" and adding, "I feel like I'm closest to God when I write. I have to leave myself open for the songs to come in or go out."[32] In a related stream of comments, she has consistently sought to maintain her appeal to religious fans while acknowledging the likely dichotomy between their moral values and her sexy persona. For example, when discussing her cover image for a 1978 *Playboy* magazine interview, during the challenges of her crossover to mainstream American appeal, she declared, "It might not offend *me*, but I was afraid maybe a lot of my country fans and some of the people who love me who are of a religious nature might not understand."[33] The interview inside speaks to her attention to any conservative fans who might condemn either her appearance in the publication or her efforts to expand her audience. Similarly concerned about her film *The Best Little Whorehouse in Texas*, Parton opined, "It's a shame the title sounds so risqué because certain people in the Moral Majority who should see it may be turned off."[34] One can discern a whiff of criticism here—should these fundamentalist members of the Moral Majority see the film to recognize themselves as hypocrites similar to those who would shut down the eponymous brothel?—but Parton couches these sentiments in an inviting manner, hoping that all will come see her latest project.

Along with refusing to divulge her religious convictions while presenting herself as deeply spiritual, Parton has long demurred from endorsing feminism while embodying its ethos. In a 1979 interview with Margo Jefferson, as the Equal Rights Amendment to the U.S. Constitution was debated throughout the nation, Parton simultaneously proclaimed her ignorance of the movement while enacting its ideals: "I don't even understand that women's liberation stuff, don't know what it's all about. I'm a lucky person. I'm liberated, free-spirited, free-minded, but it's not something I promote or push—just a natural way I've always lived." Considering these words, Jefferson wrote, "I doubt the emotional as well as the political truth of [Parton's] pronouncement," in a compelling example of a spectator projecting her own vision of Parton onto Parton, despite the surface meaning of the star's words.[35] In a similar example of these dynamics, Parton denied *9 to 5*—an explicitly feminist, if comic, film—imparted a feminist message: "I wouldn't have been involved if I'd thought it was gonna be a sermon of some sort. Not that I'm not for rights for everybody. I'm just sayin' I didn't want to get involved in a political thing."[36] Despite such disavowals, many people view Parton as a feminist and, more so, as a feminist icon. Indeed, *Ms.* magazine honored her as one of its 1986 Women of the Year, along with Winnie Mandela, Maryland senator Barbara Mikulski, and Sharon Gless and Tyne Daly, the stars of *Cagney and Lacey* (1981–88). In her editorial introduction to Parton, Gloria Steinem contemplated the seeming mismatch between Parton and feminism while extolling her unique manifestation of its principles: "People . . . may be surprised to learn that [Dolly Parton and feminism] go together. In fact, she has crossed musical class lines to bring work, real life, and strong women into a world of pop music usually dominated by unreal romance. . . . And her flamboyant style has turned all the devalued symbols of womanliness to her own ends."[37] A feminist who refuses the label of feminist but is identified as such by many feminists: the twists and turns of the Parton persona of southern authenticity become dizzying.

As a further indicator of her determined neutrality, Parton refuses to divulge her political leanings and likens battling political parties to inimical religious factions. On this point she affirmed, "But as far as gettin' politically involved, it's like bein' denominations. If you're a Democrat the Republicans hate you; if you're a member of one church, then the other ones hate you."[38] And so, akin to her ambiguous opinions on spirituality and feminism, Parton's politics serve as a Rorschach test for her fans, as they collectively attempt to interpret any telltale signs that might disclose her partisan leanings. For instance, in her autobiography she recalled her reaction upon learning of Democratic President John F. Kennedy's assassination: "I had loved John Kennedy. Not in the way a woman loves a man but in the way one idealist recognizes another and loves him for that place within themselves that they share. I didn't know a lot about politics, but I knew that a lot of things were wrong and unjust and that Kennedy wanted to change them."[39] While denying any political affinity for Kennedy, she nonetheless aligned herself with his racial politics, further explaining that her current boyfriend said, "I'm glad they shot the n——-lovin' son of a bitch!" Her autobiography notes that she soon after ended their relationship.[40] Parton referred to Phil Bredesen, the former Democratic governor of Tennessee

(2003–11), as a "very good friend,"⁴¹ but a minor brouhaha erupted when Parton suggested she would support Hillary Clinton's 2016 presidential campaign "if she gets [the Democratic Party's nomination]"; she backpedaled soon after.⁴²

The 2017 Emmy Awards tested Parton's steadfast nonpartisanship, as she was reunited with her *9 to 5* costars Fonda and Tomlin to present the award for Outstanding Supporting Actor in a miniseries. As part of their patter, Parton teased the idea of a reunion—"Personally, I have been waiting for a *9 to 5* reunion ever since we did the first one." Connecting the film to Republican president Donald Trump, Fonda stated, "Back in 1980, in that movie, we refused to be controlled by a sexist, egotistical, lying, hypocritical bigot," and Tomlin added, "And in 2017, we still refuse to be controlled by a sexist, egotistical, lying, hypocritical bigot." Parton looked dismayed by their words and sought to reframe the discussion away from politics to less controversial matters, joking about her breasts, unconvincingly suggesting that Tomlin was referring to Mr. Hart rather than to Trump, and then dismissing politics altogether: "I'm here to have a good time tonight. . . . I'm just hoping that I'm gonna get one of those *Grace and Frankie* [Fonda and Tomlin's current television program, 2015–22] vibrators in my swag bag." In a related example of her apoliticism, Parton twice declined Trump's offer of the Presidential Medal of Freedom, the nation's highest civilian honor. She also explained that she would then be unlikely to accept the award from Democratic president Joe Biden, if he were to offer it: "I couldn't accept it (from Trump) because my husband was ill and then they asked me again about it and I wouldn't travel because of the COVID," she recalled. "So now, I feel like if I take it, I'll be doing politics, so I'm not sure." She continued, "I don't work for those awards. It'd be nice, but I'm not sure that I even deserve it. But it's a nice compliment for people to think that I might deserve it."⁴³ Further along these lines, a steady stream of Parton's self-deprecating humor chuckles at the idea of her seeking political office, despite the fact that numerous entertainers, including Trump, have pursued this path. In response to the question of whether she would ever campaign for the Presidency, she replied, "Lord, no. Don't you think we've had enough boobs in the White House?"⁴⁴ In a related moment, and in a more serious tone, she deflected attention from any political ambitions to her personal goal of self-improvement: "I have seen some fun T-shirts and bumper stickers that say 'Dolly for Governor,' or even 'Dolly for President.' . . . I do not want to be governor or president. . . . I just want to be the best Dolly Parton I can be."⁴⁵

As much as Parton evinces an unflappable neutrality on matters of religion, feminism, and politics, certain issues require a response, as evident in the controversy that erupted over her Dixie Stampede tourist attraction. This dinner theater extravaganza featured singing, dancing, and pig racing while thematizing a whitewashed "War between the States," transmuting the horrors of the Civil War, fought in large part due to the South's recalcitrant defense of slavery, into ostensibly innocuous entertainment. In a blistering assessment of the venue titled "Springtime for the Confederacy," written in the aftermath of the 2017 white supremacist rallies in Charlottesville, Virginia, Aisha Harris lambasted the venue's sugarcoating of the Civil War and its erasure of racism and slavery:

> Dolly's Dixie Stampede has been a success not just because people love Dolly Parton, but because the South has always been afforded the chance to rewrite its own history—not just through its own efforts, but through the rest of the country turning a blind eye. Even though the South is built upon the foundation of slavery, a campy show produced by a well-meaning country superstar can make-believe it's not. We'd prefer to pretend, to let our deepest sins be transmuted into gauzy kitsch—and no one blinks an eye because that's what they truly want. . . . Dolly Parton is right about one thing: Dixie Stampede is as American as America gets.⁴⁶

Parton and her company soon rebranded the show as Dolly Parton's Stampede, asserting that they "recognize that attitudes change and feel that by streamlining the names of our shows, it will remove any confusion or concerns about our shows and will help our efforts to expand into new cities." Speaking a bit more bluntly, Parton commented, "There's such a thing as innocent ignorance, and so many of us are guilty of that. . . . When they said 'Dixie' was an offensive word, I thought, 'Well, I don't want to offend anybody. This is a business. We'll just call it the Stampede.' As soon as you realize that [something] is a problem, you should fix it. . . . Don't be a dumbass. That's where my heart is. I would never dream of hurting anybody on purpose."⁴⁷ Further cementing her enduring appeal, and despite some Twitter hysteria from southern conservatives, Parton's framing of the situation as both a necessary business decision and a matter of human kindness effectively defanged critics. In a related moment concerning the United States' confrontation with racial injustice following the murder of George Floyd and the rise of the Black Lives Matter movement, Parton ventured beyond her determined neutrality: "Of course Black lives matter. Do we think our little white asses are the only ones that matter? No!"[48] Thus, despite the South's merited reputation for condoning and institutionally embedding racist practices throughout its landscape, Parton ventures into political terrain by construing racism as an ongoing issue that the nation must confront and advocating racial equality as an essential premise of American culture, even when necessitating critiques of southern culture.

Complementing her star persona built on a foundation of glitz, glamour, and excess, Parton selected the butterfly as her personal logo, explaining that "they were always like little spiritual beings to me. . . . Butterflies were able to fly over the mountains and see what was there, yet they could still be content where they were."[49] Yet again Parton identifies a duality, in this instance in the creatures' limited geographic range that nonetheless allows for new vistas and possibilities, and such duality allows virtually all of her fans to see a reflection of their desires in her words, actions, and entertainment. Indeed, her fan base extends to the left and right extremes of American culture, but as Parton said of her ability to appeal to the religious right and queer communities, "It's two different worlds, and I live in both and I love them both, and I understand and accept both."[50] Dolly Parton, loved by countless fans for the authenticity of her southern star persona, simultaneously disproves the possibility of authenticity in her southern star persona, in a stunningly complex performance of the self that has stood for over seven decades. The coat of many colors that her mother made for her, the one that Parton immortalized in one of her early hits, stands as an authentic relic of her past that nonetheless provides little protection from the many fans who would fault this star for her personal beliefs, which in turn spurs the necessity for the inauthenticity of her endless dualities, in a spiraling self-construction of an impenetrable but boundlessly charismatic southern star persona.

WHICH FLORIDIANS ARE SOUTHERNERS?
Tom Petty, Gloria Estefan, and the Vagaries of Pop-Star Southernness in the 1980s

An eclectic array of southern sounds piped through the pop-music airwaves of the 1980s. As discussed in the two preceding chapters, Tina Turner staged a comeback for the ages with the soulful stirrings of her *Private Dancer* album, and Dolly Parton cemented her status as a country-crossover icon with her chart-toppers "9 to 5" and "Islands in the Stream"—a duet with fellow southerner Kenny Rogers. With their husky-toned tunes, Texas-based ZZ Top celebrated an eclectic array of topics in their hits "Legs," "Sleeping Bag," and "Velcro Fly." The B-52s and R.E.M., both founded in Athens, Georgia, moved from their roots in the alternative scene to more mainstream recognition, celebrating southernness along the way with such songs as "Love Shack" and "Deadbeat Club" for the former, with the album *Fables of the Reconstruction* for the latter. More so, southern rock had been recognized as a distinct subgenre of American music since the 1960s and 1970s with the likes of Lynyrd Skynyrd and the Allman Brothers; it continued in the 1980s with such groups as .38 Special and the Georgia Satellites. As Nick Thomas notes, this genre was rooted in "northern Florida and adjacent southern Georgia and Alabama" and "Jacksonville . . . was the epicenter of the movement."[1] This mélange of 1980s pop southern singers includes two notable and phenomenally successful Floridians—Gloria Estefan and Tom Petty—yet their diverging celebrity personas illustrate the vagaries of southern identity as mediated through the popular press. Simply put, Petty was seen and covered as a southerner whereas Estefan was seen and covered as a Cuban American or as a Miamian but rarely as a southerner, in a telling example of the ways in which the South's mythologies are perpetuated by racial and ethnic assumptions.

By any measure Petty and Estefan rank as two of the most successful pop-music artists of the late twentieth century. From 1978 to 1994, Petty and his band the Heartbreakers notched sixteen Top 40 hits, including such standouts as "Don't Do Me Like That," "Refugee," "Don't Come Around Here No More," "I Won't Back Down," and "Free Fallin,'" as well as their biggest hit, "Stop Draggin' My Heart Around," a duet with Stevie Nicks that reached No. 3 on the Billboard Hot 100 in 1981. From 1985 to 1999, Estefan registered nineteen Top 40 hits, including the No. 1 songs "Anything for You," "Don't Wanna Lose You," and "Coming Out of the Dark." That these two Floridian singers are rarely discussed together—as far as I know, this is the first such extended effort—showcases the easy stereotypes defining the South, particularly the power of whiteness to define southernness. Additional familiar southern tropes relevant to Petty's star persona include his southern accent and the redemption arc of a white man realizing his silent endorsement of the region's racist past. In contrast, Estefan offered the popular press and various cultural commentators the opportunity to reimagine the South as a whole by placing her and her music within its larger geographical context. With Estefan pigeonholed as a Miamian but with Petty never similarly delimited as a Gainesvillian, the lability of southernness, and the racial politics undergirding it, once again becomes apparent.

A SOUTHERN MAN

From his childhood years in Gainesville in the 1950s and early 1960s, Tom Petty long planned on a musical career, citing a particularly famous southern singer—Elvis Presley—as his inspiration. At eleven years old, Petty met Presley, who was filming *Follow That Dream* (1962) in nearby locations. He later recognized this encounter as a defining moment of his life: "And then suddenly I go, 'That's Elvis.' He stepped out radiant as an angel. He seemed to glow and walk above the ground. It was like *nothing* I'd ever seen in my life."[2] The Beatles inspired Petty's musical ambitions, and he has also cited the West Palm Beach

International Music and Arts Festival of November 1969 as a seminal event in his artistic development: "I got to see the Byrds . . . with the Rolling Stones. In the beginning, that was the original blueprint for the Heartbreakers—we wanted to be a mix of the Byrds and the Stones. We figured, 'What could be cooler than that?'"[3] With these influences circulating in the background, Petty formed bands during his high school years and soon gained local recognition, first with the Epics and then with Mudcrutch. Straining against the limited possibilities of regional success, Petty rhetorically pondered, "We could see it wasn't going anywhere. How big can you get in Gainesville?"[4]

And so Petty decamped to Los Angeles and, along with Mudcrutch alumni Mike Campbell and Benmont Tench, they reconstituted themselves as Tom Petty and the Heartbreakers. The band released its eponymous debut album in 1976, and each successive album—*You're Gonna Get It!* in 1978, *Damn the Torpedoes* in 1979, and *Hard Promises* in 1981—outsold the previous one, as their albums and singles consistently climbed the charts. Several songs on these albums featured southern storylines and are inextricably linked to Petty's southern upbringing, thereby alerting national audiences to the band's regional roots. As Gary Graff posits: "He began drawing from his own experiences, crafting stories about good ol' boys, strong-willed women, and rebels with 'one foot in the grave / and one foot on the pedal.'"[5] Petty set several of his songs in the South: "Magnolia" tells a boy-meets-girl story set on a "wet southern night"; "Louisiana Rain" rhapsodizes, "Louisiana rain is soaking through my shoes / I may never be the same when I reach Baton Rouge"; and "Strangered in the Night" tells a tale of an ugly racial—likely racist—confrontation: "But I saw this crazy black guy / With the demon in his eye." Noting these southern settings of the Heartbreakers' songs, Nate Bauer and Shye Gilad conclude that Petty repeatedly returned to themes of "struggle, defiance, interpersonal and social 'noise,' a subversion of uniform and superficial masculinity, and resilience, all in the context of widespread Reagan and Thatcher-era socioeconomic tumult," also positing that Petty reinforced these themes through his "resilience and life-affirming sneer."[6]

Petty bolstered the rebellious persona expressed in his music through his widely publicized battles with his record companies: as his songs celebrated everyman figures bucking the odds, so too did he cast himself in David-versus-Goliath struggles against financial predators. When MCA bought his record company and by extension his contract in 1979, Petty asked to be released, arguing that he was not a fungible asset. MCA sued him for breach of contract; Petty won the court case. Later he resisted his record company's effort to raise the price of *Hard Promises* to $9.98—a dollar more than the prevailing standard cost—even threatening to title the album *Eight Ninety-Eight*. Fighting on behalf of his fans and their pocketbooks, Petty's scrappy style aligned well with the persona projected musically. As Mara Lee Grayson documents, Petty has long been celebrated as an "everyman" figure beloved by fans and critics, and she suggests that his southernness plays a largely unacknowledged role in such accolades: "Intentionally or not, those who have assigned Petty the 'everyman' identity have also connected the rocker with one of the classic tropes of country music and the White Southern culture it is traditionally believed to reflect."[7] Such a rebellious streak is notable in the fact that a striking number of Petty's song titles feature imperative statements—e.g., "Don't Do Me Like That," "Stop Draggin' My Heart Around," "Don't Come Around Here No More"—in which the songs' lyric speakers express their impatience and frustration with their current circumstances.

Petty spoke with a southern accent, and southern accents—both his and his wife's—inflected his celebrity persona. In a chance moment that resulted in a classic song, Stevie Nicks misheard Petty's wife Jane Benyo say that she "met him at some point during the age of seventeen"; Nicks "thought [Benyo] said, 'The edge of seventeen,'" and soon released one of her biggest hits with this phrase as its title.[8] Petty stressed the significance of his southern dialect to his celebrity persona by dubbing his 1985 album *Southern Accents*. (See figure 9.) This title bespeaks the significance of the southern accent to southerners, as well as defiantly rebuking any nonsoutherners who might deride it. Indeed, the album's title track begins "There's a southern accent, where I come from / The young 'uns call it country, the Yankees call it dumb." Other songs on *Southern Accents* similarly address southern themes. The first track, "Rebels," intones, "I was born a rebel / Down in Dixie on a Sunday morning" and alludes to the destruction of southern landscapes during the Civil War—yet without concomitantly mentioning the continued enslavement of Black people as the South's objective in the conflict. That year also saw the release of the Heartbreakers' first live album, *Pack Up the Plantation: Live!*, on which he sings "Rebels" and "Southern Accents." The album was mostly recorded at the Wiltern Theatre

FIG. 9. An image from Tom Petty's *Southern Accents* tour of 1985, with the singer's image centered above a Confederate flag.

in Los Angeles, and so its title alludes not to the location of its taping but to the wider southern sensibilities expressed in the *Southern Accents* album. Lest anyone miss these defiantly southern lyrics, the Heartbreakers hung the Confederate flag as a backdrop for several performances during this era; Petty suggested that this was done to illustrate the fictional speaker of "Rebels." The line between southern white people acknowledging their heritage and endorsing racism can be razor thin under the most propitious of circumstances, but the deployment of the Confederate flag overwrites any potential complexity to signal white supremacy.

Michael Washburn, one of the leading authorities on Petty's career, sees the *Southern Accents* album as a dividing line in the singer's life, arguing that "his career in the decades following *Southern Accents* was a decided rejection of the persona and aesthetics presented during his *Southern Accents* era,"[9] and stating as well that Petty then "reframed himself as deep California."[10] Certainly, Petty toggled throughout his career between stressing and deemphasizing the southern aspects of his persona and musical style. In one interview he stated, "I'm glad we've had a chance to make people understand that we are Southern. . . . I spent more than twenty years down there. The music was formed there."[11] In another interview, however, he dismissed any assumption that the Heartbreakers' music could be identified as southern, instead insisting on its Californian vibe: "And we kind of felt, we belonged here [in L.A.]. And we always have, though we're still never referred to as an 'L.A. band.' We're always referred to as a Southern band. But the truth is every bit of music we've ever made was in L.A. We've been in L.A. for over thirty years. We're a Los Angeles band."[12] The Heartbreakers' keyboardist Benmont Tench offers a more nuanced view of their regional affiliations, noting the congruencies and incongruencies between their style and southern music in its many varieties:

> We loved the Allman Brothers but we weren't part of that scene, and deliberately because that wasn't our thing. [The Heartbreakers were] not a southern rock band, in terms of what that defines as a genre. The southernness in the Heartbreakers comes from our love of rhythm and blues, of soul music, from the fact that when we'd play gigs, when Mudcrutch would play gigs, you knew half of Wilson Pickett's greatest hits by heart. You knew Sam and Dave by heart. You know, all of the great soul music. You knew all of this stuff. You knew Carla Thomas, all this stuff. It was bred into you. So that's the kind of southern thing that we had.[13]

For many of the Heartbreakers, the South was where they were born and bred, and its influence could never be fully dissevered from their music, if that were even a possible goal. The critical distinction between the band's influences and its persona is again relevant, in that the band's southernness could have been expressed musically through the influence of Wilson Pickett, Sam and Dave, Carla

Thomas, and others without the accompanying expression of an explicitly white southern identity by lyrics, song settings, and signs such as the Confederate flag.

Following the *Southern Accents* album, Petty increasingly aligned himself with his California setting, but additional "southern accents" inflected his subsequent career. With Roy Orbison, Jeff Lynne, Bob Dylan, and George Harrison, he formed the supergroup Traveling Wilburys, whose songs often featured the rhythms and beats of country music; with Orbison, a Texan, as a fellow member, the group's membership stood at 40 percent southern. Although better known for his singing than his acting, Petty voiced the role of Elroy "Lucky" Kleinschmidt on *King of the Hill* (1997–2010), Mike Judge's Texas-set animated series, in yet another sign of the centrality of his southern accent to his career. Toward the end of his life, in a 2015 interview with *Rolling Stone*, Petty condemned the Confederate flag while concomitantly affirming his affection for the South as a whole:

> To this day, I have good feelings for the South in many ways. There's some wonderful people down there. There are people still affected by what their relatives taught them. It isn't necessarily racism. They just don't like Yankees. They don't like the North. But when they wave that flag, they aren't stopping to think how it looks to a black person. I blame myself for not doing that. I should have gone around the fence and taken a good look at it. But honestly, it all stemmed from my trying to illustrate a character. I then just let it get out of control as a marketing device for the record. It was dumb and it shouldn't have happened.[14]

With these words Petty documents the ways in which his southern persona, his efforts to "illustrate a character," circumscribed his ability to empathize with vast swaths of people alienated by southern racism and its icons. More so, he explicitly links his southern persona to the marketing apparatuses of the recording industry, in the realization that leaning into this aspect of his character would build a stronger sense of identification and alliance with the white southerners who constituted a significant portion of his fan base. Petty rightfully regretted his past emblazoning of Confederate flags, but even here evidence of a well-worn southern trope appears, in a white man's belated recognition of his participation in the region's benighted racial politics. In this redemption arc, a white man transcends his previous limitations of insight and empathy, but even so, such a storyline depends on a prior endorsement, even if mostly tacit, of the South's racist past. Despite these ethical lapses, Tom Petty's southern persona, it would appear, succeeded in enhancing his likeability and relatability for his fans, in yet another example of a white man failing up.

A SOUTHERN WOMAN

Throughout her decades in the public eye, Gloria Estefan has often been identified as a Cuban American and as a Miamian, but rarely as a southerner, and so this notable absence demands scrutiny. Absences and silences require our attention because they paradoxically speak so loudly: what is not being said often reveals quite clearly the cultural assumptions and constructions behind such loud silences. As Pierre Macherey explains in his justly famous formulation, "By speech, silence becomes the centre and principle of expression, its vanishing point. Speech eventually has nothing more to tell us: we investigate the silence, for it is the silence that is doing the speaking."[15] Within the entertainment industry such silences can play a pivotal role in the wider construction of a performer's persona. In an admittedly imperfect analogy, we might consider Estefan as "typecast" as a Cuban American or Miamian. This is not to suggest in any manner that Estefan is not a Cuban American or Miamian but to point out that she could have been seen in other, complementary ways—for the purposes of this study, as a southerner—and to consider the possibility that the cultural denotations of "southerner" would be widened by doing so. The popular press's insistence on the descriptors "Cuban American" and "Miamian" highlights the ways in which Estefan's identity, as inflected by her race, gender, ethnicity, class, and birth nation, collided with representations of her by others, in a circular process of identity and persona creation.

Gloria María Milagrose Fajardo García, born September 1, 1957, immigrated to Florida with her family during her early childhood. After Fidel Castro's Cuban Revolution of 1959, her father, José, was blacklisted for working as a military policeman under President Fulgencio Batista. In memories of her childhood, Estefan recalled both her alienation from and her embrace of American mores. She found herself marginalized at school: "In every way possible, I was set apart from my classmates. I was the only Hispanic student. I couldn't communicate in English. While the other kids ate bologna sandwiches for lunch, I ate tortillas made from scratch."[16] She enjoyed American (and British) popular culture, and so her musical education entailed her "plucking out traditional Cuban songs and Beatles hits on a guitar";[17] as she also recalled more generally, "I grew up listening to Top 40 music."[18] She met her future husband, musician Emilio Estefan, in 1975, and joined his band, Miami Latin Boys, as its lead singer; they soon changed its name to Miami Sound Machine. As Estefan also explained, she "influenced the guys to use English" owing to her exposure to mainstream American pop.[19] The group released their first major label album, *Eyes of Innocence*, in 1984; the follow-up, *Primitive Love*, was released in 1985 and scored four Top 40 hits: "Conga," "Bad Boy," "Words Get in the Way," and "Falling in Love (Uh-Oh)." With its infectious opening lyrics, "Come on, shake your body, baby, do the conga, / I know you can't control yourself any longer," "Conga" became the first single to hit the pop, Latin, Black, and dance record charts simultaneously and heralded the arrival of a distinct crossover sound embraced across large swaths of American culture. For their next album, *Let It Loose* (1987), the band was rebranded as Gloria Estefan and Miami Sound Machine. Estefan launched herself as a solo artist with the album *Cuts Both Ways* (1989).

Moving from the 1980s to the 1990s, Estefan recorded her album *Mi Tierra* in 1993, which featured songs heavily influenced by Cuban traditions and sung exclusively in Spanish. *Abriendo Puertas* (1995) branched beyond Cuba to songs representative of wider Latin traditions, including those of Colombia and Venezuela. From early in her career Estefan realized that she would need to expand rigid musical genres to fit her style: "A lot of people told me at the beginning, 'You're too Latin for the Americans, too American for the Latins. And I say, 'But that's who I am. I'm Cuban-American; I'm not one thing or the other. I have an American head and a Cuban heart."[20] And so as much as the 1990s marked Estefan's pivot to her musical roots in Cuba, this decade also saw her hit the Top 40 twice with covers of disco classics—Vicki Sue Robinson's "Turn the Beat Around" in 1994 and Carl Carlton's "Everlasting Love" in 1995. Indeed, a review of the latter song in *Network* proclaimed, "Estefan sprinkles her 'Miami' spice on the classic."[21] Spanning across cultures, languages, and musical traditions, Estefan has long created a sound that is uniquely her own, transcending musical genres and geographic boundaries that might have otherwise constrained her.

Along with her singing, Estefan has pursued an acting career and achieved greater success than many of her peers attempting this transition. One could well argue that her acting career began with her music videos, as she showcased an infectious charm in the "Bad Boy" video, in which she first spurns the sexual advances of a blond man and then flirts with a humanoid cat. (See figure 10.) In 1999 she debuted as a film star in Wes Craven's *Music of the Heart* and has since appeared in supporting roles in various television programs, including *Frasier* (1993–2004), *Glee* (2009–15), and the Netflix remake of the sitcom *One Day at a Time* (2017–20), before returning for a leading role in the recent remake of *Father of the Bride* (2022). *Music of the Heart* is set in New York City, the remakes of *One Day at a Time* and *Father of the Bride* are set in Miami, thus further testifying to the power of a rather limited geographic imaginary when Hollywood casts Hispanic actors. Of her acting ambitions, Estefan once declared, "I would love to do an ensemble piece, like *Steel Magnolias*,"[22] and this provides just one small example of how visions of the South would shift if more ecumenical visions of southernhood prevailed. The cast of this southern cinematic classic of 1989 features six female costars—Sally Field, Olympia Dukakis, Daryl Hannah, Shirley MacLaine, Julia Roberts, and Dolly Parton—all of whom were white, half of whom were southern: Parton from Tennessee, MacLaine from Virginia, and Roberts from Georgia. How would this film have looked if it had cast Estefan, a famous southern singer, in the role of Truvy, which was played by Parton, another famous southern singer?

Assessing any line between a celebrity's persona and her personality always brings risks, yet Estefan's peers throughout the entertainment industry appear to genuinely admire her for her compassion, professionalism, and ecumenical spirit. To quote one such paean, Estefan's fellow southerner Ellen DeGeneres affirmed: "Gloria Estefan is the copper plumbing of the music industry. She's beautiful, reliable, and indestructible."[23] Estefan has spoken eloquently about human rights issues and the necessity of preserving American liberties, particularly in light of her experiences as a Cuban expatriate and despite the potential blowback from a significant portion of her fanbase: "As an American, I am frightened to see our most basic liberties being trampled on in the march for political gain. As a Cuban American, I am embarrassed that non-Cubans might think that we are all of a narrow mind.... I understand the hardships that we from Cuba have experienced, but for this reason we must defend everyone's free-

FIG. 10. Gloria Estefan's music videos hinted at her acting skills, as her sly smile attests in this scene from her "Bad Boy" video.

dom, even if it means personal pain."[24] With the Gloria Estefan Foundation, Estefan has further demonstrated her ethos of compassionate concern for others: "My foundation tries to help people that fall through the cracks, that can't get help from big organizations. We try to fill in where immediate help is needed."[25]

Many admirers and entertainment reporters accentuate Estefan's role as a trailblazer, as "the first" to bring Latin music to a mainstream audience, and while her accomplishments should not be downplayed, nor should they be exaggerated. Dubbing an entertainer "the first" can be seen as a lionizing gesture, but it can also be alienating, in the inability to see this person's accomplishments against the wider backdrop of their unique culture and its positionality in the United States. Jon Secada, who wrote Estefan's blockbuster hit "Coming Out of the Dark" and sang backup for her before launching his solo career, opined, "She was the first to take Latin-influenced music, the heavy percussions sounds, mainstream.... Because of her, Latin music began to get a lot more respect."[26] Or as similarly expressed in the words of entertainment reporter Sheryl Berk: "Estefan and Miami Sound Machine were the first to bring fiery-hot rhythms and Spanish lyrics to the mainstream music charts in the '80s."[27] But, of course, they weren't, to which even a cursory overview of twentieth-century American music would attest. Desi Arnaz's band played in America's homes throughout the successful run of *I Love Lucy* (1951–57), and before his tragic death in 1959 Ritchie Valens was on the verge of superstardom with his hits "Donna" and "La Bamba." Ironically, Los Lobos scored a No. 1 hit with their cover of "La Bamba" in 1987—topping the Billboard charts several months before Estefan first accomplished this feat with "Anything for You" in 1988. Santana scored a range of hits in the early 1970s, including "Evil Ways," "Black Magic Woman," and "Oye Como Va." Estefan herself has cited the pioneering work of Xavier Cugat, Desi Arnaz, Mongo Santamaria, and Santana, as well as the crossover sounds of David Byrne and Paul Simon, as key influences on her style.

Also in the 1980s, following the so-called death of disco, Latin Freestyle music brought infectious beats to the dance floor, notably through the prolific careers of producers Jellybean Benitez and Lewis Martineé. Martineé's signature group, Exposé, scored a No. 1 hit with "Seasons Change" in 1987—again, prior to Estefan's first No. 1—as did Lisa Velez, also known as Lisa Lisa, who scored two freestyle-inspired No. 1 hits: "Head to Toe" and "Lost in Emotion," also in 1987. Furthermore, as Pablo Palomino notes, "Tracing the category of Latin American music means dealing with the wider history of the conceptualizations of Latin America as a cultural space, and with its overlapping with those of individual nations, the Western hemisphere, and the world."[28] It is beyond the scope of this brief chapter to delineate the full complexity of Latin music and its influence on American pop music, but the wider point prevails: that it is less important to see Estefan's music as a "first" than to investigate the ways in which Latin and Caribbean rhythms have permeated American culture as a whole and southern culture in particular for decades, even centuries. Quite simply, the history of Latin American music transcends regionalities and encompasses traditions from North America, Central America, the Caribbean islands, and South America, as well as from Europe and Africa. It is instructive to remember that the stalwart instrument of southern country music—the banjo—traveled to the South via the Caribbean.

In their ability to draw fans across a wider spectrum of identities than solely their birth culture, musicians can shift the ways in which various peoples see their cultures and reform them in line with exposure to new paradigms. In discussing the power of performance to affect an audience, Estefan once declared, "To reach a culture and change their actions, their usual course of being, is a very powerful and exciting thing."[29] In this context she was speaking of international audiences, specifically in Germany and Japan, but her words carry a deep resonance as well when applied to her own home in the American South. The media consistently refused to claim Estefan as a southerner, thus bolstering borders between U.S. subcultures rather than transcending them, as her music so infectiously did.

A SOUTHERN STATE

As this chapter has pondered the celebrity personas of Gloria Estefan and Tom Petty and the sense of southernness accorded them, it has tacitly raised the vexed relationship of Florida to the rest of the U.S. South. An old joke about the state's geography and demography posits that north Florida should be called southern Alabama, and south Florida should be called northern Cuba. As with many jokes, a grain of truth can be distilled from the humor, particularly because much of Florida's panhandle could well have been cordoned off into Alabama's borders. Alabama's constitutional convention of 1819 petitioned Congress to incorporate western Florida within its boundaries; several subsequent attempts to annex the panhandle occurred over the nineteenth and early twentieth centuries. With its large population of Cuban exiles following the revolution of 1959, Miami has won the nickname of "Little Havana."[30] In this regard Miami is certainly unique among southern cities, but so are other metropolises—New Orleans, Charleston, and Nashville come to mind—that are nonetheless recognized as quintessentially "southern." The diverging reputations of northern and southern Florida reveal that much of the mythic South entails overlooking the region's Spanish and Hispanic heritage, as foundationally apparent in Christopher Columbus's 1492 journey under the auspices of the Spanish crown, in Juan Ponce de León's 1513 journey seeking the Fountain of Youth, and in the travels of many other explorers and settlers thereafter. Multiple flags have flown over the state of Florida, including those of Spain, Britain, the United States, and the traitorous Confederacy, yet the prevailing mythologies of the South rarely take into account the full extent of its many intersecting cultural traditions. As Owen Furuseth and Heather Smith document of the South's history and its

Hispanic populations, "across the eleven states [Florida, Virginia, Kentucky, Tennessee, North Carolina, South Carolina, Georgia, Alabama, Mississippi, Louisiana, and Arkansas] that lie at the heart of the traditional American South, in large and small cities as well as rural crossroads and farms, Hispanics have been historically absent from the demographic, economic, cultural, and political landscape." They then propose the necessity of shifting to a new vision of the South: "In a region defined by its enduring biraciality, the rapid and large-scale introduction of Hispanics raises profound questions about the way in which new populations either force a rethinking of old precepts or lead to an entrenchment and extension of them. The degree to which the New South into which Hispanics are entering is a place of true transformation, adjustment, and acceptance or a veneer masking entrenchment is a central question" facing the region both in decades past and continuing to this moment.[31]

History (and music history) continues to be written and rewritten, and an envisioned Florida Music Hall of Fame promises to link the careers of Petty and Estefan, thus to promote a more ecumenical vision of the state's musical riches. According to the visionaries behind this project, "Visitors to the facility will enter the Museum through a grand, high-ceilinged foyer. On one wall, they'll be greeted by a collage of the most familiar faces of Florida music: Jimmy Buffett, Ray Charles, the Allman Brothers, Tom Petty, Gloria Estefan, Lynyrd Skynyrd, Jim Morrison, Stephen Stills and the like."[32] Telling the stories of Petty and Estefan together offers a more comprehensive view of the South and its celebrities, one that supplants the longstanding tendency to see a white man as inherently more "southern" than an equally—and let's be honest, likely more—talented Hispanic woman. Furthermore, as southern studies continues to broaden the borders of the South to include the Caribbean, thus to better understand the vibrant intersection of indigenous and diasporic cultures circulating throughout the region, such 1980s singers as Billy Ocean, born in Trinidad and Tobago, might also be considered southern celebrities.[33] The stories and celebrity personas of the South have for too long been defined by race and simplistic assumptions about the region's borders. In her most inspirational song, written after a horrific bus accident that almost left her paralyzed, Estefan sang of "Coming Out of the Dark"—an inspirational vision of a future that the South, by embracing the full diversity of its citizenry, both celebrities and ordinary people, might one day achieve.

9

ON SOUTHERN WOMEN'S BOOK CLUBS
Oprah Winfrey, Reese Witherspoon, Jenna Bush Hager, and the Performance of a Literary Star Persona

It may be little more than a coincidence, but nonetheless a coincidence worth exploring: three of the United States' most influential book clubs are hosted by southern women. Born and raised in neighboring states, Oprah Winfrey of Mississippi, Reese Witherspoon of Louisiana and Tennessee, and Jenna Bush Hager of Texas turned to books and bookishness at key moments of their careers, with books then serving as a distinguishing factor in the ongoing refinement of their star personas. Of course, celebrity book clubs are not limited to southern women, and in today's social media landscape, many stars, including Gwyneth Paltrow, Emma Roberts, Kerry Washington, Sarah Michelle Gellar, Shonda Rhimes, and Mindy Kaling, share reading recommendations on X (formerly Twitter), Instagram, and other such sites. Some stars edge closer to book club territory, such as Emma Watson with her (now dormant) Our Shared Self on Goodreads, or the partnership of Sarah Jessica Parker and the American Library Association's Book Club Central. Women's reading groups dominate this corner of the media landscape, although such male celebrities as Andrew Luck, the former Indiana Colts quarterback, curate book clubs envisioned for men.[1] Virtually without exception, book clubs infuse an intellectual flair into a celebrity's persona, testifying not merely to their star power but to their deeper cultural interests and their passionate engagement with the joys of reading.

In a sense, then, as much as people read books, we also interpret the ways in which others read books. As Ted Striphas affirms, books communicate bivalently through their assumed virtues and their ostensible imperviousness to crass commercialism: "The value of books would seem to lie, first and foremost, in their capacity for moral, aesthetic, and intellectual development, and only secondarily—if at all—in the marketplace. What makes a 'good' book good—or, rather, what makes *books* good—is their purported ability to transcend vulgar economic considerations for the sake of these loftier goals."[2] Such an idyllic vision of books inevitably falters against their commercial value, and Striphas further points out that the nebulous concept of "book culture" includes as well "legal codes, technical devices, institutional arrangements, social relations, and historical processes whose purpose is to help secure the everydayness of contemporary book culture."[3] Celebrity book clubs stand as a relatively recent descendant of a book club tradition that dates back decades and includes such behemoths as the Book of the Month Club and the Folio Society, as well as such niche endeavors as the Early English Text Society. In today's media- and star-saturated landscape, book clubs also illuminate the intersection of society's fixation on celebrities and the longstanding patina of intellectualism associated with literary pursuits.

Given the many denigrating assumptions circulating around the intelligence of southern women as a whole, and given the racist stereotypes particularly aimed at Black southern women, Winfrey's, Witherspoon's, and Bush Hager's affiliations with book clubs allow them to speak back to the wider cultural forces that might denigrate their intellectual acumen. As a trailblazing journalist in the 1980s, Winfrey was first celebrated more for her empathy than her intellect, with her book club thus allowing her audience a wider view of her interests and tastes. Witherspoon built her acting career by acknowledging and challenging "dumb blonde" and "dumb belle" stereotypes; her book club further assists her in demonstrating her formidable acuity in an industry built upon the exploitation of women's beauty. Bush Hager, haunted by charges of nepotism in her early career, likewise employed her book club to build a community of readers focusing on her dedication to literature rather than on the easy path to fame enabled by her family's political dynasty. For Winfrey, Witherspoon, and Bush Hager, books and book clubs challenge perceptions of women's shallow cerebral pursuits, at the same time that their reading selections ironically provide fodder for demeaning women's literary interests. That is to say, book clubs allow women to affirm their intellectualism but then their selections require them to defend their tastes, in a circular process demonstrating the ways in which women's intelligence, seemingly inevitably, becomes a topic of debate. Regardless of these dynamics, Winfrey, Witherspoon, and Bush Hager affirm themselves and their fans through the simple love of reading, all the while coordinating its complexities as a reflection of their star power.

OPRAH WINFREY

Few celebrities can date their rise to superstardom as specifically as Oprah Winfrey: on September 8, 1986, her eponymous talk show, *The Oprah Winfrey Show* (1986–2011), debuted nationally. She (and it) quickly soared to first place in the daytime rankings, and her fame has never dimmed in the decades since. As noted by numerous cultural commentators, Winfrey's empathy initially defined her star persona. Whereas most talk show hosts prior to *The Oprah Winfrey Show* maintained a sense of reserved and dispassionate distance from their interviewees, Winfrey intimately connected with her guests by sharing the traumas of her life, including the challenges of her childhood in rural Mississippi and urban Wisconsin, most notably the sexual abuse she suffered as a child and her teen pregnancy. Through her candor and her emotional insights, Winfrey forged a deep bond with her fans, as Richard Zoglin documents: "What she lacks in journalistic toughness, however, she makes up in plainspoken curiosity, robust humor and, above all, empathy. Guests with sad stories to tell are apt to rouse a tear in Oprah's eye or get a comforting arm around the shoulder."[4] In memorable episodes spanning an eclectic and ecumenical range of topics—for example, the Rodney King verdict, the all-white county of Forsyth, Georgia, her personal journey with weight loss and weight gain, and groundbreaking interviews with Michael Jackson and Ellen DeGeneres, among hundreds more—Oprah's fans knew that she would connect with her interviewees, and by doing so, connect with them as well.

Yet as much as empathy defined Oprah's persona for so many cultural critics and fans in the formative years of her international celebrity, she simultaneously displayed her literary and intellectual acumen by acting in several films and television programs adapted from the works of Black authors, thus foreshadowing the foundation of her book club. She debuted as an actor in Steven Spielberg's adaptation of Alice Walker's *The Color Purple* (1985), garnering an Academy Award nomination for Best Supporting Actress for her efforts. Subsequently she appeared in adaptations of Richard Wright's *Native Son* (1986) and Gloria Naylor's *The Women of Brewster Place* (1989). Over the decades she has frequently returned to scripted film and television roles. Notably, she starred as Sethe in Jonathan Demme's adaptation of Toni Morrison's *Beloved* (book 1987, film 1998), concurrent with her book club's selection of Morrison's *Paradise* (1998, fifteenth selection). Furthermore, many of these vehicles expanded her star persona by evincing her commitment to civil rights and progressive values, as evident in her roles in such films by Black directors as Lee Daniels's *The Butler* (2013), Ava DuVernay's *Selma* (2014), and George C. Wolfe's *The Immortal Life of Henrietta Lacks* (2017). As much as *The Oprah Winfrey Show* dominated the production and maintenance of her star persona, her films and television appearances have consistently allowed her to widen her cultural presence in a progressive and readerly direction.

After dominating the ratings in the late 1980s and early 1990s, *The Oprah Winfrey Show* faced a spirited battle for viewer supremacy as many talk shows steadily devolved into tabloid sensationalism, evident in the burgeoning popularity of such programs as Geraldo Rivera's *Geraldo* (1987–98), Jerry Springer's *The Jerry Springer Show* (1991–2018), Maury Povich's *Maury* (1991–2022), and Ricki Lake's *Ricki Lake* (1992–2004). Eschewing empathy for derision, these programs treated their guests as carnival sideshow attractions, encouraging audiences to laugh at them and disparage their problems. Winfrey leaned into this sensationalistic trend for a few seasons but soon found herself frustrated by it, to the extent that she considered ending *The Oprah Winfrey Show* approximately ten years into its run. Instead, rather than capitulating to current trends, she decided that she could redirect them: "And I realized that I had no right to quit coming from a history of people who had no voice, who had no power, and that I have been given this—this blessed opportunity to speak to people, to influence them in ways that can make a difference in their lives, and to just use that. So I came back, committed to not be subtle about it, just to use the show to change people's lives wherever I could, and do it, and just come out and say it."[5] At this pivotal moment in her career, when she might have retired at a relatively young age with a robust fortune, books and her book club redirected the course of her program, her career, and her southern star persona.

Winfrey launched Oprah's Book Club on September 17, 1996, selecting Jacquelyn Mitchard's *The Deep End of the Ocean* (1996) as its inaugural offering. (See figure 11.) In this moment she concomitantly rebranded herself as a devoted bibliophile: "This is one of my all-time favorite moments I'm having on television right now. . . . You are witnessing it—mainly because I love books." She also stated that reading is "one of the great pleasures I have right now in life" and that she relished the pleasure of "reading a good book and to know I have a really, really good book after that book to read."[6] A common paean to reading celebrates its unique ability to expand readers' personal vistas, and Winfrey echoed these thoughts: "I feel strongly that, no matter who you are, reading opens doors and provides, in your own personal sanctuary, an opportunity to explore and feel things, the way other forms of media cannot."[7] A slight paradox arises in the overlap of books themselves (as part of a personal sanctuary) and of book clubs (as part of a communal event), for the latter opens up personal experiences into shared ones, yet Winfrey smoothly segued between the personal and the communal aspects of her book club. The typical format of a book club episode of *The Oprah Winfrey Show* featured a brief documentary about the author's life and career, followed by a discussion of the novel over a dinner shared by the author, Winfrey, and several viewers. In her new role as cultural commentator and book club impresario, Winfrey still demonstrated her remarkable empathy, even when the format of a given episode featured literary discussions.

Toni Morrison's *Song of Solomon* (1977) and Jane Hamilton's *The Book of Ruth* (1988) followed *The Deep End of the Ocean,* and thus Oprah's Book Club established its early focus on women writers and their works. As Winfrey opined of her first three selections, "I chose these books because they are readable, poignant, and thought-provoking. Our audience is predominantly female; all three books I've picked are strong stories with strong women."[8] Also, many of Winfrey's selections were based on her personal relationships with books and their authors. For instance, she has declared passionately that reading provided a lifeline during her difficult childhood, at one point recounting the ways in which she strongly identified with Maya Angelou's autobiography *I Know Why*

FIG. 11. Oprah Winfrey discusses Jacquelyn Mitchard's *The Deep End of the Ocean*, thereby launching her revolutionary intervention into the publishing industry and forever shifting her star persona.

the Caged Bird Sings (1969). Seeing herself in Angelou's troubled southern upbringing, Winfrey also discerned the possibility of triumphing over challenging circumstances: "Maya Angelou grew up to be Maya Angelou. It was my life—it was the possibility for *my* life."[9] Angelou's *The Heart of a Woman* (1981)—the fourth in the author's series of seven autobiographies—was the book club's eighth selection.

Owing to Oprah's Book Club, Winfrey's star persona shifted in key ways, as Cecilia Konchar Farr assesses: "Here Oprah's role was not just the therapist/talk show host, the smart entrepreneur, or the wildly successful capitalist. She didn't play the perky cheerleader for popular fiction or the humble devotee for a well-known author. The Book Club placed Oprah in the role of cultural critic and arbiter of taste."[10] With Winfrey now reigning as a "cultural critic and arbiter of taste," her opinions irrevocably altered the publishing industry, as her selections boosted sales by hundreds of thousands of copies. As Carmen Wong Ulrich documents, "Winfrey's book club recommendation had a greater influence on book sales than anything else in the history of modern publishing."[11] Such success sparked criticisms that she selected only lightweight fiction and was thus complicit with a "dumbing-down" of American culture, and Kathy

Rooney summarizes additional criticisms directed at Oprah's book club: "that it superficially treated fictional works as Things That Really Happen; that the narratives of the books themselves were flattened by the pandering, shallow narrative of the television program; that it drew an inordinate amount of attention to the personality of the authors."[12] The very existence of the word *bluestocking* testifies to men's disparaging view of women readers, a specimen of sexism that dates back centuries, and these fatiguing dynamics reemerged to denigrate Oprah's Book Club as various critics, mostly male, launched broadsides against its purported shallowness.

Responding to these criticisms, Winfrey selected several authors of unquestioned literary merit. She praised Toni Morrison as "the greatest living American writer, male or female, white or black,"[13] and, after *Song of Solomon*, selected more of Morrison's books for her readers: *Paradise* (1997; fifteenth selection), *The Bluest Eye* (1970; thirty-fifth selection), and *Sula* (1973; forty-eighth selection). By foregrounding Morrison's significance both in Western literature and for her book club, Winfrey tacitly argued against any critics who denigrated her selections as "light reading" or "beach reading." In a telling exchange in which Winfrey acknowledged some of her readers' difficulty in interpreting Morrison's prose, she asked Morrison, "Do people tell you they have to keep going over the words sometimes?" The author coolly replied, "That, my dear, is called reading."[14] Not all of Winfrey's selections were as challenging as *Paradise*, but this exchange nonetheless highlights that any aspersions against Oprah's Book Club as proffering escapist fare simply overlooked the extensive variety of texts selected. Winfrey increasingly selected novels whose literary reputations stand virtually unquestioned and unquestionable, including William Faulkner's *As I Lay Dying* (fifty-fifth selection), *The Sound and the Fury* (fifty-sixth selection), and *Light in August* (fifty-seventh selection); Charles Dickens's *Great Expectations* (sixty-ninth selection) and *A Tale of Two Cities* (seventieth selection); Gabriel García Márquez's *One Hundred Years of Solitude* (fifty-first selection) and *Love in the Time of Cholera* (sixty-third selection); and Leo Tolstoy's *Anna Karenina* (fifty-third selection). On the whole, Winfrey's selections balanced literary classics with contemporary voices, as represented by such authors as Janet Fitch, Maeve Binchy, Sue Monk Kidd, Elizabeth Berg, and Sue Miller, all the while implicitly questioning the imposition of the borders between so-called literature and genre fiction, serious reading and light reading, and the always unsteady yet rigorously enforced barrier between "high" and "low" culture.

In a strikingly illustrative example of the tensions between a Black woman's book club and the (mostly white male) cultural critics denigrating her reading selections, these issues percolated in the book club's background until simmering over when Winfrey selected Jonathan Franzen's *The Corrections* (2001). Most authors craved Winfrey's imprimatur, but Franzen responded ambivalently, discerning in his book's selection the potential for it to be devalued as a literary work: "The problem in this case is some of Oprah's picks. She's picked some good books, but she's picked enough schmaltzy, one-dimensional ones that I cringe, myself, even though I think she's really smart and she's really fighting the good fight.... But as far as being popular ... of course everybody who's sold out and been co-opted, as I obviously have, says the same thing, and it makes for a pathetic spectacle."[15] He stated that he "considered turning [Oprah] down ... because I'm an independent writer and I didn't want that corporate logo on my book." In an interview with Terry Gross, he further declared, "At the Oprah show, they have no idea how they are going to arrange the show because they've never done a book like this."[16] Given his statements dismissive of her, her book club, and at least implicitly of the hundreds of thousands of female readers she would bring to his novel, Winfrey disinvited Franzen from her program. Approximately a decade later, she selected Franzen's *Freedom* (2010, sixty-eighth selection) for her book club, he accepted the offer, and thus ended their so-called feud.

In 2002 Winfrey temporarily ended Oprah's Book Club, stating "the truth is, it has just become harder and harder for me to find books on a monthly basis that I am really passionate about,"[17] while simultaneously affirming its importance to her personal growth: "Doing this book club has given me the courage to pursue the things I care about."[18] It was soon revived in an evolved format, shifting from a monthly to an irregularly scheduled event. Oprah's Book Club has further metamorphosed over the years, but its primary cultural role in enhancing this key aspect of Winfrey's celebrity remains. The intellectualism associated with reading—no matter whether the books be highbrow, middlebrow, or lowbrow—eclipses more troubling aspects of Winfrey's celebrity endorsements, such as her star-making ability with problematic protégés Dr. Phil McGraw and Dr. Mehmet Oz, as well as her own endorsement of some pseudoscientific curses and remedies.[19] Few book lovers can claim to have shifted

America's reading habits and publishing protocols as dramatically as Winfrey, with their patina effectively enhancing her star appeal first based on empathy but then also based on her status as a Renaissance woman of varied interests and literary pursuits.

REESE WITHERSPOON

From her adolescent cinematic debut to the present, Reese Witherspoon has built her career by reframing and expanding cultural visions of southern and professional womanhood. This aspect of her star persona shines forth most clearly in the film roles she selects, yet her book club assists in this aspiration, attesting to her intellectual interests in fiction that her production company often leverages into film opportunities. Witherspoon's many entrepreneurial ambitions are well tailored to the vision of modern womanhood she projects through her star persona, as they also, somewhat counterintuitively, have allowed her to accentuate the southern aspects of her celebrity. In contrast to the many southern actors who shuck themselves of their hometown roots in their quest for stardom, Witherspoon has leaned in, then against, and then back into her southernness at various stages of her career, illuminating the ways in which her acting career, and her book club as well, establish her unique star persona of entrepreneurial ambition often encased in a southern wrapping. As she has stated of her film roles, "I also feel a responsibility as an actress to represent women in a way that I want to be represented,"[20] with this sensibility extending to a range of her other ventures.

Witherspoon's first spoken line on film—"I love Elvis so much!" from Robert Mulligan's *The Man in the Moon* (1991)—heralded the rise of a breakthrough new talent. In this coming-of-age drama set in 1950s rural Louisiana, these words bespeak her character's adoration of the South's greatest star, and this role allowed Witherspoon to trade on her dual southern roots, in that she was born in New Orleans and then raised in Nashville. For this memorable debut, Witherspoon won a 1992 Chicago Film Critics Association Award for Most Promising Actress, which launched her steady rise to Hollywood's elite. In this foundational decade of her career, however, Witherspoon did not subsequently accentuate her southern roots. Instead, she played characters from a range of U.S. settings, including the Pacific Northwest (*Fear*, 1996) and the vaguely midwestern (*Pleasantville*, 1998). Many critics see her breakout role as overachiever Tracy Flick, a Nebraskan, in *Election* (1999), and if *Election* won Witherspoon critical accolades, her following role as Elle Woods in *Legally Blonde* (2001) won her countless devoted fans. In this smash hit that spawned a sequel (*Legally Blonde 2: Red, White, and Blonde*, 2003) and a Broadway musical, Witherspoon charmed audiences by playing a woman dismissed as an intellectual lightweight who, plotting to win her boyfriend back, gains admission to Harvard Law School, where she outsmarts her smart but snobbish peers. Elle Woods, in a sense, became a metonym for Witherspoon herself: a sugar-coated and affable warning not to confuse the actor with any "dumb blonde" or "dumb belle" stereotypes that the character so effortlessly eluded.[21] (See figure 12.)

Long before launching her book club, Witherspoon deployed books and bookishness as a key component of her celebrity persona to accentuate her intelligence and ambition. Accepted into Stanford University, although she soon left to pursue her acting career, Witherspoon embraced the ostensible contradiction, as also embodied by Elle Woods, of being an extraordinarily bright woman whom others might dismiss owing to her blonde hair. In an indication of her efforts to embody her acumen and professionalism, she dubbed her first production company Type A Films, clearly aligning her star persona with this personality type characterized by ambition, organization, and competitiveness. She also highlighted her intelligence in several interviews of the time, perhaps most notably in Sean M. Smith's "Reese Witherspoon Lets Down Her Hair," an article published in *Premiere* magazine as part of the marketing campaign for *Legally Blonde*. Most celebrity interviews are carefully curated events, but the façade fell at least slightly in this publication, in which Smith probed the underlying tensions of a celebrity interview while undertaking one. The article's lead photo of Witherspoon portrays her as a Rapunzel figure, bedecked with floor-length hair, and the caption underneath reads: "Once upon a time, there was a southern belle who led a fairy-tale life in Hollywood. But . . . this is one princess who packs a punch."[22] In the star-serving economy of entertainment journalism—where access is typically granted on the presumption, if not the requirement, that the portrait will flatter—Smith instead adopts the position of two equally matched competitors engaged in a game of wits, in which the celebrity seeks to present herself in the best possible light while the journalist attempts to peer beneath the star persona camouflaging the actual person.

FIG. 12. In a career-defining performance in *Legally Blonde*, Reese Witherspoon plays Elle Woods, who disproves any assumption of her unintelligence by hitting the books and gaining acceptance to Harvard Law School.

During their jaunt around Los Angeles, Witherspoon purchased a copy of the legendary French actor Sarah Bernhardt's biography from a rare book store. Surely one must presume Witherspoon staged the opportunity to buy a biography of a legendary actor in front of a celebrity reporter, or perhaps stumbled across it by happenstance but then took advantage of the opportunity. In the same interview, Witherspoon also mentions the importance of books in her attraction to her then-husband, actor Ryan Philippe: "He's always studying, reading a different book on a person I've never heard of."[23] Through media appearances such as this one, Witherspoon fashioned her intelligence and literary tastes as key aspects of her star persona, even if, as in this instance, the interviewer realized he was being used as a pawn.

As evident from the first decade of her career, Witherspoon, like so many actors from the South, mostly eschewed southern roles owing to the potential for typecasting, but with *Election* and *Legally Blonde* firmly establishing her career, the following decade witnessed her embrace of southern roles. In the romantic comedy *Sweet Home Alabama* (2002), she played Melanie Smooter, a fashion designer from Pigeon Creek, Alabama, now working in New York City, and Witherspoon noted their similarities: "This is the first character that I've played that I've felt is really close to my own life story and my own personality. . . . She's a Southern girl who moves away and makes an entirely new life for herself in this urban world, then has to go home. Eventually, she grows to love what's beautiful about the place she came from and recognizes it as part of herself, maybe the best part of herself."[24] In another contemporaneous interview, she credited the South for her success in Hollywood: "My Southern upbringing has been real beneficial to me in this industry: being conscientious about people's feelings, being polite, being responsible and never taking for granted what you have in your life."[25] Leaning into her southern roots led to her Oscar-winning role as June Carter Cash in James Mangold's *Walk the Line* (2005), the biography of country singer Johnny Cash. Witherspoon discerned in this role the opportunity to explore the gender dynamics of the South: "For me, it's an interesting study of a Southern woman . . . in that she had so much potential and used it not only for herself but to make the man in her life shine and become the most important voice in country music."[26]

In forming her production company Hello Sunshine, of which Reese's Book Club is a subsidiary, Witherspoon has spoken candidly about her desire to foreground women writers, women readers, and women entrepreneurs. In this move she has increasingly framed herself not only as an entrepreneur but as a social reformer dedicated to increasing women's power throughout the entertainment industry. As Witherspoon says of Hello Sunshine, "It's about storytelling for women, by women, and about getting more women behind the camera,"[27] in a clear indication that she seeks to enhance women's opportunities both on the screen and in the boardrooms where films are greenlit. More succinctly, she has stated, "I want to make a lot of women a lot of money."[28]

Ambition without accomplishment means little, but Hello Sunshine has succeeded on numerous fronts, as Lucy Feldman notes: "Celebrating books through her book club—and adapting them for the screen—is now the foundation of Witherspoon's business at Hello Sunshine, the media company she founded in 2016, where's she established a track record for spotting, and making, hits."[29] Reese's Book Club opened with Gail Honeyman's *Eleanor Oliphant Is Completely Fine* (2017), which was followed by Kate Quinn's *The Alice Network* (2017) and Ruth Ware's *The Lying Game* (2017). When introducing a selection, Witherspoon typically shares her reaction to it, often in terse but effusive statements. "This book gives me all the feels!," she exclaimed of Tembi Locke's *From Scratch: A Memoir of Love, Sicily, and Finding Home* (2019); "I can't even express how much I love this book! I didn't want this story to end!," she gushed of Delia Owens's *Where the Crawdads Sing* (2018).[30] Of course, Reese's Book Club constitutes merely one of Hello Sunshine's ventures, and as Lucy Feldman observes, "Witherspoon doesn't want to run a vanity shingle—she wants to build a media empire."[31] Some selections that have been adapted for film and television include Celeste Ng's *Little Fires Everywhere* (2017), Owens's *Where the Crawdads Sing*, Taylor Jenkins Reid's *Daisy Jones & the Six* (2019), and Cheryl Strayed's *Tiny Beautiful Things* (2012). Witherspoon's media empire fields a range of successful television productions starring Witherspoon herself, including *The Morning Show* (2019–) and *Big Little Lies* (2017–19), for which she was nominated for an Emmy Award for Outstanding Lead Actress in a Limited Series or Movie (although losing to her costar Nicole Kidman).

As evident from the publication dates of these selections, Reese's Book Club directs her readers' attention to contemporary works. More so, through its LitUp scholarship program for members of diverse communities, described as a "writer's fellowship for unpublished, underrepresented women,"[32] Reese's Book Club nurtures a new generation of talent. Another venture, the talk show *Shine On with Reese*, features Witherspoon discussing with women how they achieved their dreams. The inaugural episode featured Dolly Parton as her guest, and Witherspoon has spoken about Parton's influence on her self-perception as a southerner: "When I was probably 5 years old, I wanted to be Dolly Parton. . . . And you made me feel proud about being from a place that other people made fun of."[33] On *Shine On with Reese* Witherspoon has interviewed several other southerners, including country singer Kacey Musgraves and entrepreneur Sara Blakely (the creator of Spanx), among a range of women succeeding in their professional ambitions.

Whereas Witherspoon's book club does not limit itself to a southern milieu in curating authors, she has increasingly leaned into her southern roots in establishing herself as a lifestyle brand. Beyond her wide-ranging career in media, Reese founded the clothing line Draper James. In this endeavor she further builds on the southern aspects of her star persona, as evident in the brand's description on its webpage: "Founded by Reese Witherspoon, Draper James is classic American style, steeped in Southern charm, feminine and pretty. We're so happy you're here."[34] Witherspoon named this company in honor of her grandparents, Dorothea Draper and William James Witherspoon, to whom she dedicated her book *Whiskey in a Teacup: What Growing Up in the South Taught Me about Life, Love, and Baking Biscuits* (2018), declaring, "Thanks to you, I'm a good friend and a great cook, and I never wear sweatpants on airplanes."[35] In a striking example of cross-content marketing, *Whiskey in a Teacup* includes chapters focused on Witherspoon's love of books: "The Perfect Book Club" and "The Perfect Book Club Menu." In the former chapter, Witherspoon divulges her love of reading, "From the minute I could read, I always had my nose in a book,"[36] and again accentuates the southern aspects of her persona, mentioning that "the South has contributed a great deal to literature."[37] The chapter "The Perfect Book Club Menu" recommends red and white wine, baked brie, hot spinach-artichoke dip, an olive medley, crackers, cheese, and fruit as tasty tidbits to accompany discussing novels.[38]

Witherspoon rarely acknowledges the troubles of the South, but in one telling moment, she recognized, if simultaneously diminished, its history of prejudice and discrimination: "I grew up . . . in the South, and there is amazing, wonderful connectivity and people are loving and communitive. . . . But there is a tiny aspect of it, people [who] use parts of the Bible in order to express their intolerance and their hate."[39] The ostensible "tininess" of this aspect of the South depends largely upon one's position in the region's hierarchies of race, class, gender, and sexual orientation, and so it remains to be seen whether Witherspoon's new vision of southern womanhood will fully vanquish its hoary stereotypes. Jenna Bush Hager, the third southern woman with a book club discussed in this chapter, has interviewed Witherspoon several times over her career, stating that the actor "embodies the 'new Southern woman,'" one who is "opinionated with a fiery sense of humor and friendly disposition."[40] With her defiantly entrepreneurial vision, Witherspoon, with the assistance of her book club and its associated bookishness, might finally dispel the anti-intellectual stereotypes that have for too long overshadowed southern women. Hello Sunshine, indeed.

JENNA BUSH HAGER

The diminutive and diminishing term *nepo baby* has only recently entered the American pop-culture lexicon, but nepotism has long buoyed the scions of society's moneyed and privileged elite, ensconcing them ever more deeply into the gilded world into which they were born, regardless of their individual talents—or lack thereof. Nepotism opens doors that remain shut for those with less fortunate backgrounds, but the door that opens owing to family privilege often leaves lingering doubts concerning the beneficiary's talent and qualifications. These dynamics cannot be overlooked in the star persona of Jenna Bush Hager, who holds, with her twin sister Barbara Pierce Bush, the noteworthy distinction of being the only living granddaughters and daughters of U.S. presidents—the forty-first (George Herbert Walker Bush) and the forty-third (George W. Bush).[41] In establishing her unique southern star persona by leaning into the literary arts, Bush Hager parries against nepotistic allegations that might haunt her, all the while her many breakthroughs in publishing and journalism bespeak her continuing exploitation of this ostensible "birthright."

As with virtually all bookish celebrities, Bush Hager professes that her childhood love for reading foreshadowed her adult pursuit of the literary arts. As David Canfield records, "Hager . . . says she was a born reader. She grew up without a TV in her room—'The book was the only choice!'—and vividly recalls her mother reading *Little Women* to her and her twin sister, Barbara, when they were 5 or 6 years old. Other pre-adulthood obsessions include *The Baby-Sitters Club* and Toni Morrison's *The Bluest Eye*."[42] One could hardly imagine an odder pairing of beloved childhood texts than Ann M. Martin's tween series involving the trials and tribulations facing suburban babysitters and Morrison's searing account of a young Black girl's experience of racism and other traumas, yet they certainly suggest an ecumenical range of tastes. Moving from childhood to late adolescence and early adulthood, Bush Hager pursued an English major during her undergraduate studies at the University of Texas at Austin. As an adult reader, as Canfield writes, "she counts Donna Tartt, Ann Patchett, and Hanya Yanagihara (author of *A Little Life*) as all-time favorites."[43] Bush Hager has also praised Isabel Allende's *Daughter of Fortune* as one of her most beloved novels and observes of her tastes in fiction, "All of the books I read have strong women characters going out and conquering and becoming independent, and they don't care about men."[44]

Surely one should not doubt Bush Hager's passion for reading, nor should one dismiss her pursuit of it as an intellectually challenging academic endeavor during her undergraduate years, but one would nonetheless need to be rather shockingly naïve to overlook the nepotism that garnered her early successes in publishing and broadcasting. In 2007 she published *Ana's Story: A Journey of Hope*, the account of a seventeen-year-old mother with HIV whom she met while working as a UNICEF intern in Latin America. Ben McGrath's snarky account of her book launch, published in the *New Yorker*, documents the shortcuts available to a U.S. president's daughter: "Jane Friedman, the president and C.E.O. of HarperCollins, got a call from her friend Robert Barnett, the lawyer in Washington, D.C., last January. He said, 'Jenna Bush is doing a book,' and offered to arrange a meeting."[45] (As widely known in the publishing industry, Barnett "specializes in securing book deals for Beltway VIPS.")[46] Name recognition rather than literary artistry would appear to be the motivating factor for HarperCollins to sign this neophyte author, evident in Friedman's assessment of Bush Hager's style: "From what I gather, she's a very facile writer."[47] Few authors would appreciate the word "facile" being applied to their talents. It is hardly surprising that the *New Yorker*, a leftward-leaning and rather snooty publication, pilloried Bush Hager's efforts, such as in McGrath's observation, "She has a weakness for dubious ethnic analogies: 'His eyes were wild, like those of the pumas that lived in the jungles,' and 'A nurse wrapped Beatriz in a blanket—like a burrito.'" Even her admirers, however, damned her with faint praise: "Still, as Nils Kastberg, UNICEF's regional director for Latin America and the Caribbean, and Jenna's old boss, said, 'It's a million times better than the many memorandums that we write.'"[48] Certainly, *Ana's Story* benefited from a full-court publicity junket from Harper Collins. Bush Hager won a $300,000 advance, and her novel benefited from an eye-popping first printing of 500,000 copies.⁴⁹ As Amy Argetsinger records, "After a major publicity rollout by publisher HarperCollins—including interviews this week in *People* magazine, *The Washington Post*, and on ABC's *20/20*—Bush's first bookstore appearance in a three-month, 25-city tour was an unusual test of the 25-year-old's star power."⁵⁰ Argetsinger rightly refers to Bush Hager's "star power," with the slight irony that the author's stardom arose from kinship rather than from any previous accomplishment.

Bush Hager followed her successful debut novel with *Read All about It!*, a children's book cowritten with her mother, Laura Bush. *Read All about It!* tells the tale of Tyrone Brown, a reluctant reader who learns from his teacher an important lesson: "You never know who you are going to meet in a book!"⁵¹ In a note on the back cover, the authors write, "Discovering a good book can change our lives forever. Books offer a world of adventure, new friends, and a lifetime of learning. We hope *Read All about It!* will be a window into the power and magic of books!"⁵² Almost a decade later, mother and daughter reteamed for *Our Great Big Backyard* (2016), another children's book telling a similar story of enthusiasm overcoming truculence: Jane, an unenthusiastic traveler, comes to appreciate America's outdoor wonders after visiting Everglades National Park, Big Bend National Park, and other such sites. As with *Read All about It!*, the back cover of *Our Great Big Backyard* conveys the authors' theme for their readers: "*Our Great Big Backyard* encourages everyone—children, parents, and even grandparents—to get outdoors and find your park!"⁵³ Only an unnecessarily scurrilous critic would denigrate these optimistic tales espousing the virtues of reading and nature, yet only a woefully naïve reader would presume that they would have been published without the famed name of "Bush" twice appearing on their respective covers.

In September 2012 *Southern Living* hired Bush Hager as an editor-at-large, thus burnishing both her southern and her literary credentials. In the publicity surrounding this announcement, Bush Hager stressed her southern roots: "As a proud Texan, I grew up flipping through my mother's copy of the magazine, dreaming of the dishes. . . . I'm excited to interview influential Southerners, explore iconic places, and show how the next generation of women entertain."⁵⁴ Editor-in-chief Lindsay Bierman declared that she was "instantly charmed by Jenna's style and charisma. Her Texas roots, passion for the South, and proven reporting chops make her a natural fit for the brand."⁵⁵ Many of Bush Hager's articles for *Southern Living* profiled southern female celebrities, including Reese Witherspoon, Martina McBride, and Joanna Gaines;[56] others focused on her Texas roots and celebrated the state's culinary and holiday traditions.[57] Still, several of her essays traded on her family connections, such as her portraits of her maternal grandmother, Jenna Welch; her paternal grandmother, Barbara Bush; and her mother.[58] To state the obvious: most journalists cannot write up portraits of their mothers and grandmothers and expect them to be published.

Along with her forays in children's literature and celebrity profiles, Bush Hager has published two memoirs, *Sisters First: Stories from Our Wild and Wonderful Life* (2017), cowritten with her sister Barbara, and *Everything Beautiful in Its Time: Seasons of Love and Loss* (2020). Like the portraits of her family published in *Southern Living*, it is difficult to imagine these works being published without Bush Hager's family connections, a circumstance noted in many of the reviews. In his assessment of *Sisters First*, Frank Bruni captures this tension: "The stories that they tell are often self-serving, and they skim over the failures and wages of their father's presidency. But they do make you question the caricatures that we blithely traffic in, the assumptions that we breezily make and our reluctance to allow for how much the objects of our curiosity can change."[59] Concurrent with the publication of *Sisters First*, the Bush sisters also published an open letter in *Time* magazine to Sasha and Malia Obama, titled "Dear Sasha and Malia," offering them trite if nonetheless apt advice for their lives after leaving the White House: "Take all that you have seen, the people you have met, the lessons you have learned, and let that help guide you in making positive change."[60] Traditionally, presidents leave personal notes of encouragement and wisdom for their successors; they do not publicize these letters in national magazines. In the marketing blitz for *Sisters First*, however, the Bush sisters exploited their patrimony to dole out unsolicited and bland advice with little purpose other than to garner the limelight.

Building on her foundations in authorship and magazine writing, Bush Hager secured a position as a journalist and correspondent for NBC's *Today*. As mentioned in her memoir *Everything Beautiful in Its Time*, she was initially indisposed to a career in journalism. The media coverage of her college years, including the mini-scandals of 2001 when she was charged with underage possession of alcohol in April and then with attempting to purchase alcohol with a fake ID in May, turned a typical young adult's rebellious pastimes into a national news event, which left her with a bitter aftertaste: "If you'd asked me twenty years ago if I would one day pursue a career in media, I would have said absolutely not. This was the industry that plastered 'freshman fifteen' photos of Barbara and me everywhere after we were caught drinking underage."[61] Ultimately, she changed her mind. While working as an English teacher at a Baltimore school in her mid-twenties, "a producer at the *Today* show kept calling to ask if I would consider coming on as a correspondent."[62] Such is hardly the fate of the average Baltimore teacher, or of the average English major graduate of the University of Texas at Austin. Bush Hager signed with NBC in 2009, and her profile has widened over the years. She scored notable interviews with such figures as Michelle Obama and increasingly substituted for hosts Kathie Lee Gifford and Hoda Kotb. She has more recently been named, with Kotb, the cohost of *Today*'s fourth hour.

Bush Hager launched her book club, Read With Jenna, in March 2019, choosing Tara Conklin's *The Last Romantics* as her first selection. (See figure 13.) Many participants in celebrity book clubs assume that the host personally selects each book based on her personal tastes, and this presumption serves an essential purpose in honing the intellectual aspects of the star's persona. This vision, however, chafes against the stark reality that such labors are extremely time-extensive, to the point that many book club hosts rely on their support teams to undertake the laborious work behind each selection. These behind-the-scenes dynamics are rarely exposed to readers, but Bush Hager, in revealing Witherspoon's outsourcing of her book club to her staff, attempted to solidify her own hosting persona: "Reese Witherspoon was on the show the other day, and we were talking about it. She's like, 'I have a whole team, Jenna!' The problem is, I definitely need to read the whole book before I recommend it—and I'm a pretty picky reader." The contrast that Bush Hager establishes—Witherspoon's laissez-faire approach versus her own pickiness—subtly elevates the intellectualism she seeks to enhance.[63] More so, book clubs develop unique characteristics and traits, and readers have distinguished between Witherspoon's and Bush Hager's book clubs. Doug Jones, deputy publisher of Harper-Collins, avowed of Bush Hager's selection of Etaf Rum's *A Woman Is No Man*: "It's a brave choice because it's not an easy book. . . . It's very different, say, than some of the Reese picks. It's not a beach read"; Bush Hager added, "We should take back the term 'beach read' and have it mean anything that somebody reads compulsively on

FIG. 13. Bush Hager inaugurates her book club with Tara Conklin's *The Last Romantics*, and thus completes the evolution of her image from a President's "wild child" and nepo baby to cultural arbiter.

the beach."[64] Nonetheless, as much as Bush Hager highlights her pickiness as a reason to trust her choices, David Canfield reports both of her success and of the challenges of running a book club: "This year, no other book club has come close to Read With Jenna in sales influence. Hager is now bringing other readers into assist."[65] The profile concludes, "Still, her genuine love of reading is evident throughout our conversation."[66]

As Bush Hager's career has flourished on *Today*, her book club allows her to stake out a unique identity from the other hosts, cohosts, and reporters. The website for Read With Jenna establishes her as somewhat of a literacy expert, such as in a short article detailing her strategies for encouraging children to read: "Teaching a kid or watching a kid learn how to read is evolutionarily one of the most beautiful things that can happen as a parent," she states, as she also offers four pieces of advice to parents: Model reading, create a reading-focused space, discover and explore your children's interests, and find books with compelling adaptations.[67] In addition to Read With Jenna, she also hosts Read With Jenna Jr.—a book club guaranteeing "kid-friendly" selections.[68] Whereas many aspects of book culture shy away from consumer culture—despite the inherent paradox that books are part of consumer culture—Bush Hager leans into opportunities for cross marketing and the additional profits that it stokes, evident in such articles as "Jenna Bush Hager Recommends Five Things to Buy While Reading *Camp Zero*," in which she advocates that readers purchase a hooded terry robe, a sky projector, a bath pillow, a bathtub caddy, and a flower resin book page holder set to enhance their enjoyment of Michelle Min Sterling's novel.[69] As her success has blossomed and she has relied less on her familial connections to advance professionally, Bush Hager trumpets her love of books as the defining aspect of her professional identity: "I love reading for so many reasons, it really is sort of my escape from everyday life. It's how I calm down. It's how I detach. It's how I fall in love with other places that I will never go to. It's how I empathize with characters who are nothing like me. . . . There's nothing like falling in love with a book."[70]

Three incredibly successful southern women, three incredibly successful book clubs—again, this is a coincidence worth noting, but perhaps little more. Nonetheless, in a region where women's intelligence has long been derided and stereotyped as inferior, where prevailing gendered codes endorse men's outdoor pursuits over more cerebral pastimes, where literacy rates lag behind the rest of the nation's—it takes a certain amount of audacity to believe in the power of books to change the lives of readers but also to enhance one's own celebrity appeal.[71] Winfrey, Witherspoon, and Bush Hager, born and raised in the South, found national fame and then took to the books, even if, in a final irony, they all left the South in doing so.

10

ELLEN DeGENERES'S QUEER VOICE OF SOUTHERN (UN)KINDNESS

In a variety of national competitions ranging from spelling bees to beauty pageants, participants represent both themselves and their home states, with their victories redounding to the glory of their regional roots. Such is the case for Ellen DeGeneres, who ignited her comedy career by winning the title of Funniest Person in New Orleans. As she explained, "They taped my show that night, and my tape was sent to the contest for the whole state of Louisiana. I won and became the Funniest Person in Louisiana. I don't even think anyone else entered (maybe Al Hirt or Archie Manning)."[1] She subsequently won Showtime's Funniest Person in America competition—"Having that title and being on Showtime got me a lot of attention"[2]—and on November 28, 1986, she scored another notable career achievement when, during her first appearance on *The Tonight Show*, she became the first female comedian whom host Johnny Carson invited over to sit down and chat after her routine. Her eponymous sitcom *Ellen* debuted in 1994 and ran to 1998,[3] and DeGeneres registered a milestone moment in television history when both she and her character came out as lesbian in 1997. Although *Ellen* was canceled soon after and her career entered a period of doldrums, she skyrocketed back into the public consciousness with her phenomenally successful daytime program *The Ellen DeGeneres Show*, which premiered in 2003 and ran for nineteen seasons. A queer trailblazer and an uproarious comic talent, DeGeneres built her star persona through her honesty, her authenticity, and her consistent emphasis that all people must be treated with—and treat others with—a fundamental kindness reflective of their inherent worth as human beings. As Brenda R. Weber and Joselyn K. Leimbach explain, authenticity yoked the divergent aspects of DeGeneres's appealing star persona throughout much of her career: "Ellen DeGeneres is not famous for being famous. She is famous for being herself. Or at least . . . for conveying authenticity under the banner of a comedic Ellen-ness in which her perceived genuineness functions as the mortar that holds the house of Ellen together."[4] Quite simply, DeGeneres's countless fans appreciated her for being her honest and truthful queer self.

But then in 2020 the bubble burst, when DeGeneres's star persona collapsed under allegations that her reputation for kindness merely camouflaged her indifference and even callousness. Because she modeled a persona of authenticity and benevolence expressed through her unique identity as a queer southerner, she provides a particularly rich, if regrettable, metonym of the region as a whole. Like DeGeneres, the South has long prided itself for its kindness and manners, for its traditions collectively branded under the rubric of "southern hospitality," while evincing little concern for those marginalized by its mores. As Anthony Szczesiul summarizes in his brilliant monograph *The Southern Hospitality Myth*, "Rather than promoting an ethics of universal welcome, the discourse of southern hospitality has expressed a retrograde politics of exclusion."[5] An ultimately hollow understanding of kindness and hospitality continues to haunt the South, in its collective self-proclamations of warmth and geniality that attempt to suture over its troubled past and present, particularly in regard to the valorization of heteronormative whiteness over marginalized, nonwhite, and queer communities. DeGeneres's star persona exuded warmth and charm until the façade was stripped away, leaving many fans alienated by the disjunction between the facts and the fictions of her celebrity.

DeGeneres's southern background registers steadily in the background, and frequently in the foreground, of her performances and self-presentation. "I was born, bred, and lightly sautéed in and around New Orleans, a city steeped in tradition and marinated in history," she wrote in her first book, *My Point . . . and I Do Have One*.[6] Published in 1995 amidst the fanfare for her fledgling eponymous sitcom and thus as part of the marketing campaign both for her and for it, *My Point . . . and I Do Have One* allowed DeGeneres to introduce herself to a national audience through her regional identity as a southerner while concomitantly establishing her unique comic voice, evident in her rambling, peripatetic style. Notably, her dilatory manner includes mentioning twice in three pages that she is a native Louisianian, as she also declared, "I was born in Jefferson Parish, Louisiana, at Ochsner Hospital, January 26, 1958. I lived in a house on Haring Road in Metairie until I was . . . oh, let's say eight or nine—maybe ten . . . could've been seven or six, I don't know."[7] These lines exhibit the circular and backtracking nature of much of DeGeneres's humor, as she meanders in and around a point, perhaps to reach a conclusion of some sort or perhaps just to enjoy the meandering, for surely she would remember whether she lived on Metairie's Haring Road until she was either six or ten years old. This passage illustrates her key comic strategies of evasion, digression, and sideways approaches to her topics, as John Limon explains: "DeGeneres wants to get to her 'main point.' She wants to put her main point, exhibitionistically, in front and not aside. Except kidding is her point. Which is to say that digression itself is the point. What she does not want to put aside is the aside."[8]

As these examples also demonstrate, DeGeneres's allusions to the South in her comedy routines frequently appear, in musical terms, as grace notes to a theme she is otherwise developing, such as when she offered a "thank you" to the New Orleans Saints,[9] or when she recalled, "My dad . . . called a lot of people 'Pahdnah.' I don't know if it was a New Orleans thing or if he just couldn't remember people's names."[10] Despite the overarching kindness she espouses as a key part of her celebrity persona, DeGeneres allows herself the occasional antagonist with whom to spar, and notably, the most prominent of these figures has been her fellow New Orleanian Harry Connick Jr., such as in her advice to insomniacs: "You need to read something boring, like a story written by Harry Connick Jr. or something."[11] In transcribing her supposed journal entry for May 16, 2009, DeGeneres touched upon her southern roots and background, as well as referring to her gender nonconformity: "Today I gave the commencement speech at Tulane University in my hometown of New Orleans. I had a great time and I think I gave those kids a lot of great advice. I can't believe they let me do that even though I didn't go to no college. I meant to, but I totally forgot. I think I made my mama very proud today by making one of her dreams for me come true. I finally wore a gown."[12] A native New Orleanian rarely dressed in traditionally female attire who "forgot" to attend college: such an image captures the biographical truth of DeGeneres but wrapped within an overarching comic presentation and persona. More than merely a child of the region raised in its folkways, DeGeneres employs the South as a touchstone of core truths of her personality, as revealed in a statement about her love of dancing and southern pronouns: "If you know me personally . . . then you know I love to dance. I really do, y'all. (Y'all is a New Orleans expression that I felt obliged to include at least once in this book to show that I haven't 'Gone Hollywood.' There, I've used it. Now no highfalutin' critic can say that I've forgotten where I came from)."[13] A southern-accented "y'all" proves the truth of DeGeneres's southern star persona—notwithstanding the inherent paradox of an authentic persona—as well as counterbalancing the possibility of a "highfalutin' critic" accusing her of inauthenticity.

As DeGeneres's southern upbringing inflects her star persona in a winsomely appealing manner, so does her emphasis on manners and kindness. These twin aspects of her persona—southernness and kindness—were evident from early in her career, such as in a 1994 *Primetime Live* interview that aired as part of the publicity junket surrounding the launch of *Ellen*. Host Sam Donaldson introduced the segment: "Everyone likes a good laugh, and we know a woman who's got more than enough to share. Just ask correspondent Judd Rose, who went down South with TV comedy star Ellen DeGeneres, to the place she once called home, to serve up a little after-dinner treat." Known for his somewhat stilted delivery, Donaldson nonetheless builds an appealing image of the star, stressing her regional roots in the trip "down south" and playing on the tropes of southern foodways in the image of a home-cooked meal. During the interview unfolding amidst this southern backdrop, Rose describes DeGeneres as "a friendly puppy, eager to please, if a little awkward about it" and stresses as well that "what comes across most is that she is relentlessly nice."[14] And truly, one need hardly scour the DeGeneres archives to find that she has repeatedly emphasized the importance of kindness. In *The Funny Thing Is . . .* , she admonishes, "Be nice to everyone, even though you don't want to and you may not like certain people. Be kind, friendly, and respectful even if people are not nice to you. That way, you're not dragged down to their level."[15] In another moment, when discussing a tour stop in Atlanta, DeGeneres again employed "y'all" to emphasize her affection for the South owing specifically to the region's etiquette: "It's so nice to be back in the South, back on familiar turf. . . . Everything is 'yes ma'am' and 'no ma'am.' My favorite is 'y'all' (which I still use).

It's such an economical way to talk. 'Yall goin'?' is so much easier to say than, 'Are you presently considering departing?'"[16] The references to southern manners—"'yes ma'am' and 'no ma'am'"—reinforce both her southern *bona fides* and her kindness. Chapter titles from *Seriously . . . I'm Kidding* include "Common Courtesy" and "*American Idol*, or 'If You Don't Have Anything Nice to Say, Don't Say Anything at All,'" with the latter detailing her discomfort during her stint as a judge on this reality-TV singing competition, for which she needed to candidly assess the strengths and weaknesses of each contestant. The public consensus, confirmed by DeGeneres herself, resolved that she was simply too kind to serve effectively as a judge: "As hectic as my schedule was, the bottom line is that I don't like judging people and I don't like hurting people's feelings."[17] Kindness so defined DeGeneres's persona and proclaimed worldview that it became almost axiomatic in her conversations, such as when she stated seriously and concisely, "My point is, be nice and be on time,"[18] as opposed to expressing this concept in her typical dilatory phrasings. T. J. Holmes aptly assesses DeGeneres as "a woman who has built a reputation and, in fact, an empire on the idea of us all being nice, being kind to each other."[19]

As much as authenticity, southernness, and kindness define DeGeneres's star persona, her self-presentation is also indelibly shaped by her queerness. Queer stars face a particularly complex challenge in creating an authentic persona if they are closeted, for the ostensible authenticity of their personas clashes with the required inauthenticity of a life in which they demur from divulging to fans a core aspect of their identity. DeGeneres mostly elided discussions of her sexuality during the early years of her comedy career but occasionally presented herself as straight, such as in a comic scenario in which she imagined herself flirting with a male police officer to avoid a speeding ticket and tells him, "I'm single so I feel it's important to look my best for men because that's my job as a woman. I date a lot of guys; I'm not seeing anyone seriously at this particular time."[20] Owing to such jokes and to a cultural presumption of heteronormativity, the general public simply assumed her straightness, and during the early years of her career she was frequently referred to with such terms as "America's sweetheart" and "the girl next door"—phrases fraught with the wearied expectation that she would find the right man soon enough.[21]

Given these conditions, and despite the irony of candor as a key component of her star persona, DeGeneres's early fame was burdened by the virtual impossibility of authenticity, and this dynamic sabotaged the creation and performance of her eponymous character in *Ellen*. As is well established in sitcom history, many stars play fictionalized yet recognizable versions of themselves in their series. Ray Romano is not Ray Barone of *Everybody Loves Raymond* (1996–2005); Bernie Mac is not Bernie McCullough of *The Bernie Mac Show* (2001–6); Tina Fey is not Liz Lemon of *30 Rock* (2006–13)—except for the fact that these roles featured key aspects of their comic personas and that their shows were greenlit and marketed on the premise that they would play characters approximating the public's understanding of their personalities. DeGeneres asserted her affection for a fellow southern sitcom star—"I loved Andy Griffith"[22]—thus alluding to another example of a comedic star persona that aligned smoothly with the actor's starring role. In contrast, DeGeneres publicly demarcated herself from her character: "Most people you meet on television are pretty close to their characters. They're not exactly, but they're pretty close. I just didn't think that's what I wanted to focus on on my show."[23] The establishing shot of *Ellen*'s pilot episode—a California Department of Motor Vehicles office—removes the eponymous star/character from her southern roots, and this episode's comic plot—that Ellen Morgan's driver's license photograph is so unflattering that she goes to outrageous comic lengths to replace it—allows viewers to assume her straightness. *Ellen*'s fundamental premise was that Ellen Morgan stood as the central figure of a group of four friends—evident in the program's original title as *These Friends of Mine*—but even as the show notched ratings sufficient for renewal, its storylines meandered in search of a meaningful arc—largely owing to the distance between Ellen DeGeneres and Ellen Morgan. Between the first and second seasons lead characters were dropped, new characters were introduced, and the show was retitled, but without a romantic interest or a comically conflicted work space—two of the defining narrative structures of television sitcoms—*Ellen* drifted in search of its comic *raison d'être*.

In a similar instance of the inauthenticity of the closet and its effect on her career, in 1996 DeGeneres starred in her first feature-length film, *Mr. Wrong*, as the success of *Ellen* indicated a sizable market for the star and her humorous style. The result, however, bombed at the box office and suffered a drubbing by critics. Merging black comedy with the standard tropes of romcoms, *Mr. Wrong* depicts DeGeneres's character Martha Alston realizing the grim truth behind the charming façade presented by her boyfriend Whitman Crawford

(Bill Pullman). As the critical consensus on the website Rotten Tomatoes reads, "A mean-spirited joke without a punchline, *Mr. Wrong* is so painfully unfunny that Ellen DeGeneres and Bill Pullman's lack of chemistry feels like a total drag despite being the point."[24] As with *Ellen*, *Mr. Wrong* could not suture over the inconsistencies between DeGeneres's star persona and her acting abilities,[25] nor could it overcome the disjunction between black comedy and the affable kindness for which DeGeneres was becoming known.

With *Ellen*'s ratings sagging and DeGeneres increasingly dissatisfied with life in the closet, she aligned herself more closely with Ellen Morgan when they both came out of the closet: for the star in a *Time* magazine cover story (April 14, 1997) that included the caption "Yep I'm Gay"; and for the fictional character in "The Puppy Episode." A pivotal moment in the history of queer television representation, this episode featured a parade of celebrity cameos, including Demi Moore, Billy Bob Thornton, k. d. lang, Gina Gershon, and Melissa Etheridge, and it explicitly linked the struggle for queer rights to Black Americans' struggle for civil rights. In a conversation with her therapist, played by Oprah Winfrey, Ellen Morgan says, "Society has a pretty big problem with [queer people]. . . . Do you think I want to be discriminated against? Do you think I want people to call me names to my face? To have people commit hate crimes against you just because you're not like them?" Her therapist interjects, "To have separate bathrooms and separate water fountains, sit at the back of the bus?" It is likely happenstance, but no less compelling to observe, that these two characters are played by southern women marginalized by heteronormative and white cultures, thus imbuing the scene with a tacit critique of the region and its conservatism. Later in the episode, Ellen Morgan accidentally comes out not only to her love interest Susan (Laura Dern) but to bystanders in a crowded airport waiting area: "Why am I so afraid to tell people? . . . I'm thirty-five years old. Why can't I just come out and say . . . I'm gay. You hear that? I'm gay. And it sounds pretty darn good." (See figure 14.) Although a momentous event in the history of queer television, *Ellen* was cancelled soon after, both DeGeneres and Dern struggled to find work, and Winfrey received viciously racist hate mail.

Following "The Puppy Episode," DeGeneres's star persona evolved into greater authenticity, and her emphasis on kindness evolved as well, particularly because she could speak candidly about the bigotry she faced as a lesbian, both before and after coming out of the closet. In the *Time* interview in which she

FIG. 14. In "The Puppy Episode" of her sitcom *Ellen*, Ellen DeGeneres's character Ellen Morgan (left) comes out to herself, her potential love interest Susan (Laura Dern), and the travelers sitting at an airport gate, in a pivotal moment of queer television history.

disclosed her homosexuality, she eloquently recounted the isolation of a closeted lifestyle: "I never felt like I belonged anywhere. I never felt like I belonged to the gay community, I never felt like I belonged to the straight community. I've really felt like this in-between. I watched the whole Gay Pride march in Washington in 1993, and I wept when I saw that. I mean I cried so hard, thinking, 'I wish I could be there,' because I never felt like I belonged anywhere."[26] In addition to her admission of such gut-wrenching loneliness, she divulged that she had long endured the rampant homophobia of the comedy circuit, in the many instances when she shared the stage with comics cracking antiqueer jokes and then proceeded to entertain these audiences who found such humor funny: "You can imagine the fag jokes. When I started headlining, it was always guys on before me. I would always follow somebody doing either dyke jokes or fag jokes and doing the lisp thing and the audience is going crazy and laughing.

I just thought, 'Oh God. What if they pick up that I'm gay?' It was that fear and shame."[27] Homophobic attacks did not miraculously cease when DeGeneres came out, and the *Time* interviewer added, "Jerry Falwell called you Ellen DeGenerate," to which DeGeneres coolly replied, "Really, he called me that? Ellen DeGenerate? I've been getting that since the fourth grade. I guess I'm happy I could give him work."[28] DeGeneres frequently referred to coming out as a defining moment of her life when she opted for authenticity: "It wasn't until I decided to really live my life honestly and openly and come out that I had to just be—I'm not living my life for anyone else but me, I have to live my life."[29]

Even after coming out, DeGeneres's queer persona generated considerable comment, particularly for her subversion of the butch/femme binary. She often grooms and dresses herself somewhat masculinely, evident in her short haircut and her preference for pants over skirts and dresses, but with sufficient focus on her beauty—her luminous skin and piercing blue eyes—that she landed a contract with makeup corporation CoverGirl. As she wrote with tongue in cheek, "Throughout my entire life, I have believed . . . that true beauty is not related to what color your hair is or what color your eyes are. True beauty is about who you are as a human being, your principles, your moral compass. And then in 2008 I was finally able to throw all that hogwash out the window because I was named the new face of CoverGirl cosmetics!"[30] In enacting what some might deem a homonormative version of queerness, most evidently through her marriage to Portia de Rossi and her non-inflammatory style, DeGeneres's lesbianism inflects her star persona without politicizing it, a noteworthy (although some would concomitantly argue not a praiseworthy) accomplishment. As Linda Mizejewski observes, "DeGeneres's predictable wholesomeness and upbeat nature are indeed disturbing elements that would prefer to make butch lesbianism invisible or at least abjected. DeGeneres instead makes lesbianism itself incoherent for such a worldview."[31] Yet here again, even with these critiques, one can discern an authenticity to DeGeneres's queer southern star persona as tailored to her personality and desires, not to cultural preconceptions of how lesbians, whether butch, femme, or binary-breaking, should publicly appear.

Throughout the years of *The Ellen DeGeneres Show*, DeGeneres commented on her goals and aspirations for herself and her viewers, primarily in terms of creating an entertaining experience with an ethos of social responsibility. "It's escapism from what's going on, one hour of feeling good," she declared, and then added: "At the core it's a comedy show. But if it's not funny, at least it feels good."³² Speaking more seriously, she addressed the importance of role models, particularly for female viewers: "And now that I have my own show on television I feel a sense of responsibility to follow in their footsteps and have a positive influence on the young girls and women who watch me every day. That's why I keep things light and upbeat and it's why I try to have powerful and influential women on my show to serve as examples for the people at home. I love having women like Michelle Obama and Hillary Clinton on my show."³³ Over the hundreds and hundreds of episodes of *The Ellen DeGeneres Show*, DeGeneres presented herself as a kindly authentic queer southerner, perhaps most passionately in her fundraising for New Orleans following Hurricane Katrina in 2005 and in her denunciations of antigay bullying in 2010. Speaking of her hometown, DeGeneres affirmed, "New Orleans was such a special city" and disclosed the emotional turmoil wrought by its destruction: "I didn't do a monologue. I talked about my family and my friends and I cried and tried not to cry."³⁴ She spearheaded several fundraisers for the city's citizens and its recovery efforts, thereby enacting the authentic kindness for which she was known. Following the death of Tyler Clementi, a Rutgers University undergraduate student who ended his life after his roommate secretly recorded his sexual encounters with another man, DeGeneres implored her audience to stand with her against bullying: "I am devastated over the death of eighteen-year-old Tyler Clementi. . . . My heart is breaking for their families, for their friends and for our society that continues to let this happen. These kids needed us and we have an obligation to change this."³⁵ Various other examples of DeGeneres's charitable and public service could be added to these, and they collectively demonstrate the inherent plausibility of DeGeneres's queer southern persona as invested in bringing about a kinder, gentler world for all.

As the eponymous host of *The Ellen DeGeneres Show*, DeGeneres recognized the need to present herself authentically while, somewhat ironically, modulating herself through the role of a talk show host: "The talk show is me, but I'm also playing a character of a talk-show host. There's a tiny, tiny bit of difference."³⁶ The crux of star personas, however, is that such a "tiny, tiny bit of difference" lies in the eye of the beholders—not just the star's vision of her dual selves but those of her fans, entourage, and others. Toward the end of her talk show's run, DeGeneres found herself mired in a series of small controversies that left her persona of authentic southern kindness in tatters. She was seen conversing with former President George W. Bush—who built his 2004 reelection campaign on opposing gay marriage—at a Dallas Cowboys football game, and she defended comic Kevin Hart after he was relieved of his hosting duties for the Academy Awards following several homophobic statements, leading many fans to wonder why a queer woman would socialize with and defend straight men who demonized and derided queer people. In an uncomfortable moment on her program, DeGeneres chided actor Dakota Johnson for not inviting her to her birthday party, but Johnson correctly insisted that DeGeneres had been invited. When the COVID pandemic necessitated that the population quarantine in their homes, Ellen joked of life in her palatial estate, "One thing that I've learned from being in quarantine is that people—this is like being in jail, is what it is. . . . It's mostly because I've been wearing the same clothes for ten days and everyone in here is gay."[37] The joke fell flat and suggested a person out of touch both with the seriousness of the moment and with her astounding wealth and privilege. As such controversies mounted, comedian Kevin T. Porter tweeted that DeGeneres is "notoriously one of the meanest people alive" and encouraged others to submit their accounts of her misbehavior: "Respond to this with the most insane stories you've heard about Ellen being mean & I'll match every one w/ $2 to [the Los Angeles Food Bank]."[38]

Behind the scenes of *The Ellen DeGeneres Show*, DeGeneres's employees found her persona of southern kindness a cruel joke as they endured what many described as a toxic workplace. As Hank Stuever documents, "Long-standing rumors about her backstage demeanor (don't speak directly to her, don't look her in the eye, don't let her smell you . . .) coalesced into workplace grievances. . . . Former employees and industry colleagues began sharing stories about DeGeneres's dark side. WarnerMedia launched an internal investigation; three top *Ellen* producers were fired."[39] DeGeneres apologized for the controversy—"If I ever let someone down, if I've ever hurt their feelings, I am so sorry for that. If that's ever the case, I've let myself down and I've hurt myself"[40]—although, as several commentators noted, apologies are rarely convincing when phrased conditionally, and thus the half-hearted apology apparently confirmed the illusory nature of her star persona. Notably as well, DeGeneres ruefully advised her viewers to consider carefully any personas they might be considering for themselves: "Anybody who's thinking that changing their title or giving yourself a nickname, do not go with The Be Kind Lady. Don't do it. The truth is, I am that person that you see on TV. I am also a lot of other things. I, sometimes I get sad. I get mad. I get anxious. I get frustrated. I get impatient. And I am working on all of that."[41] With these words DeGeneres obliquely alluded to her star persona: she is both "that person you see on TV" and a real human being experiencing a range of human emotions, including unpleasant ones, that the star persona could never admit.

Ultimately, the collapse of DeGeneres's southern star persona accentuates the simple fact that personas are manicured representations of people, not the people themselves. DeGeneres discerned this core truth of celebrity identity in a similar conundrum commonly facing comedians: that their fans, sometimes even their family and friends, expect them to be perpetually amusing: "As a comedian, I've learned that people expect me to be funny all the time. That is a lot of pressure, as you can imagine. I'm not the kind of person who is 'on' all the time, and I don't really like being around those types of personalities. . . . I am funny but that doesn't mean I'm always funny. I'm also sad and mad and shy and serious."[42] No one can be funny all the time, and it is equally unlikely that any person could be truly kind all the time, but as the South has long prided itself on its manners while excluding countless people from full equality, so too does DeGeneres exemplify the ultimate emptiness of southern manners. It would be too coy to end this chapter by saying, "Oh, Ellen, bless your heart" because, as southerners know, this sweet-as-honey phrase cloaks a serpent's tongue, as DeGeneres explained to British comedian James Corden. He interpreted the words positively, as "That's the nicest expression you could ever have," but DeGeneres corrected him, explaining that southerners would likely translate its meaning as something along the lines of "You poor, stupid person."[43] But bless the heart of any and all celebrities hoping the public will never discern the line between their persons and their personas.

TYLER PERRY
Atlanta's Entrepreneur and Queer Auteur

Flip the pages of any entertainment magazine, and its photographs confirm that glitzy residences, bedecked with lush furnishings and set on expansive grounds, register as one of the defining perks of the higher tiers of stardom. Despite such awe-inspiring tributes to their impeccable taste and extravagant fortunes, few stars can concomitantly claim that they have irrevocably altered a city's landscape in the manner that Tyler Perry has reshaped Atlanta, Georgia. By purchasing the grounds of Fort McPherson, a former military base, to refurbish as a film studio, Perry recalibrated the city's past, present, and future, as Oprah Winfrey documented in a portrait of her collaborator: "Tyler made history, opening the largest privately owned motion-picture studio in the U.S., set on 330 acres. The former Confederate Army base is now a state-of-the-art production facility with twelve soundstages—each named after an iconic African-American figure."[1] Perry himself pondered the historic significance of his studio's location, identifying the seismic shift in its racial significance—"The land itself was once a Confederate Army base, which meant there were people here fighting to keep my ancestors enslaved"[2]—as he also claimed its significance to his entrepreneurial ambitions: "I own the lights. I own the sets. . . . So that's where the difference is. Because I own everything, my returns are higher."[3] Throughout his decades as Atlanta's preeminent entertainment mogul, Perry has toggled seamlessly between presenting himself as a groundbreaking entrepreneur and also as what might be termed a queer auteur. As a filmmaker continually skirting borders between genders, social classes, Black and white audiences, and "high" and "low" art, Perry mediates ostensible binaries that have long dominated the South and the arts, thereby building a southern star persona uniquely invulnerable to their strictures. Queerness, in this regard, need not correlate with homosexuality, but instead with a desire to break down normative codes of art and southern life.

A New Orleanian by birth (September 13, 1969) and childhood, Perry moved to Atlanta in the early 1990s to pursue his theatrical ambitions and soon found himself inspired by the city's vibrant Black community of arts, culture, and business. As he recalled, "That world opened up to me on my first visit to Atlanta during 'Freaknik,' a sort of spring break without the beach for black college kids. I wasn't in college, but I went anyway. . . . For the first time in my life, I saw there were black people doing great things with their lives. There were black doctors, lawyers, business owners. . . . I knew Atlanta was the place for me."[4] Perry plugged away in obscurity until his play *I Know I've Been Changed* hit big with audiences in 1998 at the Atlanta House of Blues; it was then staged successfully at the nine-thousand-seat Fox Theater. Over the following years, Perry premiered a string of plays in urban theaters across the nation—the artistic descendant of the so-called "Chitlin Circuit."[5] The staggering success of these productions garnered Hollywood's attention, and in 2005 he released his first film, *Diary of a Mad Black Woman,* an adaptation of one of his earlier plays. Starring in the role of Madea, a no-nonsense, sharp-talking, elderly woman of ample proportions and towering height leavened with Christian charity, Perry launched this franchise, among many other films and television programs, that propelled him into the upper ranks of America's moneyed elite. Like so many other Black "overnight sensations," Perry had toiled tirelessly for years for Black audiences before "instantly" becoming a household name, now among Hollywood executives and white Americans as well.

Although many filmmakers present themselves as artists first, and ones often impatient and frustrated by the ways in which Hollywood economics might frustrate or curtail their artistic vision, Perry portrays himself dually as an artist and a businessman. In this latter aspect of his star persona, he frequently stresses his belief in the power of ownership, such as in the example of his realization that his father, a constructor, "would get his $800 a week and be ecstatic, and then I'd watch the man who owned the house sell it and make

$80,000 in profit." He then expounded on the significance of this anecdote: "So what I learned early on was, 'Be the man who owns the house.'"[6] Throughout his interviews in the popular press, Perry reiterates such themes, such as when he—a man of great wealth but thrifty nonetheless—ponders the fleeting value of some assets: "Cars and bling-bling—none of that crap is going to be worth anything. I could teach a class on what not to buy."[7] Many stars enjoy sufficient coverage from entertainment magazines, but Perry further expands the reach of his celebrity through profiles in business journals, such as in an article in *Forbes* that theorized, "Perry has succeeded for two reasons: He has honed a product that too many others viewed as destined for the discount bin. And he made sure to control it all."[8] In a similarly focused story, Drew Jubera summarized Perry's entrepreneurial philosophy under the heading of "Tyler Perry's Business School," with the following four guidelines outlining his business advice: "Use Your Own Money," "Learn to Sell," "See the Big Picture," and "Ration Your Assets."[9] In another such publication, he succinctly stated, "Ownership changes everything."[10]

In his self-presentation as a shrewd and thrifty businessman, Perry also establishes himself as a Hollywood outsider, one who discerns the pitfalls of businesses entrenched in wasteful practices. Fulminating against such profligacy, Perry extols the virtue of his cost-cutting measures and compares his frugal production methods to those of Hollywood executives: "I can do it efficiently at a fraction of what it costs in Hollywood because there are not 20 executives telling you, 'Move the cup to the left' or 'I don't like the color of her sweater.' . . . I go down, look at everything. I like it. We shoot the show. I don't have all those people trying to justify their jobs."[11] Margena Christian documents Perry's paradigm-shifting creative process—"The innovative filmmaker has built a system that enables him to produce his film and television projects in half the time and often at a fraction of the cost of a typical Hollywood production"—and confirms the eye-popping profits from his projects: "A Tyler Perry film . . . makes for investors 120 percent return on their money."[12] Both sufficiently wealthy to embody Hollywood excess yet sufficiently alienated from its mores to condemn its decadence, Perry elevates himself through his entrepreneurial ethos of wealth earned from a combination of artistic talent and financial acumen.

Fans of any race would likely find his financial advice helpful, but Perry also acknowledges the particular challenges facing Black entrepreneurs and the importance of Black wealth. While not directly addressing the racism he likely encountered during negotiations with Hollywood studios, Perry once stated, "I was able to make some incredible deals by allowing people to underestimate me,"[13] presumably white executives assuming their intellectual superiority over a Black man who did not graduate high school (although he subsequently earned his GED). Perhaps most importantly, Perry sees ownership as the key method for eradicating the racist legacy of the United States, as evident in these slightly coded words: "I do not think change comes from asking people to let you in. I think change comes by becoming owners of studios, owners of projects, owners of content."[14] As an owner, Perry wields the power to change American entertainment, and more specifically, Atlanta's economy and landscape, in a manner exponentially more powerful than most entertainers.

In another key inflection of his entrepreneurial persona, Perry has pursued numerous humanitarian efforts, and thus the benevolent effects of philanthropy temper any potential vision of him as yet another man of immoderate wealth disconnected from his wider communities. In 2021 the Academy of Motion Picture Arts and Sciences—which, to date, has never acknowledged his cinematic oeuvre with an award or even an award nomination—paid tribute to his famed generosity with the Jean Hersholt Humanitarian Award, an honorary Oscar, acknowledging his "cultural influence extending far beyond his work as a filmmaker" in his many charitable endeavors.[15] As a further inflection of his humanitarian persona, Perry studiously attempts to create films promulgating positive messages and images, evident in the slight controversy that arose in depictions of Madea with a pistol. Responding to the concerns of his fans, Perry reenvisioned his star-making character: "There are no pistols in this one because of the children. . . . When we know better, we do better."[16] With these simple but powerful words, Perry acknowledges his ongoing resolution to improve his understanding of issues of representation and their cultural power, as well as his role in disseminating them.

Related to his humanitarian pursuits, and owing to the rags-to-riches arc of his life, Perry serves as a role model for countless young fans, and he regularly seasons his entrepreneurial persona by equally stressing his compassion for others. He has spoken forthrightly about the cruel mistreatment that he suffered during his childhood, disclosing that his father, Emmitt, abused him both mentally and physically. (Indeed, to distance himself from his father's legacy, and in another example of his efforts to shape himself and his persona, he changed his name from Emmitt Perry, Jr., to Tyler Perry.) Likewise, he has candidly discussed the sexual abuse he endured between the ages of five and twelve.[17] In response to these traumatic events, he repeatedly and passionately emphasizes the need to forgive others: "It's nothing like real forgiveness, a deep-down forgiveness where you don't hold any grudges against people. . . . I forgave [everybody] for the things they didn't know and for the things they didn't know to do."[18] Perry is equally frank about his attempted suicide: "I tell people, if you're thinking about suicide, all that stuff I've attempted and thought about it. . . . The key to life when it gets tough is to keep moving. Just keep moving."[19] By overcoming these and a variety of other personal and professional obstacles, Perry holds himself up as a role model for others to emulate: "If I can come out of New Orleans and be the person I am and have some level of success, I think it speaks to every person who was displaced, every person who had to struggle."[20] An entrepreneur of immense wealth and a humanitarian of great generosity, Perry burnishes his star persona equally by presenting his life story as an example of the possibility of overcoming an impoverished southern childhood to achieve meteoric success.

Owing to the blockbuster grosses of his films, Perry, without question, merits the designation as an entrepreneur, but his cinematic achievements complicate the artistic aspect of his southern star persona, for the simple fact that many have received critical drubbings. Thus, as a filmmaker whose art is dismissed by many critics, Perry faces the challenge of modulating the creative aspect of his persona despite frequent aspersions. Whereas the term *auteur* is typically applied to revered filmmakers such as Jane Campion, Alfred Hitchcock, and Spike Lee, those whose work is esteemed for its artistic merit and insightful vision, its application to Perry generates a critical tempest, as strikingly evident in discussions among Black artists about the merits of his work. Roxane Gay witheringly dismissed him as "a small man with a limited imagination."[21] Malcolm-Jamal Warner rued his theatrical corpus—"I would really hate for it to come to the point where Tyler Perry type plays become the new Black theatre standard"—with Daniel Beaty agreeing, "There are definitely things in it, you know, that are kind of lowbrow."[22] Perry responded by defending the right of his audiences to choose entertainment that they find appealing: "I think traditional Black theatre is suffering because of comments like that one. . . .

It's insulting on so many levels, not just me, but to the millions of Black, the hard-working folk, that want to go out and laugh and have a good time."[23] In a similarly spirited back-and-forth, Spike Lee derided Perry's films as part of his excursus bemoaning the state of Black cinema—"Each artist should be allowed to pursue their artistic endeavors, but I still think there is a lot of stuff out today that is coonery and buffoonery"—to which Perry passionately rebutted, "Spike can go straight to hell! You can print that. I am sick of him talking about me, I am sick of him saying, 'this is a coon, this is a buffoon.' I am sick of him talking about black people going to see movies. This is what he said: 'you vote by what you see,' as if black people don't know what they want to see."[24] Many of Perry's films are indeed poorly reviewed, with critics bemoaning their melodramatic plots, farcical humor, and simplistic resolutions.[25] It should be noted as well, however, that some critics see talent in his work, even if hoping this auteur might refine his skills further, as evident in A. O. Scott's review of *Madea Goes to Jail* (2009): "Mr. Perry dutifully gives his audience what it wants, but you can't help feeling that he might also have more to offer: more coherent narratives, smoother direction, better movies."[26] Even sympathetic critics, it would appear, face challenges in mustering encouraging words about Perry's artistic output.

Any discussions of the aesthetic value of Perry's plays and films or his status as an auteur cannot avoid longstanding debates about purported distinctions between high art and popular culture, those that stir up critical imbroglios but rarely affect filmgoers' choices. That is to say, to assess Perry's corpus against those of Campion, Hitchcock, and Lee, for instance, profoundly misreads his artistic objectives and the stories he seeks to tell. Sounding a more positive note, Pulitzer- and Tony-Award-winning playwright August Wilson encouraged Perry to value his unique contributions to American culture: "If that's your gift, then that's what you do and do it."[27] Critics might bemoan his productions, but, given the size and scope of his output that speaks powerfully to large swaths of American audiences, it is worthwhile to recognize that the term *auteur* can more ecumenically refer to any director who employs a consistent set of tropes transcending individual titles in their corpus to create a coherent gestalt, as Andrew Sarris outlines: "Over a group of films, a director must exhibit certain recurring characteristics of style, which serve as his signature. The way a film looks and moves should have some relationship to the way a director thinks and feels."[28] Perry certainly fits this conception of an auteur, for so many of his films evince similarities in their southern settings, sincere religiosity, and evocative emotionality. Auteurs often buck Hollywood's prevailing norms, and Perry has spoken openly about his disdain for the industry's creative processes: "Hollywood would smother me. It would kill my creativity. Out there you just deal with all the foolishness."[29]

This cleft between Perry's roles as an auteur and an entrepreneur emblematizes the ways in which his career and his southern star persona negotiate a range of tensions, resulting in his status as a queerly entrepreneurial auteur. In suggesting his position as a queer auteur, I am not proposing that Perry is gay but that his star persona and his works destabilize purportedly rigid boundaries between genders, sexual orientations, and a range of other cultural binaries. As Alexander Doty proposes of queer auteurship, "another way queer auteurs are 'made' happens when the films of non-queer-identified directors become interesting to queerly positioned spectators for their queer (sub)texts."[30] In key ways, Perry invites queer readings both of his films and of himself. Most obviously, playing the role of Madea requires him to dress in drag, and virtually all drag performances carry a whiff of queerness in their comic gender play. Further along these lines, in several scenes of the Madea franchise Perry encodes a queer subtext to his performances of this already over-the-top figure. For example, in *Diary of a Mad Black Woman* Madea screams, "A wire hanger" when looking through Helen's closet and its fabulous designer clothes—in an obvious allusion to Faye Dunaway's over-the-top performance in the camp classic *Mommie Dearest* (1981). In *Don't Make a Black Woman Take Off Her Earrings* (2006), his character's ersatz memoir and self-help book, Perry ventriloquizes of himself through Madea, "We were really worried one day. We saw him with a pink dress on. He said it was because it was Mardi Gras, but I don't know. We were all very concerned."[31] At the very least, Perry appears sufficiently comfortable with queerness to depict himself as the young object of a gay panic. Prior to his long-term relationship with Gelila Bekele, with whom he fathered his son, many articles in the popular press portrayed Perry as an eligible bachelor for the ladies, but Denene Millner broached the open secret of the many queer rumors circulating around him: "Perry is still by his damn self, despite persistent rumors about his romantic life—everything from relationships with African-American starlets . . . to the suggestion that he's gay."[32] Pointing to the many handsome male actors cast in his films and the many lingering shots of their chiseled abdominal muscles, Wesley Morris espies a queer subtext to Perry's films featuring predominantly heteroerotic storylines: "Perry isn't openly gay, but his movies are."[33] Responding to these swirling queer rumors, Perry simply asserted his comfort in his gendered identity: "It used to bother me a whole lot in the beginning . . . but what it's done is give me firm seating in my manhood."[34]

Gender's inherent malleability allows Perry to inhabit a range of roles traditionally coded as feminine or masculine, no matter the unlikelihood of this very physically masculine man—he stands six feet, five inches tall on a robust frame—embodying femininity. As Perry explains of his gender-switching role, Madea represents a nostalgic view of a past time when neighbors knew one another and, more significantly, allows him to position himself in this maternal role: "Her name is the southern term for 'mother dear.' Madea used to be on every corner in every neighborhood when I was growing up and generations before."[35] "Madea" also echoes "Medea," the mythological figure who murdered her children with Jason, thus imbuing the character with a sharper edge. Acknowledging the ways that Madea allows Perry to bridge the boundaries between genders, he avows, "I think Madea has an opportunity to say everything that I can't say because, number one, I'm a man, and women get away with saying things a lot more than a man would. In our society, women are given much more latitude to have emotions and to express them. And, number two, she has been around for more than a few decades, so she can get away with stating some opinions I'd be afraid to say."[36] Madea thus allows a man to voice his viewpoints through a woman, and such performances undercut any sense of gender's intransigence.

These gendered dynamics, and Perry's queer play with them, are evident in his debut film, *Diary of a Mad Black Woman*, a foundational moment in introducing himself (and his star persona) to a national audience. The opening credits announce its lead stars, including Kimberly Elise and Steve Harris, and then add, "And introducing Tyler Perry." Following the film's publicity campaign, even viewers new to Perry's work likely realized that he played the role of Madea; what many new viewers would likely not have foreseen, however, is that Perry plays two additional roles in the film: Madea's brother Joe and nephew Brian. Perry requires similarly excessive, if masculine, costuming to play the role of elderly Joe, and much of the humor of this flatulent old-timer arises in his bawdy repartee with Madea. "You're huge, you're big," he declares; "And that's something you'll never in your life hear a woman say," she replies. In his role as Brian, however, Perry eschews any costuming excess and plays the part "straight," with this character often attempting to tamp down the chaos unleashed by his aunt. (See figure 15.) In the mix of Madea, Joe, and Brian, Perry proves himself a master of disguise in his films and also a strikingly protean figure in his real life. That is to say, to see Perry is sometimes to see a funhouse image of comic excess, whether female or male; or to see a staid comic foil; and other times simply to see Perry. In these overlapping, conflicting, but ultimately coherent personas, to see Perry is thus to recognize the inherent flux of his artistic (and entrepreneurial) self.

As these examples show, Madea plays a central role in Perry's ability to subvert any strictures of gender, and she also allows him to disintegrate borders between genres. Perry's films toggle between comedy and drama, as evident in his consistent insertion of serious themes into otherwise lighthearted comedies. Perry describes Madea as "bait [because she is] disarming, charming, make-you-laugh; so I can slap Madea in something and talk about God, love, faith, forgiveness, family . . . any of those things."[37] Further to these points, Perry argues that Madea allows him to mediate the genres of drama and comedy,

FIG. 15. In *Diary of a Mad Black Woman* Tyler Perry plays both Brian Simmons, a button-down attorney, and his aunt Mabel Simmons, also known as Madea. This split-screen image captures the queer duality of many of Perry's performances.

stating, "It's hard for Black dramas to get made because people don't think that anybody will support them. . . . It's very important for me to have a dramatic story inside a comedic story. It's important for me to give both sides a taste."[38] In effect, Madea allows Perry—both the auteur and the entrepreneur—to tell the stories that he wants to tell, sidestepping any perceived commercial liabilities to Black dramas by encasing them in comic shells. Perry's Madea follows in a line of Black comics playing larger-than-life women in drag—Flip Wilson's "Geraldine," Eddie Murphy's "Grandma Klump" in *The Nutty Professor* (1996), Martin Lawrence's "Big Momma" in *Big Momma's House* (2000)—with the key distinction of his deployment of her to bridge the genres of comedy and drama.

As much as Madea assists Perry in dissolving borders of genders and genres, critics have sharply debated her multiple and conflicting significations, and thus attempted to decode Perry's sensibilities through their readings of her. As a curious amalgam that simultaneously pays homage to and parodies femininity, female drag and its performers are often celebrated for subverting cultural constructions of gender but can also be accused of reinforcing the gender politics they ostensibly undermine. Alison Rose Reed offers such a critique of Madea: "Perry's infamous, and highly profitable, drag performances enable him to instrumentalize Black women's pain while simultaneously exploiting and abjecting queerness."[39] Additionally problematic, Madea evokes for some viewers racist images of the Mammy tradition, a pernicious narrative and cinematic legacy that overwrites the horrors of slavery through images of Black women devotedly nurturing white families. Although it should be acknowledged that Madea summons complex issues of race and representation, and not entirely positive ones, Perry employs Black stereotypes for the enjoyment of Black audiences, as Kwakiutl L. Dreher proposes: "Perry takes these stock characters from the plantation genre and places them amid the *Black* community to care for *Black* families generally and, specifically, to preserve those value systems that have sustained Black communities."[40] Whereas Mammy characters have traditionally upheld images of benevolent whiteness despite the atrocities of slavery, this charge cannot apply to Madea, given the investment of Perry's films in depicting the lives of Black characters in southern communities.

In another line of criticism, some viewers see Perry's films as advocating conservative religious viewpoints that coincide with Black respectability politics. Certainly, the Madea films evince strong Christian themes as his characters turn to spiritual outlets to assist in resolving their problems. In an apt example of these dynamics from *Diary of Mad Black Woman,* Myrtle (Cicely Tyson), Helen's mother, espouses her belief that "God is everything!" and that, in observing her daughter's challenges, she should turn to her faith: "You got the strength God gave us women to survive." Kaila Adia Story sees in Perry's oeuvre the endorsement of Black respectability politics, in their disapproving shots of, for instance, Black men gambling or Black women wearing sexy outfits: "Perry's films update the politics of black respectability for contemporary times.... His poor and black female protagonists become pawns of his black respectability rhetoric in the cultural marketplace of sameness where he shops and barters for his own cultural capital."[41] Notwithstanding the queer elements of Perry's performances as Madea, Robert J. Patterson espies an investment in normative sexual and gender roles throughout the star's corpus: "Perry presents marriage as a requisite for black women's happiness." Patterson further suggests that these storylines reflect the filmmaker's "deep investment in heteropatriarchy."[42]

As Perry has admitted that he can voice his more controversial opinions through the prism effect of Madea's gender and age, her words in *Don't Make a Black Woman Take Off Her Earrings* also indicate that he endorses various aspects of respectability politics. For example, in the subsection titled, "What in Hell Is 'Acting White' Supposed to Mean?," Madea implores her readers, "Oh, please! Get off this white-black thing, just be! Education is a good thing no matter who you are. Bill and Camille Cosby and Barack Obama—they've made us proud."[43] In a similar vein, Madea laments that rappers "just want to talk about 'this bitch,' this 'ho,' . . . and 'where your booty is' . . . and all that foolishness. It's crazy."[44] Of course the irony should not be overlooked: Perry, whose work Lee denounced for its "coonery and buffoonery," denounces, through the voice of Madea, hip-hop lyrics for their "foolishness." Both the target of and the espouser of Black respectability politics, Perry locates himself in an uncomfortable middle space that highlights the ways in which Black art continues to be examined in terms of its representation of Blackness in a manner largely irrelevant to representations of whiteness.

Finally, as much as Perry embodies a new vision of southern Black artistry and entrepreneurialism, he also depicts a hitherto seldom seen and increasingly innovative view of the South. Through the southern settings of his films, mostly shot in and around the Atlanta area, Perry acknowledges the region's racism while celebrating the richness of its Black community. In an ode to his mother's love for him, Perry condemned southern racism while pointing to it as the reason why his works foreground southern Blackness: "I grew up in Louisiana, and my mother grew up in the Jim Crow South. She didn't have a healthy trust of white people. Because of the things she had endured—horrific things—she wanted me to know the value I had within me. I never felt like I needed to look outside of my own race for success. I knew that if I mined what was in our community, what I had in me, it would work."[45] The horrific Jim Crow South that Perry's mother endured is, in her son's oeuvre, now portrayed as a region filled with successful Black people and their families. As Perry credited his exposure to Atlanta's Freaknik celebration as key to his enhanced vision of Black potential, so too do his films capture this possibility, notwithstanding any problematic tropes they might also carry. As Miriam J. Petty explains of these conflicting dynamics: "Like . . . other artists of the blackface minstrel drama, Perry routinely produces work that invokes the iconic, idealized, and quasi-historical American South while simultaneously mobilizing black bodies as living symbols of southern space. . . . If minstrelsy worked to consolidate white identity by playing with whiteness's 'opposite,' Perry's films likewise work to create and consolidate a 'real' black identity by mobilizing and trafficking in classed, gendered, and regionally specific ideas about blackness."[46] His depiction of the South, like his southern star persona, is highly contested and queerly protean, but notwithstanding any valid concerns expressed by fans, critics, and scholars, it is, at the very least, a vision of Black southern life remarkably and refreshingly different from the vision of Black southern life proffered by white entertainment executives over the twentieth and early twenty-first centuries. For too long, films about the South, even those explicitly invoking the Civil Rights struggle, cast white actors in their lead roles, as exemplified by such performances as Gene Hackman in *Mississippi Burning* (1988), Alec Baldwin in *Ghosts of Mississippi* (1996), and Emma Stone in *The Help* (2011).

As Atlanta's preeminent entrepreneurial auteur, Perry has broken boundaries between genders, genres, and races, and in so doing has reshaped not solely his southern star persona but Atlanta's as well. Many descendants of participants in the early twentieth-century's Great Migration northward are now returning to their families' southern roots, and so Atlanta has increasingly become the face of the New Black South. Perry represents not merely the city's commercial and entrepreneurial ambitions but its artistic ones as well. With this queer auteur leading the way and reshaping the landscape from its Confederate roots, Atlanta's future will be remarkably different from its past, in a welcome shift to a more inclusive future. As a final example of these dynamics, and in one of the sharper moments from *A Madea Christmas* (2013), a white character asks Madea, "Did you hear the one about the two rabbis and the black dude?," to which she sharply replies, "Did you hear the one about the stray bullet who killed the redneck for telling the story about the two rabbis and the black dude?," in a clear indication of her impatience with anti-Black and antisemitic humor. As Perry reconstitutes Atlanta's landscape from its Confederate past and Madea recodes southern comedies from their racist tropes, it is fitting to imagine this queer auteur and his exaggerated alter-ego enjoying the last word. Madea, concealing Perry as her queer auteur inside, might finally be able to sit back, laugh, and leave her earrings on.

12

MATTHEW McCONAUGHEY CROWNS HIMSELF TEXAS'S PHILOSOPHER KING

When contemplating the galaxy of stars hailing from the Lone Star State—including Sissy Spacek, Tommy Lee Jones, Woody Harrelson, Jennifer Garner, Jennifer Love Hewitt, Eva Longoria, Renée Zellweger, Jamie Foxx, Luke and Owen Wilson, Hilary Duff, and Patrick Swayze, among dozens more—certainly many would agree that Matthew McConaughey stands tall as the most Texan of them all. "If you want a modern day actor who personifies the true Texan spirit, look no further than Matthew McConaughey," asserts Neil Daniels in his biography of the star.[1] McConaughey's confident swagger, his sonorous twang, and his masculine bravado impart a regional flair that is stereotypical yet unique to his stardom and star persona, thus imbuing his many southern roles with an authenticity born from his upbringing. McConaughey has further complemented his Texas star persona by presenting himself as a plain-speaking, cowboy philosopher of the contemporary era. "Paradox is my jam," he asserted, as well as referring to himself as "a self-Socratic griot," "a folk-singing philosopher poet,"[2] and "an armchair anthropologist . . . and truth-seeking street poet."[3] From the foundational moment of his career in Richard Linklater's *Dazed and Confused* (1993), McConaughey has defined himself as an authentic Texan and an amateur philosopher, merging these two aspects of his persona into a seamless, if simultaneously disjointed, whole. Musing over the star's career and southern self-presentation leads to an interpretive conundrum that can be aptly phrased through a uniquely Texas aphorism: is McConaughey simply all hat, no cattle?

Born November 4, 1969, McConaughey grew up in Uvalde, Texas, raised by his parents (who divorced each other twice and married three times) and two older brothers. First planning a career in law, he instead began pursuing a film degree at the University of Texas at Austin, graduating in 1993. The definitive Hollywood story of the unwitting ingenue plucked from obscurity and launched into stardom still belongs to Lana Turner (discovered at fifteen years old at the Top Hat Malt Shop in Hollywood), but McConaughey's meteoric rise began similarly, in an Austin hotel where he encountered Don Phillips, the casting director of *Dazed and Confused*. As Phillips later assessed of his protégé, "Matthew has three things that make you a star: you've got to be smart, you've got to have talent, and the girls have got to want to go to bed with you. He scores on all counts but at the same time he has a natural cool and humility about him."[4] Winning the role of Wooderson, a high-school graduate still partying with high-school students, McConaughey delivered a memorable performance through the Texas-accented cadence of his words. After asking a freshman for a joint, McConaughey-as-Wooderson intones his iconic lines, "All right, all right, all right," in a steady rhythm of laid-back cool, and soon dispenses his appreciative, comically inflected assessment of dating teenagers: "That's what I love about these high school girls, man. I get older, they stay the same age." (See figure 16.) Although these words hint at predatory behavior, the film is uninterested in pursuing the issue of whether Wooderson's interest in teen girls flirts with statutory rape, instead imbuing his perspective with an aura of erotic folk wisdom. Any troubling aspects of this character notwithstanding, Wooderson clearly stands as the film's role model when he advises the lead character, Randall "Pink" Floyd, not to pledge to abstain from drugs so that he can continue playing on his school's football team: "You gotta do what Randall 'Pink' Floyd wants to do. Let me tell you this. The older you do get, the more rules they're gonna try to get you to follow. You just gotta keep livin,' man. L-I-V-I-N." "Pink" Floyd follows Wooderson's sage advice, and the film's predominant storyline thus ends with a celebration of the stoner counterculture's inherent virtue, as well as its triumph over the conformity demanded by suburban high-school authorities.

More than merely a character that he once played, Wooderson complemented, if not inspired, McConaughey's self-perception as a folk philosopher. As he commented on NPR's *Fresh Air*, referring specifically to Wooderson's words about high school girls: "That was the piece for Wooderson that I was

FIG. 16. In his breakout role as Wooderson in *Dazed and Confused,* Matthew McConaughey (second from left) found a character who inspired, or at least coincided with, many of his personal philosophical viewpoints.

like, That's not a line, that's his being. That's his philosophy. He has it figured out."[5] Many might counterargue that erotic desire for teen girls hardly constitutes a philosophical outlook on life, but McConaughey also found inspiration in Wooderson's statement to "Pink" Floyd, "You just gotta keep livin,' man. L-I-V-I-N," for these words have immeasurably colored his self-presentation and star persona. His voicemail message reportedly iterated Wooderson's philosophy—"Hey, this is McConaughey. . . . Just keep livin' along the way. Talk to you later"[6]—and as his career blossomed he named his production company j.k. livin productions. *Above the Bones,* the debut album of reggae musician Mishka that was released through j.k. livin, includes a statement of the label's ethos: "As life continued forward, [McConaughey] found that the j.k. livin approach to each day helped him navigate through the good times and bad, stay true to his ideals along the way and make the best out of this adventure we call life. j.k. livin is not a rulebook, it's a lifestyle."[7] Eschewing the constraints of a "rulebook" while establishing the exemplary nature of McConaughey's celebrity regime as a "lifestyle," the j.k. livin philosophy preaches a simple gospel of self-sufficiency packaged as adherence to ideals that remain tantalizingly undefined. McConaughey later shuttered his production company but rebranded its name for his foundation, as explained in the Author's Note of his memoir *Greenlights*: "In 2009, Matthew and his wife, Camila, founded the j.k. livin Foundation afterschool curriculum, which helps at-risk kids in over fifty-two Title 1 high schools across the nation make healthier mind, body, and spirit choices."[8] When casting directors and producers scrutinize actors for roles in their films, the performers are evaluated according to a range of defined and ineffable physical and performative congruencies that make them the best choice for the role, yet only rarely is a shared philosophy one of the points of similitude considered. The symbiosis between McConaughey and Wooderson, however, imbued his performance with the authenticity of their shared viewpoints, as it also influenced his star persona over the ensuing decades.

Following the success of *Dazed and Confused* and his scene-stealing performance as Wooderson, McConaughey's star rose steadily, and he soon found himself cast in supporting roles in such major Hollywood productions as *Angels in the Outfield* (1994) and Herbert Ross's *Boys on the Side* (1995), as well as such Texas-set films as *Texas Chainsaw Massacre: The Next Generation* (1994) and John Sayles's *Lone Star* (1996). Joel Schumacher's *A Time to Kill* (1996), an adaptation of John Grisham's novel about a white lawyer in Mississippi defending a Black man accused of murdering his daughter's rapists, heralded his breakthrough into Hollywood's A-list. Grisham reportedly rejected such top stars as Brad Pitt, Val Kilmer, and Woody Harrelson, instead choosing McConaughey. For the most part, critics applauded his selection. In Peter Travers's words, McConaughey delivered a "performance of smarts, sexiness, scrappy humor and unmistakable star sizzle,"[9] and Roger Ebert similarly applauded his "strong and convincing" acting.[10] Most importantly for the trajectory of McConaughey's career, *A Time to Kill* ranked as a box-office smash, finishing among the year's ten highest grossing films.

Following the blowout success of *A Time to Kill*, McConaughey registered as one of Hollywood's elite stars, but he surprised many of the industry's cognoscenti by accepting the secondary role of Palmer Joss in Robert Zemeckis's *Contact* (1997), ceding top billing to Jodie Foster as protagonist Eleanor Arroway. Here too emerges McConaughey's interest in imbuing his Texas star persona with philosophical depth, for the film, based on Carl Sagan's novel of the same name, depicts humanity's search for intelligent extraterrestrial life, with Arroway allegorically aligned with Science and Joss with Religion. In *Greenlights* McConaughey commented on the factors that drew him to this role, construing himself as similarly inclined to ponder life's mysteries: "After my spiritual journey on the Amazon, my choice to inhabit a man who believed in God in a world of science was very close to the truth of where I was in my own life and where I wanted to spend my time in front of the camera. Jodie Foster was the clear lead and people questioned why I took 'the girl's role,' as they called it at the time, instead of taking other *leading* roles I was being offered. But I was more than satisfied with my choice, as I was interested in what I termed 'philanthropic roles and stories of self discovery,' as well as working with great directors."[11] *Contact* received lukewarm reviews, and many critics agreed that McConaughey appeared strikingly miscast, as in David Ansen's *Newsweek* assessment: "Just about every scene with the philosophical reverend is a clinker, and he keeps popping up in implausible places to continue his debate with Ellie about the existence of God. It's a role that could make any actor look bad, and McConaughey, too young and too pretty for it, cuts a ludicrous figure."[12] Although one can certainly ponder the justness of any blanket assessment that young, attractive men should not be cast as philosophers, this opinion prevailed in the industry, although it did not notably diminish McConaughey's rising star power throughout the late 1990s, during which he worked with several of Hollywood's top directors. In addition to *Contact* with Zemeckis, McConaughey played the role of Roger Sherman Baldwin, a white lawyer defending Africans who rebelled against their enslavement, in Steven Spielberg's *Amistad* (1997) and reunited with Richard Linklater for *The Newton Boys* (1998). He also starred in Ron Howard's *EdTV* (1999). In 1999, in a key moment in which his irreverent sensibility coincided with his media persona, the police, investigating a noise complaint from neighbors, found McConaughey playing bongo drums naked while smoking marijuana; they arrested him for marijuana possession and resisting arrest.

During the next stage of his career in the first decade of the 2000s, McConaughey costarred in a string of romantic comedies: *The Wedding Planner* (2001) with Jennifer Lopez, *How to Lose a Guy in 10 Days* (2003) with Kate Hudson, *Failure to Launch* (2006) with Sarah Jessica Parker, *Fool's Gold* (2008) again with Kate Hudson, and *Ghosts of Girlfriends Past* (2009) with Jennifer Garner. Without doubt, McConaughey's southern roots and the legendary figure of the southern gentleman influenced these casting decisions. In a mixed review of *The Wedding Planner* in *Variety*, Robert Koehler nonetheless lauded McConaughey's performance: "McConaughey has never been sexier or more charming, generating a warmth that seems much more his métier than his various unsatisfying action characters."[13] Similarly, Christine Peters, the producer of *How to Lose a Guy in 10 Days*, stated of casting McConaughey as the male lead: "We needed sexy, hot, charming, intelligent—really, how many guys are there out there like that? . . . He's a true Southern gentleman."[14] The line between a southern gentleman and a smarmy roué often lies in the eye of the beholder, and Lisa Schwarzbaum's review of *Failure to Launch* captured her impatience with McConaughey's accentuated performance: "If, for example, you like McConaughey's affect of sexy, sleepy-eyed drawl—is he toasted, or just a sun-kissed Texan—then you are meant to like Tripp."[15] As Natasha Stoynoff concluded of McConaughey's roles for much of his career, and as particularly relevant for his romcom phase, "Still, his looks and Southern charm made typecasting inevitable."[16] Typecasting, even when generously remunerative, can remarkably constrict any actor's ambitions, and McConaughey tired of the genre, describing his romcom roles as "Saturday characters" because "they need a buoyancy. . . . You're not supposed to get . . . Hamletian about it." Notable as well, McConaughey discerned in the narrative structures of romcoms, with their longstanding prioritization of female protagonists dating back at least to Shakespeare's *As You Like It* and *Twelfth Night*, a potential effeminization of the male character, which he resisted: "I had fun doing that and also trying to do those [roles] without emasculating the male, which can be done in those romantic comedies often."[17] Also of note during this era, McConaughey was named *People* magazine's Sexiest Man Alive in 2005, further cementing his reputation for personal magnetism and allure.

Ghosts of Girlfriends Past marked the end of McConaughey's romcom phase, and for the most part, the closing of the aughts also marked the end of his starring roles in such adventure films as *Reign of Fire* (2002) and *Sahara* (2005), as he then turned to a series of more dramatic characters. Indeed, when McConaughey was dubbed Sexiest Man Alive, he joked about his new title: "I like the 'Alive' part. . . . Now I've made it. Wait until you see the roles I could take after this. You're going to see my gut hanging over, plus 22 (lbs.). It'll be a whole new kind of sexy!"[18] These comic words ironically foreshadowed his subsequent transition from romcoms and rakish sexiness to meatier roles, even if these roles did not require him to gain twenty-two pounds. The so-called "McConaissance" began in 2011 with his performances in Brad Furman's *The Lincoln Lawyer*, Richard Linklater's *Bernie*, and William Friedkin's *Killer Joe*. Over the course of his career McConaughey has played lawyers in several films, notably *A Time to Kill*, *Amistad*, *The Lincoln Lawyer*, and *Bernie*, and here too he has connected his roles to his philosophizing. As he stated in an interview, "I've always been fascinated with the system . . . and how the system works and lawyers are great characters 'cause they get to be the tour guide between guilt and innocence. How the system works is very interesting and it's not as idealistic as I used to think it was. There is a lot of deal making that goes on."[19] The "McConaissance" continued in 2012 with performances in Lee Daniels's *The Paperboy*, Jeff Nichols's *Mud*, and Steven Soderbergh's *Magic Mike*, and reached its heights in 2013 with a supporting role in Martin Scorsese's *The Wolf of Wall Street* and the starring role of Ron Woodroof in Jean-Marc Vallée's *Dallas Buyers Club*. To play the role of Woodroof, a Texas man who contracted HIV and fought the Centers for Disease Control and Prevention for wider accessibility of experimental treatments, McConaughey lost more than the twenty-two pounds he earlier joked about gaining, and his performance garnered him the Academy Award for Best Actor. More accolades accrued in 2014 for his lead performance in the HBO series *True Detective*.

It is noteworthy that many of the productions from the "McConaissance" era occur in southern landscapes, thus allowing McConaughey to build upon his Texas background and star persona: *Bernie*, *Killer Joe*, and *Dallas Buyers Club* are set in Texas, *True Detective* in Louisiana, *Mud* in Arkansas, and *The Paperboy* and *Magic Mike* in Florida, with the additional southern touch that McConaughey's character in the latter film is named Dallas. Interviewing McConaughey for the southern lifestyle magazine *Garden & Gun*, Joe Bargmann noted this trend and asked the actor, "You're playing a lot of Southern characters these days. Is that deliberate?," to which he replied: "Well, I never really looked at it like playing a Southern role was going against the grain. I also never chose a role because I said, 'Hey, this is a Southern character.' I always looked at it as 'This is a great character who happens to be from the South.' I'm comfortable in nature. . . . I'm not specifically trying to 'play Southern.' It just so happens that some of the greatest characters are from the South."[20] He further explained his distaste for southern stereotypes: "But about the Southern movie—you sure can tell when someone decides to play the stereotype. That can be good for a comedy, I guess. Part of the stereotype is that we're slow."[21] Virtually all southerners recognize the regional stereotypes bandied about the wider U.S. culture, and McConaughey's words indicate both his awareness of the limitations inflicted by stereotypes but also the potential of "playing Southern" in an authentic manner arising from his uniquely Texan identity.

Whereas his romcom years threatened to limit his star persona to that of a charming romantic partner and the "McConaissance" undeniably enhanced his reputation as a serious dramatic actor, both stages of his career reveal McConaughey's cagy appraisal of his star persona. Foremost, one can discern the preeminent role of self-branding in McConaughey's career, as he credited himself for coining the term "McConaissance" as a necessary strategy for shifting the course of his career:

> Did you know I made up, coined, and created the term *McConaissance?* I did. I was at Sundance with *Mud* in 2013 when I sat down for an interview with MTV. I'd been on a pretty good career run and I figured it needed a campaign slogan, an anthem, a bumpersticker, but I knew it couldn't come from me.
>
> "You've been on quite the run, Mr. McConaughey. *Killer Joe, Bernie, Magic Mike,* and now *Mud.* Congratulations," the journalist said.
>
> "Thank you, yeah, I'm on a great ride, I actually did an interview the other day and the journalist called it a 'McConaissance,'" I replied.
>
> "Oh my gosh, the 'McConaissance.' That's brilliant. That may stick." It did.
>
> I've never told anybody that story until now.[22]

He has also stated of this period of his career that "it was an unbranding phrase, not a rebranding phase. I was away. You didn't see me shirtless on the beach."[23] The difference between an unbranding and a rebranding may elude all but the savviest of marketing experts, but the creation and promotion of the "McConaissance" speaks directly to the actor's attention to his star persona, the necessity to recalibrate it, and the achievement of this goal through a range of southern roles. More so, the branding of the "McConaissance" speaks to Mc-

Conaughey's interest in crediting to himself a strategy previously employed by a range of female romcom stars, notably Julia Roberts and Sandra Bullock, who built their careers on romcom foundations before winning Oscars for dramatic roles, respectively in *Erin Brockovich* (2000) and *The Blind Side* (2009).

Despite the acclaim McConaughey received during the years of the "McConaissance," his subsequent films have, on the whole, delivered disappointing box office receipts, including *The Sea of Trees* (2015), *Free State of Jones* (2016), *Gold* (2016), and *White Boy Rick* (2018). Even the best of actors can be connected to the most disappointing of films, and the convoluted, virtually incoherent, plot of the genre- and mind-bending movie *Serenity* (2019), in which McConaughey's character Dill realizes that he is a character in a video game created by his son, alienated audiences. Counterbalancing his Best Actor Oscar, McConaughey earned a nomination for the Razzie Award for Worst Actor, losing—or is it winning by losing?—to John Travolta for *The Fanatic* (2019) and *Trading Paint* (2019). Among the disappointments of these years, he registered his greatest success voicing the role of Buster Moon in the animated films *Sing* (2016) and *Sing 2* (2021).

Away from the cinematic world, in 2020 McConaughey published his memoir *Greenlights*, an account of his life simultaneously packaged as a how-to manual for maximizing one's potential. David Marchese observes McConaughey's "reinvention as a sort of down-home Texan psychedelic self-help guru"[24] and quotes the star as declaring, "I believe if you just live the truth, that's as dynamic as it can get. It's the meta idea of 'Star in your own movie, and that's life.'"[25] As McConaughey outlined of his ambitions for *Greenlights*, "This is an approach book. I am here to share stories, insights, and philosophies that can be objectively understood, and if you choose, subjectively adopted, by either changing your reality, or changing how you see it."[26] One can hardly quibble with much of the self-help advice that McConaughey doles out, as it typically focuses on the intersection of personal responsibility and ambition. Key to the book's message is the definition of the term *greenlight*, and, as he explains, "Greenlights mean go—advance, carry on, continue. On the road, they are set up to give the flow of traffic the right of way, and when scheduled properly, more vehicles catch more greenlights in succession. **They say proceed.**"[27] After recounting an anecdote from his life, he summarizes the lessons to be learned: "We have to **prepare** to have freedom. We have to do the **work** to then do the job. We have to prepare for the job so we can be **free** to do the work."²⁸ As these passages indicate, McConaughey tends to stress his points with boldface typesetting, and the word *greenlights* is always printed in green ink. In another passage, he expresses similar ideas, if more poetically: "Reach beyond your grasp, have immortal finish lines, and turn your red light green, because a roof is a man-made thing."²⁹ Not surprisingly for an actor, film metaphors riddle his imagery and imperatives: "Time to get rid of the filters. Make my life my favorite movie. Live my favorite character. Write my own script. Direct my own story. Be my biography. Make my own documentary, on me. Nonfiction. Live, not recorded. Time to **catch that hero I've been chasing.**"³⁰ Occasional passages indulge in such garbled self-help speak that they resist interpretation, as in the admonition that "the soul objective is the pursuit of the singular finish with only the arrival in sight. This is what brings us together."³¹

For the most part *Greenlights* paints an appealing picture of its author and his life experiences. McConaughey often invites readers to chuckle at his missteps, such as the fitness regime that he undertook to prepare for playing dragon hunter Denton Van Zan in *Reign of Fire*, which included downing a double shot of tequila every morning, running barefoot five miles across the desert, keeping his heart rate below sixty beats per minute while standing on a rooftop's edge, and tackling sleeping cows at midnight. The physical toll proved too taxing, but McConaughey cheerily concludes of the experience, "My *dragon slayer workout regime* had failed miserably, but the upside was that I experienced a lot of pain, as any good dragon slayer would."³² Also, it is likely unparalleled in the history of memoirs that the author thrice discloses the mystical consequences of his nocturnal emissions, but McConaughey shares the subconscious eroticisms that led to profound life decisions. "*All the elements of a nightmare but it was a wet dream,*" he avows of the vision that led to his hiking the Andes in Peru along the Urubamba River into Machu Pichu.³³ Another such revelation—"I had a wet dream"—catalyzes an excursion on the Niger River.³⁴ The third wet dream "reminded me that *all I ever knew I wanted to be in life was a father.* . . . The red light vision of being a lifelong bachelor had come to me in a greenlight wet dream. It was a spiritual sign, a message to surrender."³⁵ Such is the fecundity of McConaughey's nocturnal emissions.

As much as McConaughey recalls his life in the manner of a fellow randomly encountered at a dive bar spinning an enjoyable yarn, an undercurrent of violent masculinity troubles the assumption of philosophical guru that McConaughey otherwise assumes. In recalling a bar fight, he explicitly links the violence of the night to his personal evolution from boyhood to manhood, as witnessed by his father's approving eyes: "I pounded down on him with vicious right fists until the drunken jeers of a good bar fight slowly turned to murmurs. ... That night was *my* rite of passage. Dad let me in. It was the night I became *his boy, a man* in his eyes."[36] The ideal of the Renaissance thinker is worthy of admiration, yet McConaughey envisions an explicitly masculine incarnation of this paradigm, as he extols "real Renaissance men, well versed in *the art of livin* [sic]," extolling them as "upright, strong, and sturdy men who carried themselves with honor, constitution, and a manner of earned aristocracy. Lumberjacks by day, conductors of the philharmonic by night."[37] In the acknowledgments of *Greenlights*, McConaughey thanks Jordan Peterson "for the clarity."[38] Peterson's brand of self-help crystallizes the complexity of life into anodyne packaging similar to McConaughey's *Greenlights*, as evident in the chapter titles from his bestselling book *12 Rules for Life: An Antidote to Chaos*. Maxims such as "Compare yourself to who you were yesterday, not to who someone else is today" and "Pet a cat when you encounter one on the street" will surely help many, yet Peterson's connections to a range of controversies, particularly his unique brand of toxic masculinity, call into question McConaughey's philosophical credentials.[39]

Complementing his interest in self-help philosophizing, McConaughey has also referred to himself as a "philosopher poet statesman,"[40] with such words hinting that he might follow the lead of such actors and entertainers as Ronald Reagan, Jesse Ventura, and Donald Trump by swerving into a political career. Notably, he dangled the possibility of campaigning for Texas's gubernatorial office by aligning this aspiration with that of starring in a western: "Now, I've never done a Western—not sure why. I did *The Newton Boys*, but they were more bank robbers. Governor of Texas? Yeah. That'd be kind of a Western, for sure. So I see a Western in my future, one way or another."[41] McConaughey ultimately opted not to run for office, but during his flirtation with a potential campaign, he refused to divulge any sort of political platform beyond banal platitudes. In an interview with *Esquire*, he sketched his political philosophy: "The far left doesn't seem to want to ever be able to admit the evil that mankind can possess, and the far right doesn't want to think past tomorrow. . . .

I want to propose meeting in the middle as a dare. I dare you to meet in the middle, instead of like *Oh, that's a place of great compromise*. I dare you to come over here and have a look, to have to meet in the middle, at least have to look at the opposition in the eye. At least shake their hand and go, *Well what can we agree on?*"[42] In another interview he stated, "I'm interested in finding our common denominators" and "Coming together—that's the radical move right now. That's the dare."[43] Construing his proposition that voters converge around their commonalities as "radical" and as a "dare" imparts a soupçon of Texas bravado into this otherwise tepid proposal that all Americans should simply agree on what we can agree on. On a range of controversial issues—abortion, immigration, education—McConaughey demurred from taking clear positions, and as Julian Mark commented, he also "never revealed which party he would have run under, and in interviews he tended not to take strong positions on big issues."[44] Many voters and even politicians would likely concede the inherent limitations of the United States' two-party system, but refusing to align with either of them, or refusing to stake out an Independent status liberated from them, simply elides meaningful questions about McConaughey's stances on the issues. In the end, he chose not to run.

But in many ways, the most devastatingly tactical persona for politicians is to mirror the beliefs of as many voters as possible, whether accurately or not, by constructing themselves as an open slate upon whom voters can project their desires, from which the politicians profit but then for which they can never be held to account. Jerzy Kosinski's brilliant satire *Being There* (1971) illustrates the implausible heights to which a person can rise simply by never expressing a determinate viewpoint, which appears a strikingly apt metaphor for McConaughey's approach to politics. An actor's star persona benefits from specific intersections of the person and their roles, but a politician's persona in many ways benefits more from the very imprecision of their character. And so, to answer the question with which this chapter began—is McConaughey all hat and no cattle?—sometimes the hat can do the job just fine on its own. A hat is a costume and thus part of a persona, and maybe that's all that is needed, as evident in the extraordinary career of one of the South's biggest stars.

AZIZ ANSARI
Comic Star of the Postsouthern South

"There's no easy path to stand-up [comedy], but an Indian kid from South Carolina? That is some journey," commented comic legend Chris Rock on comedian Aziz Ansari's meteoric career.[1] Hailing from Bennettsville, South Carolina, a small town located on the Great Pee Dee River in a predominantly rural county of a very conservative state, Ansari frequently ruminates over his life experiences as the child of subcontinental Indian immigrants, embracing the ironic disjunction between stereotypes of the South and of Indian Americans. By accentuating and performing his southernness in his comedy, whether stand-up or scripted, Ansari shatters numerous stereotypes of the region's citizens and thus in some ways heralds the arrival of a "postsouthern" South, one that might finally break with its troubled history of racism. In brief, a postsouthern South would overcome the troubling legacies of its past—its devotion to the malicious myths of a supposedly glorious "Lost Cause," its celebration of antiquated gender roles, its thinly veiled (if veiled at all) veneration of white supremacy—and emerge into a more enlightened era of embracing its many inhabitants who embody a wide variety of racial, ethnic, gender, and erotic identities. Both alienated from the South's mores and enamored of some of its traditions while simultaneously heralding this possibility of a postsouthern South, Ansari models an ironic relationship to the region that forthrightly condemns the region's racial prejudices while perpetuating some of its other troubling tropes, through the creation of his uniquely humorous, complex, and even contradictory southern star persona.

Born February 23, 1983, Ansari spent his childhood as a person of Asian descent in a region largely populated by white and Black residents. Following the well-worn path of many native-born southerners who leave their constricting hometowns for the greater freedoms of multiethnic metropolises, he migrated north after graduating high school to attend New York University. Such a pattern is well established for Black southerners, notably through the Great Migration, but also for a variety of other individuals who find the region's mores stifling, including liberals, queer people, and members of a range of ethnic minorities. Once in New York City, Ansari quickly climbed the ladder of stardom. He began performing in comedy clubs and soon prospered on the national circuit, notably by winning the Best Stand-Up award at HBO's 2006 U.S. Comedy Arts Festival. Small roles followed both in films, including *School for Scoundrels* (2006) and *I Love You, Man* (2009), and in television programs, including *Scrubs* (2001–10) and *Reno 911!* (2003–). With fellow comics Rob Huebel and Paul Scheer, Ansari starred in the sketch comedy program *Human Giant* (2007–8). He achieved his break-out role in *Parks and Recreation* (2009–15) by playing Tom Haverford, an aspiring entrepreneur employed as a low-level bureaucrat in the program's eponymous government agency. Next Ansari cocreated and starred in *Master of None* (2015–21), a critically acclaimed series for which he won two Emmy Awards for Outstanding Writing for a Comedy Series (with Alan Yang for the "Parents" episode in 2016, and with Lena Waithe for the "Thanksgiving" episode in 2017). Along with these scripted roles, Ansari has continued performing stand-up, touring nationally and internationally in such shows as *Intimate Moments for a Sensual Evening* (2010), *Aziz Ansari: Buried Alive* (2013), *Aziz Ansari: Live at Madison Square Garden* (2015), and *Aziz Ansari: Right Now* (2019). Through these many acclaimed performances and programs, Ansari has positioned himself as one of the defining comic talents of his generation.

As star studies has matured as a field, it has increasingly taken into account the ways in which nonwhite celebrities must negotiate the landmines of white culture.[2] As is well known, Asian American boys and men face a range of stereotypes as the so-called "model minority," including assumptions of their superior intelligence, sexual effeminacy, and physical weakness.[3] Rupam Saran documents the effects of such stereotyping and concludes that even "positive stereotyping of Indian immigrants and their children . . . masks their needs and educational issues"; she details further its role in creating class divides and other antagonistic social relationships.[4] Such pressures extend into the professional lives of Indian American performers, particularly because their skin tones potentially affect an audience's reception of their personas. Leilani Nishime explains the ways in which race is treated "as if it originates in bodies and as if it could be understood in the same way across space and historical period," but in actuality "audiences read . . . bodies differently across contexts."[5] Ansari faced these additional pressures in building his star persona, alongside the already challenging issue of how to, or even whether to, integrate southernness into a persona of Americanness.

Ansari's southernness is only one aspect of his star persona, through which he primarily presents himself as a cosmopolitan millennial and as a male feminist. If not precisely declaring himself an expert, Ansari convincingly casts himself as well-versed in the complexities of contemporary courtship, as evident in his book *Modern Romance*, which his publishers tout as "an unforgettable tour of our new romantic world."[6] A soupçon of endearing bravado enlivens his self-presentation, as he is both strikingly hip and slightly nerdy. Jason Woliner, who collaborated with Ansari on several projects, affirms, "From the beginning . . . I think Aziz had this fully formed persona—he knew who he was, and had this confidence, or swagger, that people really could latch on to."[7] Mixed in with these elements of his persona, Ansari also represents the United States' increasing ethnic diversity, and he projects this multifaceted persona both in his stand-up routines and, more surprisingly, in his two major scripted television roles—Tom Haverford in *Parks and Recreation* and Dev Shah in *Master of None*—in which a steady stream of comedy flows from his identity as a southerner, as both characters allow him the opportunity to play characters based to some degree on himself.

On a certain level, this congruency between the actor and his roles is not surprising, as a number of comedians and actors have starred as fictionalized versions of themselves in sitcoms (as discussed in this volume's chapters on Andy Griffith, Ellen DeGeneres, and Miley Cyrus). Intriguingly, in *Parks and Recreation*, Tom Haverford, a supporting role, hails from Ansari's hometown of Bennettsville, South Carolina, in contrast to the other actors and their charac-

FIG. 17. Obviously not a "redneck," Aziz Ansari, in the role of Tom Haverford in *Parks and Recreation,* cheekily proclaims himself one owing to his southern heritage.

ters, who do not share such a hometown link. Also, both programs include running comic themes hinging on Ansari's southern identity, illustrated by a short joke in *Parks and Recreation.* Ansari as Haverford quips, "I am from Bennettsville, South Carolina. I am what you might call a redneck."[8] (See figure 17.) The joke hinges on Ansari applying the stereotype of the southern redneck (white, racist, uneducated, beer belly) to himself (Brown, antiracist, well-educated, trim). In a contrapuntal scene, Tom shares with his boss, Ron, the challenges of growing up as a person of color in the U.S. South: "I was a skinny Indian kid in South Carolina, and it sucked. It took me twelve years, but I reinvented myself."[9] *Master of None* similarly builds the character of Dev from biographical features of Ansari's life, as evident in this exchange between Dev and his girlfriend Rachel while traveling to Nashville:

> RACHEL: You're from South Carolina, you have a younger brother, your dad's a doctor, and you went to a public high school for students . . . gifted in math and science.

DEV: Yeah, but don't you feel like those are just assumptions you can make about any Indian person?[10]

Rachel's description of Dev's life matches Ansari's biography, and Dev, who could not recall Rachel's life history in similar detail, turns the singularity of his life into a humorous recasting of stereotyping. Indeed, even if these biographical elements were not included in Ansari's scripted roles, his voice reveals his southern accent, as noted by fans who see his southern mannerisms as part of his appeal. Kelefa Sanneh declares that Ansari "speaks with a faint but noticeable Southern accent,"[11] and Patrick Smith, reviewing one of Ansari's stand-up routines, similarly states, "There's also an energetic cadence to his mild Southern accent that makes whatever he says almost impossible not to laugh at."[12]

By accentuating his southern roots in his scripted performances and stand-up routines, Ansari shatters numerous stereotypes of the region's citizens and thus in some ways heralds the arrival of a "postsouthern South," a long-anticipated shift in the region's demography and mores in which rural whites would no longer stand as its default representation in the wider cultural imaginary. For many southerners, waiting for the South to change is simply a disappointing, nonfiction version of Samuel Beckett's *Waiting for Godot*: one can wait all one wants, as patiently as one wants, but doing so does not guarantee the arrival of meaningful social change in the South. Indeed, a New South has been promised since the Civil War and the ensuing Reconstruction Era, such as in Henry W. Grady's words of 1890. "The new South is simply the old South under new conditions," he writes, with words that could be construed as a promise or a threat.[13] More recently, scholars in the field of southern studies have employed the concept of a postsouthern South to theorize its cultural transformations. Thomas F. Haddox suggests that the adjective *postsouthern* captures the evanescent potential "when belief in 'traditional' southern ways and possibly even in the reality of 'the South' begins to wane."[14] From this perspective, a postsouthern South would lose its virtually hegemonic construction of its past, and in so doing, allow the possibility for the overarching vision of a "solid South" of racist ideologies to dissipate. At the same time, Haddox rightly cautions that the concept of postsouthernness "preserves earlier notions of the South in the very act of calling them into question,"[15] and, as we shall see, this repackaging of the horrors of the South in a postsouthern framework haunts Ansari's humor. As Martyn Bone observes, the South cannot help but shift, even if only marginally, in response to the vertiginous dynamics of a networked and interconnected world: "'the South' increasingly is integrated into a dizzying network of global or 'transnational' flows—not only of capital, but also of immigrants and their cultures."[16] United States citizens move in and out of the South for a host of reasons, including job opportunities and family responsibilities, and international immigrants, including Ansari's parents, have also contributed greatly to the breakdown of a seemingly monolithic southern culture.

As much as some white southerners might resist these shifting tides of postsouthernism, demographic trends point to an increasingly multicultural and multiethnic U.S. South. Whereas subcontinental Indians migrated to the United States in relatively small numbers throughout much of its history, these trends shifted in the mid-1960s when Indian migration swelled following a series of legislative changes removing national-origin quotas, commencing temporary skilled worker programs, and creating employment-based permanent visas, as Jie Zong and Jeanne Batalova document.[17] Doctors willing to practice in underserved areas were particularly welcomed to the United States following the passage of Medicare in 1966. Ansari's parents—his father, Shoukath, is a gastroenterologist and his mother, Fatima, manages Shoukath's practice—availed themselves of these migratory trends. As Ansari documents in his acts, his parents regularly encountered racism in the South, in a clear indication of its failure to live up to the promise of postsouthernism. For instance, Ansari tells a story concerning the bigoted head of his father's hospital who refused to refer patients to him.[18] Despite the racist challenges his parents faced upon arriving in the U.S. South, Ansari frequently likens their new home nation to their former one, such as when he talks of his family's roots in Tamil Nadu, India, and demonstrates the universality of good cuisine and outmoded mores: "It's the South Carolina of India. The southern part with good food that no one goes to."[19] With a similar barb he states that his family is "from like the South Carolina of India. It's pretty rough."[20] South Carolinas, it would seem, are global phenomena.

In the dream of a postsouthern South, racism would have died the ignominious death it so richly deserves, and in much of his comedy, Ansari downplays the possibility of southern racial animus. For those who feel its brute and abject force, racism is terrifying, not humorous, but comedians are faced with the difficult task of acknowledging racism while simultaneously finding a latent humor to exploit. In a statement recognizing the ways in which whiteness stands as the default assumption of much American culture, Ansari has proclaimed, "The goal when you're a minority in comedy is to get people to treat you like a White person."[21] To be treated like a white person, however, at times requires adopting the perspective of white people, which can entail reformulating racism into comic premises. Further to this point, Ansari provocatively claims: "I kind of love racism, in a way, because I'm fascinated by it."[22] One should not hold Ansari too literally to his words—it is unlikely that he truly "loves" racism—but this line nevertheless speaks to the complex conflation of identities, regionalisms, untested beliefs, and personal prejudices that surface when discussing race and its repercussions in the modern United States. Along these lines Ansari downplays the prevalence of racism in the U.S. South in many of his jokes. Of his childhood years in South Carolina, he has stated simply, "Most of the time it was pretty fine,"[23] and in an anecdote drawn from his schoolyard experiences he recalls a teacher's intervention when he was bullied: "I remember one time when I was a kid and someone actually physically hit me when I was growing up in South Carolina. . . . Teacher goes over to the kid immediately and just goes, [*as he adopts an exaggerated southern accent for this female teacher*], 'If you touch him again, I will end you.' And that was it. Bullying done."[24] Notably, race is not mentioned as a motivating factor in this attack, and the teacher—presumably white—is presented both as defending young Aziz and as condemning his attacker. Although not one of Ansari's more humorous anecdotes, it nonetheless contains an ironic reversal—the bully bullied—and Ansari's exaggerated performance of southern femininity reconceptualizes it as menacing rather than nurturing, and with the ultimate purpose of protecting a young, nonwhite child. In another such joke, Ansari compares any racialist teasing he endured to the suffering of fat white children: "You read that I was the only minority in school, you envision this little Brown boy sitting in a corner by himself. It wasn't like that—the level of teasing I got was on par with what a fat White kid would go through." He pauses and then adds, "Sixty-five percent of what a fat White kid would go through."[25] In Ansari's depiction of the South, fat white children merit more sympathy than a person of color surrounded by whiteness.

Although Ansari presents his childhood years as relatively free from racial discrimination, other jokes hint at more troubling incidents, and he frequently twists recognizably southern scenarios and stereotypes to create a unique vision of a postsouthern South, notably through his redneck jokes. As much as the redneck is connected to the violence of racism, racism is by definition not funny, and so cannot easily be recuperated into a comic routine.[26] In the following sequence, Ansari first establishes the fear that rednecks instill in people of color: "I'm originally from South Carolina, and . . . my brother sent me something that really reminded me of how crazy it is down there. It was a promo video for this thing called the Simple Man cruise. And this was this cruise ship where they get all these southern rock bands, like .38 Special, the Marshall Tucker Band, Lynyrd Skynyrd, and they throw 'em on a boat. All these rednecks get on board, they set out to sea, and it's *scary as shit*. 'Cause I've never seen rednecks like this before. I lived in South Carolina for eighteen years—never saw people like this."[27] Ansari first leans into the stereotype of the redneck and paints these cruisers as its most extreme and frightening exemplars, the likes of which he never witnessed during his childhood. While I certainly do not intend to downplay the fear that many people of color would experience when finding themselves surrounded by white people, it is important to remember that Ansari is building a joke in establishing this setting, which toggles between these rednecks appearing first as "*scary as shit*" but soon as utterly harmless. He then recounts the words of one of these redneck men: "This one dude gets on this cruise, [and] is like, [*adopts an exaggerated southern accent*] 'Ah, hell, man, you can swing a dead cat around here, you bound to hit a good guitar player.'" Ansari pauses to allow this odd statement to register and then jauntily exclaims, "What the hell does that mean? I don't know, but I like the way this guy talks."[28] The joke is less about the *meaning* of this man's words—he is clearly communicating that, with so many famous bands on board, many excellent musicians will be found among them—than about Ansari's performance of his words, complete with cornpone accent. The threat posed by a boatload of rednecks dissipates, and Ansari segues into his appreciation of white southern colloquialisms by impersonating this man's voice in a variety of comic situations.

Master of None offers a similar example of Ansari's efforts to dissipate the threat of racism and southern rednecks when Dev and his girlfriend Rachel discuss whether they will patronize a honkytonk as part of their Nashville getaway. They begin discussing this rather odd word—*honkytonk*—and Dev states, "I know *honky* is like a semi-racist term for white people." They banter back and forth on the word's derivation and meaning until Rachel concludes, "So, wait, *honky-tonk* means white people hitting it hard?" Based on this humorous but spurious definition, Dev states: "As a minority, I'll admit I'm a little bit nervous about a situation where a large group of white people are 'hitting it hard.' But I'll take my chances. All right, honky. Let's go tonk."[29] In this example of the postsouthern South, Ansari again acknowledges but dismisses racism. Of course, one could well argue that dismissing the South's racism is highly problematic, even unethical, but this is precisely the comic hope that Ansari identifies in a postsouthern South: even the horrors of racism can be transmuted into humor.

On other occasions, Ansari employs incidents of southern racism to highlight the rampant racism of American culture as a whole. In one such riff, he first discusses his experience as a student in Bennettsville's predominantly white elementary school: "I remember being in the first grade. Every single kid in the class was white, except for me and this little Asian girl. And even back then, people used to be like, 'All right, Aziz! What's going on with you and Christine Li, man? I see you two. What's going on over there? Come on, man. You look weird. She looks weird.'"[30] For most audience members, this joke affords the opportunity to condemn the South for its backward mores, but Ansari segues to demonstrate its continued relevance. More recently, a variety of voices has presumed that he should date second-generation, Indian American comedian Mindy Kaling, with the reasoning behind this proposal identical to that of his first-grade, southern classmates.[31] From this perspective, the modern United States as a whole strikingly resembles the South of decades ago. For many southerners, the region's seemingly eternal bigotries merit strong and necessary condemnation, yet the tendency of nonsouthern Americans to view racism as a uniquely southern problem also chafes.

In another strikingly postsouthern rhetorical move, Ansari aligns the stereotypes levied against white southerners with those levied against minorities. Not all stereotypes carry the same brute force as racist ones, yet all stereotypes pigeonhole individuals as representatives of a wider class, as Ansari explains of the epithet "red-staters": "When you say 'red-staters,' you're saying, like, 'dumb, racist people,' and there are plenty of white people there who are not dumb, racist people. Maybe I'm just very quick to react when, as a culture, we try to paint this whole large group of people as one specific thing. Because that's what, as a minority, you deal with all the time. It's just people looking at you and being like, 'You're this. I know exactly what you are.' And you're like, 'Shut up! That's not me. You don't know me.'"[32] Yet a paradox emerges in these otherwise uplifting words because white southerners are not a minority; in treating them as such, Ansari flattens all stereotypes as equally dehumanizing, despite the great disparity between racial epithets and those directed at "red-staters."

For the most part, Ansari's sitcom *Parks and Recreation* won widespread acclaim for its gentle, offbeat humor, in its primary storyline of earnest do-gooder Leslie Knope (Amy Poehler) and her indefatigable efforts to fight bureaucracy and red tape on behalf of the citizens of the fictional town Pawnee, Indiana. Its early seasons, however, feature a string of racist jokes in which Leslie refuses to believe that Tom is a native-born southerner. In one such moment, Leslie comments on Tom, "I think he's a Libyan"[33]—as if no Brown man could be a native-born American—and later Leslie invites Tom to a dinner party so her friends can meet her boyfriend Justin. "Oh, hey, Tom! I'm having an A-list dinner party for Justin. And you, out of all my friends, come from the most distant and exotic land," she says; Tom replies ironically, "South Carolina?" Leslie laughs and dismisses his implicit rejoinder, "Save it for the party."[34] Here the cultural stereotype of the southerner clashes with the cultural stereotypes accorded to brown-skinned men. Such themes are extended in the following dialogue:

LESLIE: You're not from here, right?

TOM: No, I'm from South Carolina.

LESLIE: But you moved to South Carolina from where?

TOM: My mother's uterus.

LESLIE: But you were conceived in Libya, right?

TOM: Wow. No. I was conceived in America. My parents are Indian.

LESLIE: Where did the name Haverford come from?

TOM: My birth name is Darwish David Ismael Gani, and I changed it to Tom Haverford because, you know, brown guys with funny-sounding Muslim names don't make it really far in politics.[35]

The ostensible humor of this encounter hinges upon Leslie's utter inability to believe that a Brown man is a natal citizen of the United States, and more so, of the South. Jokes of this sort occurred relatively frequently in the first two seasons of *Parks and Recreation* but were then abruptly dropped, likely because they do not fit within its overarching genial themes of pleasant characters engaging in offbeat antics with good-natured motivations. On the contrary, the attempted humor of these jokes depends on construing Tom as unrecognizable as an American, and specifically as a southern, citizen.

The vision of a postsouthern South promises necessary change but in some ways simply repackages the region's troubled history, and Ansari's postsouthern star persona likewise sutures over contradictions in his self-presentation. Another aspect of Ansari's star persona that aligns with his southern roots arises when he nostalgically envisions a past of genteel manners in heteroerotic relationships: "If you want me to be honest, I really feel like all guys of this generation is kind of a sad state of affairs. Like, gentlemen are gone. We just have 'dudes.'"[36] Throughout *Modern Romance* he idealizes the dating rituals of a halcyon yesteryear. "To be honest, I tend to romanticize the past," he declares, as he then describes his romantic vision of a date: "I take a girl to a drive-in movie, we go have a cheeseburger and a malt at the diner, and then we make out under the stars in my old-timey convertible." Lest this romantic vision of the past descend into pure sentimentalism, Ansari segues sharply by reminding his audience of nostalgia's tendency to gloss over history's troubling elements: "Granted, this might have been tough in the fifties given my brown skin tone and racial tensions at the time, but in my fantasy, racial harmony is also part of the deal."[37] As he further details the travails of modern romance in this book, he categorizes men as "gentlemen" and "bozos," with the gentlemen exhibiting manners, sophistication, and generosity, whereas the bozos exhibit boorishness, crudity, and selfishness.[38] Although one could certainly argue that nostalgia for a bygone era of more courteous courtship is not an exclusively southern value, Ansari's vision of a gentleman, while not strictly demarcated as a southern archetype, aligns strikingly well with the longstanding figure of the South's chivalrous gentleman. This mythic figure unites nostalgia with an appealing vision of masculinity that nonetheless masks the paradoxes, deceptions, and even cruelties at its heart.[39]

As "southern gentlemen" often employed a façade of gentility to hide more nefarious purposes, particularly against Black people but also against white women and others who crossed their paths, so too was Ansari's persona of enlightened masculinity called into question as part of the reckonings of the #MeToo movement. In an essay titled "I Went on a Date with Aziz Ansari. It Turned into the Worst Night of My Life," Katie Way documents a troubling encounter between Ansari and "Grace," the pseudonym of a young woman who briefly dated Ansari.[40] Over the course of their evening together he determinedly pursued her sexually despite her increasing discomfort. Their text-message exchanges capture their conflicting views of the evening. Ansari wrote, "It was fun meeting you last night," to which "Grace" responded, "You ignored clear non-verbal cues; you kept going with advances. . . . I want to make sure you're aware so maybe the next girl doesn't have to cry on the ride home." Ansari apologized: "Clearly, I misread things in the moment and I'm truly sorry." As with so many cultural controversies, Way's article presented a Rorschach test to the nation, with some seeing Ansari as a predator and others wondering why "Grace" did not simply end the date. At the very least, however, the encounter between Ansari and "Grace" highlights the ways in which men's performances of etiquette often camouflage ulterior motives. Within the mythologies of the U.S. South, men's chivalry stands as one of the region's defining virtues, yet chivalry often masks deeper truths about power and privilege, and also about denying power and privilege to others. Following "Grace's" accusations, Ansari stepped away from public appearances for approximately a year, returning with his comedy special *Right Now*, in which he addressed the controversy: "I just felt terrible that this person felt this way. And after a year or so, I just hope it was a step forward. It moved things forward for me, and made me think about a lot. I hope I've become a better person."[41] For Ansari, this "better person" might be one less invested in tropes of the southern gentlemen that seek to override female autonomy.

In another sign of the ways in which southern tropes troublingly contribute to Ansari's star persona, critics have suggested that he both appropriates and marginalizes Black culture. Kelefa Sanneh summarizes this dual effect: "His jokes and stories about black celebrities allow him to acknowledge his own status as an anomaly in the mainly white world of alt comedy. In this way, he can identify with the white people in the audience, chuckling at the excesses of African-American culture, while simultaneously allying himself with the ambition and eccentricity of these nonwhite performers."[42] For example, Ansari has declared that his "favorite racial stereotype ever" is "Black men having explosive reactions to magic tricks"—a stereotype construing Black men as gullible and overemotive.[43] Examining Ansari's performance as Tom Haverford, Michelle Ann Abate notes striking parallels to minstrelsy and blackface performances: "Tom's signature facial expression mirrors that of minstrel performers. . . . Although the character does not blacken his face with burned cork or accentuate his mouth with red makeup, he does have the same bulging eyes, wide grin, and arched eyebrows."[44] Abate compares several images from minstrel shows and *Parks and Recreation*, detailing the ways in which exaggerated facial features draw on a long history of racist performances. As she further explains, "The fact that actor Aziz Ansari . . . is nonwhite only further complicates the way in which race, identity, and humor function through his character. Indeed, one might make the case that . . . the show uses his brownness as a proxy for blackness."[45] Growing up in the South entails witnessing countless acts of racist humor and stereotypes, all of which, for non-Black people, require determined attention to extirpate lest one reproduce them.

At the risk of concluding this chapter with a cliché, it is essential to emphasize that Ansari, like all stars and all humans, continues to grow, evolve, mature, and change, and so will his presentation of himself as a native southerner. In early shows, he repeatedly derided his chubby cousin Harris; now he is embarrassed that he publicly mocked his young relative. As the South, both in its past and in its promised progression into postsouthernism, is itself a place of contradictions, of savage racism and downhome hospitality, so too are the people born and bred in it, even those who leave it far behind. Ansari's younger brother Aniz remembers his brother's urgent advice when he (Aniz) mentioned moving to Atlanta: "Just get the fuck out of South Carolina. Number one, man, just get the fuck out of South Carolina."[46] As much as Ansari's words construe South Carolina as a hellhole to be escaped from at any cost, Aniz also credits their southern roots for their successful careers in creative industries: "Growing up where we grew up is 100 percent the reason why our perspective is the way it is, and even why we ended up being creative people and doing TV and comedy. . . . It wasn't like we were going to school every day and getting bullied by redneck kids. Bennettsville was our hometown, and we were part of the town."[47] The South is a central part of Aziz Ansari's biography, a steady theme in his humor, and a key part of his star persona; the contradictions of the postsouthern South, as they do for so many of its citizens, have become his own.

14

MILEY CYRUS'S QUEERLY AUTHENTIC SOUTHERN INNOCENCE

Young southern actor and singer Miley Cyrus skyrocketed to fame owing to her starring role in the phenomenally popular family sitcom *Hannah Montana* (2006–11), in which she played the role of Miley Stewart, a self-admittedly dorky teen living in all respects a normal life—except for her secret alter-identity as international pop-sensation Hannah Montana.[1] With vivacious Miley Stewart as its appealing protagonist, *Hannah Montana* followed a long tradition of foregrounding plucky teens, and Bill Osgerby discerns the cultural popularity of a "teen girl TV tradition whose accent on freedom and fun *always* gestured towards a femininity that was independent and active."[2] Without doubt, Miley embodies this archetypal character whom Cyrus seamlessly performs. Southern stereotypes and the creation and maintenance of Cyrus's southern star persona also played an outsized role in the program's popularity, for many of its plot lines hinged on dualities: Hannah Montana is an internationally famous pop singer living a life of glitz and glamour, whereas Miley Stewart is an average tweenager living with her family and experiencing the daily tribulations of adolescence. These and other dualities are entrenched by geographies: Hannah's fame coincides with her residence in California, a state representative of celebrities, big cities, and cosmopolitanism, whereas Miley hails from Tennessee, a state representative of everyday people, rural communities, and homespun values. The red state / blue state dichotomy thus registers in the background of this program, as it has continually reverberated throughout the construction and reformulations of Cyrus's southern star persona.

Also paralleling Cyrus's career, *Hannah Montana* evokes the presumed innocence of the tween sitcom genre on its surface level of narration, yet the program, toward the end of its run, concomitantly allegorized Cyrus's controversial transition into a sexual provocateur. These storylines prepared young viewers to accompany the protagonist/actor as she segued out of the show and into her career as a solo artist, and in so doing, they undermined Cyrus's fundamental duality by enhancing her cosmopolitan appeal at the expense of her roots in the conservative South. The presumed innocence of tween sexuality established another level of duality within the program's marketing and narratology: through the core value of Cyrus's personal authenticity as a southerner, *Hannah Montana* hid sexuality from parental view and depicted its protagonist as an age-appropriate role model, thus paradoxically marketing an absence of sexuality that later merged seamlessly into Cyrus's marketing of herself as a queer advocate and icon. In this light, Cyrus's post-*Hannah* declaration of her pansexuality encodes another queer meaning to her sitcom and her southern star persona, encouraging an allegorical reading of Miley's "coming out" as Hannah Montana as equivalent to Cyrus's revelations of her adult erotic interests.[3]

A guiding trope of contemporary celebrity is founded on the presumption of a star's authenticity and, as a corollary to this authenticity, her relatability. As Jo Littler proposes, stars such as Jennifer Lopez proclaim their authenticity by rewriting the Cinderella myth, allowing them to revel in glamour while highlighting their impoverished roots: "Instead of merely luxuriating in her palatial excess, Cinderella now has to show that she can still remember that she started out in the kitchen. This knowledge or awareness structures her character; it stops her 'getting above herself,' it keeps her 'real.'"[4] Such stars appear to be not just rich and famous (and thus distanced from their fans) but also grounded and authentic; they consequently remain relatable to their audiences, despite vast disparities in income and lifestyle. For *Hannah Montana* the tween viewer should be able to identify equally with Miley Cyrus, Miley Stewart, and Hannah Montana, with the actor and her character's dual identities facilitating this process. Melanie Kennedy outlines how *Hannah Montana* modulates between celebrity and tween culture, fusing a hybrid reality cognizant of the myriad and contradictory ideologies related to tweendom: "*Hannah Montana*, and the broader tween media landscape, should be understood as products of the contemporary postfeminist, neoliberal, pop-cultural moment, highly invested in celebrity as well as the attendant discourses of the self, the real, and the authentic."[5] Authenticity is key to the narrative adventures of *Hannah Montana* in creating an appealing character for tween viewers, one who strives to maintain her genuine, grounded self as she juggles her everyday and superstar lives, as it is also key to marketing related merchandise to the demographic she represents.

To enhance their appeal, family sitcoms have long exploited the thin line between their stars and their protagonists, and *Hannah Montana* blurs the distinction between fiction and reality in numerous ways—most obviously in the razor-thin line between star Miley Cyrus and protagonist Miley Stewart, as both actor and character hail from Tennessee and have won international acclaim as pop stars. Cyrus's father, Billy Ray, a country singer best known for his hit single "Achy Breaky Heart" (1992), plays Miley's father, with this character similarly experiencing a successful singing career in his past and now writing songs for his daughter. Even Miley's horse correlates with Cyrus's childhood pet—a connection acknowledged in an episode's dedication to "Roam-Man (1988–2009)."[6] The marketing of Miley/Cyrus/Hannah consistently obfuscates the borders between them, such as in the "Back Home Again with Miley" minidocumentary, which follows Cyrus and her father on a journey to their Tennessee residence. A caption reads, "Even though it's across the country from their Hollywood home, this farm is the heart of the Cyrus family," and Miley's return to Tennessee catalyzes the plot of *Hannah Montana: The Movie* (2009). Further enhancing the fictional authenticity of *Hannah Montana*, many guest stars play thinly disguised versions of themselves or simply themselves, such as country superstar Dolly Parton who plays the recurring role of Miley's Aunt Dolly and, in real life, is Cyrus's godmother. Cyrus asserts of the overlap between herself and her character: "Most people know me as Hannah Montana, but Hannah is a television character. She's fiction. Sure, I've put a lot of myself in her. I've tried to make her come to life. But that doesn't make her real, and it doesn't make her *me*."[7] This duality between Miley's and Cyrus's lives is key to the construction of Cyrus's star persona, for it builds levels of discourse and metadiscourse that both obfuscate and escalate the program's treatment of sexuality. In the ensuing play between virginal innocence and sexual maturation, the character and the celebrity are both rendered relatably "authentic" while denuding this authenticity, rooted in southernness, of its purported meaning. The result is a queer authenticity, in the sense that Cyrus stands simultaneously as both authentic and inauthentic, as both an innocent tweenager and a provocateur, depending on the particular moment of her career's evolution.

Certainly, the executives, marketers, and writers of *Hannah Montana* consistently foreground Miley's need to maintain her authenticity, as they concomitantly trumpet her relatability to the program's tween viewers. As the program's sell sheet declares, "It is about everyday girls with secret, superstar lives both real and imagined. . . . All girls can relate to girl next door Miley Stewart, but they want to be like her alter ego, Hannah Montana."[8] Rich Ross, the Disney executive who greenlit *Hannah Montana*, agrees: "It's not just that she's a rock star; . . . it's that she's relatable, too. She's someone you want to be friends with. And she's working to balance what she has in her intense life."[9] Relatable to her tween viewers while demonstrating her appropriate (southern) values to adults, Miley models an authenticity attractive to disparate strands of her audience yet one that must ultimately collapse beneath its inherent paradox. As regressive as such a viewpoint might be, some see tween (and even adult) sexuality as incompatible with adolescent virtue, and thus Cyrus could hardly mature into adult sexuality, with the eyes of the world upon her, without at least tweaking the expectations of her more conservatively minded fans (and their parents).

For Cyrus/Miley to assert herself as a moral authority, she must remain true to her authentic self, a theme introduced in the series' first episode through the lyrics of "This Is the Life," in which she sings "I'm going to take my time, I'm still getting it right." Given this credo, Miley's mistakes become the means for viewers to learn alongside her, and her authenticity is evident in the fact that she is disarmingly candid with friends and family, often blurting out a version of her "say what" catchphrase when another character states something unexpected.[10] Also key to the character's relatability and authenticity is her outsider status in her everyday life as Miley Stewart. The program frequently stresses Miley's southern roots, establishing a red state / blue state dichotomy that she bridges effortlessly: southern in her upbringing and values ("I can't. I'm from Tennessee. We don't do that," Miley pleads to her friend Lilly), yet Californian in her celebrity subculture ("Well, you're in California now, and we do do that," Lilly replies).[11] To stress Miley's credibility as an average teen, she and Lilly are victims of school mean girls Ashley and Amber, with the former mocking her southern roots, "Could you be any more of a hillbilly?"[12] As in fiction, so in life, and Cyrus recalls in her autobiography her sixth-grade struggles with friends and foes, thereby establishing her relatability to her tween audience in their joint struggles for acceptance among classmates: "The cool people find each other. The smart people find each other. Me and all the other in-between artsy people realize we'd better join forces and make the best of it."[13]

Ironically, even Hannah's and Cyrus's assumptions of their diva personas deepen their core authenticity and thus foreshadow its queer fissures. This evolution occurs in *Hannah Montana: The Movie* when Robby Ray takes Miley to Tennessee to "detox" her from her Hollywood airs. As her grandmother (Margo Martindale) tells Miley after she sulkily arrives in Tennessee, "Look, missy. You may be Hannah Montana back home, but here we're britches and boots. And if that ain't good enough for you, maybe you should just pack up and git." With life again conscripted to imitate art, Cyrus mentions in her autobiography that at one point she "was being a brat. Stardom had changed me. I wasn't Miley anymore. I was Hollywood. Something *had* to shift."[14] Hollywood transforms Miley and Cyrus into glamorous narcissists, yet both the character and the actor, reminded of their core values, shift back to their authentic selves grounded in southern values—all the while maintaining their Hollywood lifestyles of celebrity excess.

Miley's authenticity is directly tied to *Hannah Montana*'s merchandising, which is not solely a lucrative revenue stream but key to the program itself, as it dramatizes Hannah's likeable persona while stressing her status as a marketing icon. With disarming candor, Cyrus writes in her autobiography, "The show had proven so successful that Hannah Montana had gone from being a character to being a brand."[15] Carissa Rosenberg, *Seventeen* magazine's entertainment director, echoes this sentiment yet switches the actor for the character: "Miley Cyrus herself is a brand, not just Hannah Montana."[16] Developing this consumerist motif, *Hannah Montana* stages numerous scenes emphasizing Hannah's appeal in marketing products. As her publicist, Vita (Vanessa Williams), tells her: "Do you know what a well-placed photo of you shopping is worth? You're a star, an icon. You look at it, touch it, wear it, and the whole world has to have it."[17] Several episodes of *Hannah Montana* portray young fans eagerly purchasing merchandise endorsed by their icon, evident when Lilly reads Hannah's email aloud to her, which includes a fan's determination to emulate her pop idol:

"Dear Hannah, I love, love, love that scarf you wore at the video awards. Where, where, where can I get one?"[18] The show refrains from providing the answer—Walmart—yet this bifurcation of worlds—down-home simplicity and celebrity glamour—extends to Cyrus's description of the fashions in her two closets: "Both are stuffed with more clothes than I could wear in a year. Half of the stuff is clothes I bought at Forever 21 and Walmart, and half is gifts from designers like Chanel, Gucci, and Prada that I began to get as the show took off."[19] While few celebrities would admit to hanging Walmart fashions in their wardrobes, this corporation sells the Hannah Montana line of clothing, and Cyrus describes of its creation: "We look at what I wear, and then we try to make it for $16."[20]

Yet at the same time that Hannah is depicted as part of the marketing industry behind her success, the authenticity that is core to the Miley/Hannah dyad often emerges to trouble her image as a celebrity pitchperson—and, consequently, to strengthen it. The episode "Smells Like Teen Sellout" extends Hannah's credibility to the commercial realm, with its title alerting young fans to the possibility that their icon could exploit her celebrity by endorsing inferior products. While shooting a commercial for "Eau Wow" perfume, Hannah discovers, to her dismay, that it smells like raspberries, as she then recalls winning a raspberry-pie-eating contest and vomiting on the governor of Tennessee. Colin Lassiter, a recurring character in the role of a Larry King–style interviewer, declares, "I'm glad you're not one of those celebrities who goes out and pushes something she doesn't believe in." Hannah realizes she cannot sabotage her integrity by endorsing Eau Wow, even though the company gave her a car in appreciation of her marketing appeal; she tells Robby Ray, "The truth is always the best thing. Even though sometimes it hurts." Within the standard narratology of a family sitcom, such moralizing indicates that the protagonist has learned a valuable lesson, with viewers at home learning one as well: that Hannah Montana—and Miley Cyrus—are trusted voices within the commercial milieu.

Many parents fret that children will find television's candid depictions of sexuality confusing and upsetting and so seek out "family-friendly programming"—that emptiest of television signifiers—to shield their children from sexually mature themes. On its surface, *Hannah Montana* shies away from candid depictions of eroticism, and within its tween world, girls' interests are divided between shopping and boys, with these twin desires dramatized when Lilly suggests that "the mall has cute clothes," but Miley replies that "the beach has cute boys"—and in this instance, the beach wins.[21] Many similar storylines dramatize Miley's crushes and dating relationships with boys, yet these hints of adolescent sexuality rarely disrupt the series' vigilant innocence. When the possibility of light eroticism for these adolescent characters becomes too real, *Hannah Montana* often slips into fantasy, such as when Miley kisses a cookie jar while thinking of her love interest Jesse or when her brother Jackson declares, "Prepare to be kissed, as you've never been kissed before"—with the camera revealing that he is addressing Miley's toy pig.[22]

Cookie jars and stuffed animals aside, *Hannah Montana* must confront the likelihood of its protagonist kissing, yet it does so gently, and camera cuts and other evasive editing techniques consistently delay depicting Miley's sexual maturation. Hannah thinks that she will kiss her crush, Jake, as they shoot a film, and Jake advises her how to stage their embrace: "Just close your eyes, and count to sixty. It'll be over before you know it." Intimidated by the possibility of a kiss lasting so long, Hannah replies in shock, "Sixty?" Even this staged embrace is never seen, for the director stops filming at the moment before their lips meet.[23] Given *Hannah Montana*'s hesitation to depict teen sexuality beyond brief kisses, parents of tween viewers know they need not be concerned about escalating depictions of eroticism. Even the slightest possibility that Miley/Hannah could lose her virginity—which, of course, would never be allowed to happen—is rendered impossible by the many layers of surveillance to which she is subjected. One of the many security personnel who guard Hannah says, "It's my job to keep that southern belle from getting dinged"—with the double entendre of "getting dinged" suggestive of the intercourse that cannot occur within the program's fictions.[24] Concerning the construction of her southern celebrity persona that complements her screen character, Cyrus affirmed her commitment to maintaining her virginity: "When I got old enough and there were boys in the picture, I asked if it was time for me to get my own [purity] ring. My mom gave me one that has a circle on it, to represent the circle of marriage."[25] Within both its discourse and metadiscourse, *Hannah Montana* treats teen sexuality so lightly and endorses virginity so earnestly that many parents would likely applaud its Disneyfication of sexuality for young viewers.

In line with this ethos of innocence, *Hannah Montana* flirts with issues of tween sexuality only obliquely, yet in casting Brooke Shields as Miley's deceased mother, it encodes a queer layer of sexual transgression and commercialism that it concomitantly purifies. Shields burst into the limelight in the 1970s and early 1980s in a string of provocative films featuring frank depictions of teen eroticism, notably *The Blue Lagoon* (1980) and *Endless Love* (1981). Additional controversy accompanied her commercials for Calvin Klein jeans, including one in which she purred, "Do you know what comes between me and my Calvins? Nothing." *Hannah Montana* reminds its parental audience of this connection when they learn the name of Miley's horse: Blue Jeans. The risqué blue jeans of Shields's past are resignified into a reminder of Miley's simpler life in Tennessee, washing away the lingering aura of pedophilia that many viewers found so unsettling in Shields's adolescent commercial career. With the specter of her past behind her and now donning a maternal image, Shields imparts loving wisdom to Miley from beyond the grave, such as in her comforting declaration, "You were loved before you were Hannah Montana, and you'll be loved long after Hannah's on one of those 'Where are they now?' shows."[26] Child viewers are unlikely to know of Shields's career highlights from the early 1980s, yet in recoding her sexually charged past through the wholesome image of Miley's deceased mother, *Hannah Montana* also rewrites the scripts of Cyrus's sexually incendiary stunts, suggesting it is a phase that she will grow out of, just as her television mother did. From this vantage point, Miley's determined innocence reveals its queer subtext, for viewers realize that, just like her fictional mother, a provocative sense of adolescent sexuality is hiding beneath her plucky exterior.

Whereas *Hannah Montana* disavows teen sexuality throughout its storylines, its cagey thematizing of marketing and of Miley's and Cyrus's authenticity prepares its young audience to accompany Cyrus through her post-Hannah metamorphosis into an openly queer pop star. This transition into a sexual provocateur, as well as her later coming out as pansexual, coincides with, and becomes allegorized into, Hannah's quest for authenticity as an artist. The litany of Cyrus's sexually titillating, headline-grabbing acts during and following her years as Hannah Montana bespeaks her continuous efforts to align her star persona with her changing age and audience. Midway through the show's run, she posed for a June 2008 *Vanity Fair* photo shoot with Annie Leibovitz that portrayed her draped in bed sheets, her bare back suggesting nudity. An additional photo with her father, Billy Ray—featuring her bare midriff, his bare shoulders, and she leaning into his lap as they hold hands—struck some readers as disturbingly incestuous. The manufactured controversy worked as intended, as Camille Paglia sardonically pointed out: "They knew perfectly well it would cause a storm.... I'm so tired of Annie Leibovitz."[27] Cyrus dutifully apologized: "I took part in a photo shoot that was supposed to be 'artistic' and now, seeing the photographs and reading the story, I feel so embarrassed.... I never intended for any of this to happen and I apologize to my fans who I care so deeply about."[28] Gary Marsh, the president of entertainment for Disney Channel Worldwide, chided his star, warning her to maintain her all-American image: "For Miley Cyrus to be a 'good girl' is now a business decision for her. Parents have invested in her a godliness. If she violates that trust, she won't get it back."[29]

Negotiating among children's innocence, adolescent maturation, and adult provocation, Cyrus detailed her muddled understanding of the intersection of her southern star persona and her status as a children's role model: "My job is to be a role model, and that's what I want to do, but my job isn't to be a parent. . . . My job isn't to tell your kids how to act or how not to act, because I'm still figuring that out for myself. So to take that away from me is a bit selfish. Your kids are going to make mistakes whether I do or not. That's just life."[30] Cyrus's jumbled words bespeak the difficulty of pinning down a coherent celebrity identity for her throughout her many personas. She claims her responsibility to be a role model—presumably one of whom parents would approve—but then asserts for herself the right to be a typical adolescent who will make frequent mistakes—thus distancing herself from the position of role model that she has previously claimed. Many public appearances continued to shock some fans, including her August 2009 performance at the Teen Choice Awards, in which she spun around a stripper pole while singing "Party in the USA." Anticipating the conclusion of *Hannah Montana*, the June 2010 release of her "Can't Be Tamed" single, with the lyrics "I go through guys like money flyin' out the hands" and a video with risqué costuming, announced a striking shift in her celebrity persona. The controversies continued—even escalated—following the conclusion of *Hannah Montana* in 2011. Her August 2013 performance at MTV's Video Music Awards, in which she twerked—a dance move symbolic of anal sex—with Robin Thicke ignited incendiary commentary. (See figure 18.) The backlash included such comments as news host Mika Brzezinski's pointed criticism: "There's pushing the envelope and there's porn—there's raunchy porn that's disgusting and disturbing."[31] Various other incidents extensively covered

FIG. 18. Many fans were shocked by Miley Cyrus's sexually provocative performance with Robin Thicke at the 2013 Video Music Awards, testifying to the challenges of tween stars maintaining personas of childhood innocence as they mature into adulthood.

in the entertainment media—penis birthday cakes, daring haircuts, selfies in various stages of dishabille with her surprisingly nimble tongue in exaggerated display—testify to Cyrus's strategic marketing of herself to a public always eager to learn of her latest escapades. Unsurprisingly, many children and their parents, taken aback by this new image, castigated her for her actions, particularly while she still inhabited the tween-friendly role of Hannah Montana.

Yet because the lines between Cyrus, Miley, and Hannah were drawn with such cagey ambiguity, parents who would discourage their children from following the post–*Hannah Montana* version of Cyrus were cast as, in effect, stifling their children's psychosexual development—at least within the moral universe of the program, which frequently emphasizes the need to let children assume responsibility for themselves. Two contrasting episodes—"Yet Another Side of Me" and "Hannah's Gonna Get This"—dramatize the quandary Hannah faces in developing as an artist: whether to remain true to her musical roots and her current fans or to experiment with new genres and risk alienating these fans, with these storylines allegorically framing the issue of her increasingly sexual star persona. In "Yet Another Side of Me," Hannah encounters Isis, the longstanding queen of pop obviously modeled on Madonna. Convinced by Isis's advice to be perpetually preparing her next incarnation, Miley abandons her musical roots for a thrash metal sound, singing about her former days as a "nice girl"—one who obeyed her parents but now finds herself bored by such youthful innocence. By this episode's end, Hannah seeks Robby Ray's guidance. "There's got to be a way to keep them interested and still be me," she laments; her father advises authenticity as the solution to her dilemma: "As long as you're true to yourself, your fans will always be there." Hannah rejects the sexually suggestive aspects of this new persona, telling her costume designer, "I won't be needing the torn fishnets, the combat boots, or the bullwhip," with these accessories hinting at a dominatrix outfit. The episode ends as Hannah discovers that Isis has fashioned herself into a Hannah Montana clone for her latest reincarnation, so Hannah's authenticity contrasts with Isis's inauthenticity, proving the superiority of the adolescent who knows herself and, in this instance, rejects a hypersexualized persona in favor of continued innocence.

While it is easy to mock Madonna, it is not so easy to enjoy her striking career longevity in a pop-culture arena where the vast majority of performers maintain their fame for only a few years. So as much as Hannah refuses to change her act in "Yet Another Side of Me," she updates her sound and image in "Hannah's Gonna Get This." Further testifying to the sitcom's interest in the marketing of pop stars, pop songs, and pop merchandise, her producer hires a focus group of young fans to discuss their reactions to her new release. This song pulses to a techno beat that metonymically represents sexuality—in contrast to the innocent, bubble-gum pop of traditional Hannah fare. Of the focus group member who appreciates her artistic evolution, Hannah declares, "See, somebody's not afraid to let an artist grow. I mean, clearly my audience is wise beyond their years." She encourages the children who voted against her new sound to embrace change: "Now, look, I know change can be scary, but it's a part of growing up. It's how we find out who we are and who we're gonna be." One little girl whimpers, "I don't want you to change. I love you just the way you are." With Hannah caught in the double bind of pleasing some fans and displeasing others, Robby Ray again advises her to pursue authenticity as her primary goal: "Any time an artist tries to grow, there's always gonna be people who don't like it. You just gotta ask yourself, are you gonna listen to the naysayers, or are you gonna listen to your heart?" Miley offers an unenthusiastic rebuttal—"Well, when the naysayers are crying seven year olds, your heart kinda gets torn"—but the evolution that the sitcom has evaded in its surface treatment of sexuality now approaches, as Robby Ray again encourages her to be true to herself: "Well, I'm proud of you, honey, for trying to make all your fans happy, but since you can't do that, the one that you really need to make happy is you."

As she maintains her authenticity as an artist by moving in a new musical direction, Hannah sparks a controversy when she publicly confesses her alter ego of Miley Stewart, which parallels Cyrus's assumption of her risqué and increasingly queer and pansexual celebrity persona. These "coming out" episodes function on the narrative level as the climax of the series' story arc, yet they concomitantly assume queer inflections within the metadiscourse concerning Cyrus's celebrity persona. On Colin Lassiter's interview program in the "Kiss It Goodbye" episode, adults voice their outrage over Miley's revelation. One tells her, "You ought to be ashamed of yourself," to which Miley responds: "What? All I did was tell the truth." The episode continues as Miley defends herself to Lassiter, declaring "I was just trying to do what felt right for me," and he consoles her, "Well, don't worry, sweetheart. Some parents are just a little overprotective." The next caller argues that Hannah Montana—like Santa Claus and the Tooth Fairy—is a beloved children's fantasy that must be preserved, and so Miley's position of honesty is ironically validated. Within the sitcom's allegorical metadiscourse, Cyrus's sexualized performances are naturalized as part of her growth as an artist. As the analogy implies, just as parents cannot preserve their children in the eternal stasis of believing in Santa Claus and the Tooth Fairy, they must allow their children to enjoy Hannah's artistic metamorphosis to better appreciate Cyrus's queer transition into adult stardom.

Hannah Montana then depicts Miley moving past these criticisms to perform again, as Aunt Dolly, hosting a musical special, introduces Hannah to the audience: "Well, I want to introduce somebody to you now that's been getting a lot of criticism lately, but she is not gonna let that stop her from doing what she loves to do, and that is singing for you." The children in the audience cry out "We love you, Hannah," proving her endurable appeal as she sings "Kiss It Goodbye," a song of personal transformation that includes the lyric "I'm a different girl."[32] With real life again echoing the program, Parton defended Cyrus's controversial transition. Guy Trebay documents that "when asked whether she was shocked by Ms. Cyrus's rapid shift from . . . a 'wholesome teenager' to a 'raunchy performer,' Ms. Parton said, 'Well, yeah, but in a good way.'"[33] For Cyrus's star to continue rising, she must convince tween viewers to accept her "coming out" as a different girl, with her show promoting this sexual evolution within the muted tones of a family sitcom reticent to address teen sexuality. In contrast to Parton's defense of Cyrus, singer Sinéad O'Connor urged her to rethink the ways in which marketing forces were constructing her career: "As for the shedding of the Hannah Montana image . . . whoever is telling you getting naked is the way to do that does absolutely NOT respect your talent, or you as a young lady."[34] In this manner Cyrus's sexuality became a subject of debate and critical discussion, no matter the prurience of monitoring a young woman's evolution into adulthood. Her southern star persona of plucky innocence, as modulated by California cool, constructed her as a girl to protect rather than as an independent agent of her own erotic destiny.

Even light kisses rarely appear on *Hannah Montana*, yet Miley/Hannah effectively laid the groundwork for Cyrus's sexual and celebrity metamorphosis through the power of marketing. In constructing the character's relatability to her fans, her ethical values as a spokesperson, and her authenticity and outsider status through her southern roots and star persona, Miley won over young viewers and their parents through her surface authenticity that allows queer countercurrents to overcome tween innocence. And as Cyrus's career has flourished in the years since *Hannah Montana*'s conclusion, she has continually shifted her erotic image while maintaining the pseudo-authenticity key to her enduring success, particularly in her advocacy for homeless queer youth. The *New York Times* praised her as "a natural avatar for a post-gender generation,"[35] and she recently declared her ecumenical erotic interests: "I'm very open about my sexuality—I am pansexual."[36] She also proclaimed of herself, "Everything I've ever done has been true to me at that minute," a statement of eternal authenticity that bedazzles with its chameleon play of time, image, and truth, in its collapsing of tween innocence and provocative queerness.[37] As *Hannah Montana* proceeded from its tween roots and its star began emphasizing her sexuality and her desire to evolve as an artist, the southern roots of her star persona increasingly faded, demonstrating the malleability of southern signifiers in the expression of an inauthentic authenticity that might possibly have told the truth.

With *Hannah Montana* now over a decade behind her, Cyrus's star persona appears increasingly cosmopolitan, still queer, less southern. Her tours and albums continue to draw strong responses from fans, and recent successes include the single "Flowers," the best-selling global single of 2023. She continues to stress her queerness and her support for the broader queer community. Following her marriage to Liam Hemsworth (2018–20), she pointed out that marrying a man did not erase her pansexual identity, but merely showcased one aspect of it. Also, she established the Happy Hippie Foundation, an organization whose mission is "to fight injustice facing homeless youth, LGBTQ youth and other vulnerable populations."[38] In relation to the southern aspects of her star persona, her album *Bangerz* (2013) merged country music with hip-hop in several tracks, and she still maintains a home in Franklin, Tennessee. Also, she appeared in her godmother Dolly Parton's Christmas special, *Dolly Parton's Mountain Magic Christmas* (2022), demonstrating the lasting bonds of her southern connections. Hannah Montana, that winsome Tennessee tween and California diva of bubble-gum pop, died when the series ended in 2011; Miley Cyrus survived the transition from child star to adult star, with her sense of queer southernness surviving, if shifting, along with her.

CODA
Southern Stargazing as the Universe Expands

"Jolene, I know I'm a queen, Jolene / I'm still a Creole banjee bitch from Louisiane," sings Beyoncé in her cover of Dolly Parton's classic country song "Jolene," a track on her newly released *Cowboy Carter* album (2024). In Parton's original recording, the lyric speaker whimpers in desperation, begging the siren Jolene not to steal her man; in this remake, Beyoncé warns Jolene away, defiantly identifying her strength as a southern woman. Notwithstanding the many notable and persistent contributions of Black artists over the years (including Tina Turner's *Tina Turns the Country On!* album, as discussed previously), country music has long been dominated by white artists, and so the release of Beyoncé's *Cowboy Carter* album marks a watershed moment in the history of the genre, as well as a watershed moment in the history of Beyoncé's construction of her celebrity persona. The star's fans were likely less surprised by this album than the general public: as Francesca Royster points out, Beyoncé performed with the Dixie Chicks on the Country Music Awards in November 2016, and the rhythms of her *Lemonade* album demonstrate the star's longstanding interest in rewriting the codes of country music.[1] But with *Cowboy Carter* the artist magnified this aspect of her star persona, amplifying its meaning for her career and reimagining the racial codes of country music as a whole. And so it is clear that a chapter on Beyoncé would immeasurably strengthen this book, but even then, it would remain incomplete.

Indeed, as this book concludes, it is important to note that it should not end; indeed, it never *could* end. Like contemplating the stars in the skies above, stargazing at celebrity culture continues to unfold before our very eyes, in real time, with ebbs and flows of identity, performance, and audience. Prior to, during, and after I drafted the contents of *Southerners Acting Southern: On Celebrities and Their Star Personas in the Imagined South*, new possibilities for chapters popped up before me, displaying the deep-space vastness of the subject of southern stars, as so many events and discoveries prompted the possibilities of new chapters. Country music stars define a central aspect of southern celebrity, yet the topic remains underrepresented in this book: other than the coverage of Dolly Parton, no chapters address such country music superstars as Patsy Cline, Loretta Lynn, Charlie Pride, or Reba McEntire. Following the reckoning over systemic racial injustice after George Floyd's murder in May 2020, several country music stars reexamined their use of southern tropes in their acts and reconfigured their personas: the Dixie Chicks renamed themselves as The Chicks, Lady Antebellum renamed themselves as Lady A. During a March 2023 trip to Nashville, my husband and I visited the Grand Ole Opry, where married couple Garth Brooks and Trisha Yearwood staged a surprise finale celebrating Women's History Month, which left me pondering how this country-music power couple negotiated their stardom within Nashville and beyond. Toby Keith died on February 5, 2024, and reading his obituaries, it occurred to me that an essay addressing his particular brand of southern masculinity would illuminate the deeper complexities of the so-called redneck stereotype. As country music has long been viewed as a redoubt of whiteness, so too is it viewed as intransigently heteronormative, but a new crop of queer country singers—such as Ty Herndon, Chely Wright, and Shane McAnally—are breaking down formidable barriers to queer representation—as is Lil Nas X, who fuses hip-hop, pop, and country while striking a southern queer Black identity uniquely his own. All of these topics related to country music celebrity, and more, deserve deeper scrutiny.

Other possible chapters that I considered but did not pursue, and now regret, include one addressing drag queen superstar RuPaul. I knew that RuPaul resided in Atlanta as a teenager and rose to the heights of the city's club scene in the 1980s, but I knew as well that he was born and raised in San Diego, and so I ultimately decided against a chapter addressing this most extraordinary of divas:

Coda

San Diego may be in southern California, but it is most certainly not southern. Upon reading RuPaul's autobiography *The House of Hidden Meanings,* my eyes popped upon learning that both of his parents hail from Louisiana—his mother from St. Martinville, his father from Minden[2]—for his drag diva-ness makes so much more sense as a product of the South than of his natal hometown of San Diego. Also missing is a chapter on any such transgender stars as Laverne Cox (Mobile, Alabama), Hunter Schafer (born in New Jersey but attended high school in Raleigh, North Carolina), Tommy Dorfman (Atlanta, Georgia), and Jazz Jennings (Florida). When one travels beyond the borders of the South, one invariably runs into folks who believe they know the "truth" of the South from the genre of so-called "reality television," and whatever their faults, these programs feature the exploits of a range of striking southern personalities, and so this book could have addressed as well such stars and shows as the Duggar family of *19 Kids and Counting* (2008–15), the Robertson family of *Duck Dynasty* (2012–17), the Shannon family of *Here Comes Honey Boo Boo* (2012–17), Chip and Joanna Gaines of *Fixer Upper* (2013–18), and the dueling divas of *Real Housewives of Atlanta* (2008–). It is an interesting coincidence—but possibly not a coincidence?—that the three drag queens of the reality program *We're Here* (2020–24) hail from the South: Bob the Drag Queen (Columbus, Georgia), Eureka (Bristol, Tennessee), and Shangela (Lamar County, Texas). In another moment when a current event inspired a reevaluation of this book's Table of Contents, former President Jimmy Carter checked into a hospice facility on February 18, 2023—and died over a year later on December 29, 2024—which prompted me to consider the celebrity personas of southern politicians, including Lyndon B. Johnson, Bill Clinton, George W. Bush, and Stacey Abrams.

Finally, it must be admitted that the stars selected for this study necessarily reflect, to some degree, my own experiences as a southerner (Louisianian by birth and upraising, Floridian for over two decades) of a certain age (born 1970) and of a queer orientation, and as a white person growing up in Baton Rouge, a city that remains notably segregated by neighborhood to this very day. Is it a coincidence, then, that Louisiana is the most represented home state of these stars, including Louis Armstrong, Truman Capote, Ellen DeGeneres, Tyler Perry, and Reese Witherspoon? Another such "coincidence" could be identified in the fact that several of the singers addressed in these pages—Tina Turner, Dolly Parton, Gloria Estefan, and Tom Petty—enjoyed their greatest success on the pop charts in the 1980s, the period of my life when I was most attuned to pop music. My affinity for queer stars is evident in the appearance of Truman Capote (whose writings I voraciously devoured in high school), Tennessee Williams (whose films I obsessively watched in my twenties), Ellen DeGeneres (whom I cheered as she broke down homophobic barriers in the 1990s), and Miley Cyrus (whose *Hannah Montana* I watched, first reluctantly but then found surprisingly charming, while writing a book on television sitcoms). Further along these queer lines, I confess to a certain suspicion of my own motives in mentioning Brooklyn-born diva Barbra Streisand in a book on southern stars, but when the opportunity arose, I seized it. In most of my cultural analysis I assume an air of impartiality—one that, for the most part, was maintained in this volume—but assessing the southernness of various stars wanders into an inherently subjective field of analysis. I was staring so long into the heavens of southern stars, but like the night sky itself, the field eluded me in its entirety even if, as I hope, I have identified some notable constellations to ponder while leaving others open to further exploration.

And so this Coda must serve multiple purposes: a *mea culpa*, a farewell, and an exhortation to keep searching the stars of the southern skies, to see farther than I did, or could possibly.

NOTES

INTRODUCTION: SOUTHERN STARS AND SOUTHERN MYTHS

1. The Ava Gardner Museum, Smithfield, NC, "The Discovery of Ava" Exhibit, visited and viewed 5 Dec. 2022. See also Ava Gardner, *Ava,* for a similar account of this moment, in which she adds, "People used to say I dropped my g's like magnolia blossoms, and I guess I did" (32).
2. Dyer, *Stars,* 22.
3. Dyer, *Heavenly Bodies,* 2–3.
4. Redmond, *Celebrity,* 3–4.
5. Wojcik, "Typecasting," 224.
6. Billy Bob Thornton, qtd. in Hunt, "Southerners Aren't Always at Home in Hollywood."
7. Egan and Thomas, "Introduction: Star-Making, Cult-Making and Forms of Authenticity," 8.
8. See Rushing, "Region," for an overview of regionalism in the U.S. South.
9. Greeson, *Our South,* 1.
10. McPherson, *Reconstructing Dixie,* 11.

1. LOUIS ARMSTRONG'S SMILE VERSUS NEW ORLEANS'S CONFEDERATE MONUMENTS

1. Armstrong's nickname "Satchmo" is a portmanteau of "satchel mouth." See Bergreen, *Louis Armstrong,* 4–5.
2. Bergreen, *Louis Armstrong,* 103.
3. Bergreen, *Louis Armstrong,* 6.
4. Landrieu, *In the Shadow of Statues,* 222.
5. Armstrong, *Satchmo,* 7.
6. Bergreen, *Louis Armstrong,* 81.
7. For a thorough discography of Armstrong's recordings, see the "List of Recordings" in Bergreen, *Louis Armstrong,* 499–518.
8. Borshuk, "'So Black, So Blue,'" 262–63.

9. Sanders, "Louis Armstrong: The Reluctant Millionaire," 142.
10. Gillespie, *To Be, or Not . . . to Bop*, 295–96.
11. Davis, *Miles: The Autobiography*, 313.
12. Ellison, *Invisible Man*, 8.
13. Salamone, "Laughin' Louie," 48.
14. Bergreen, *Louis Armstrong*, 4.
15. *Satchmo in East Berlin*, 22 Mar. 1965.
16. Armstrong, *Louis Armstrong in His Own Words*, 166.
17. Wald, "Louis Armstrong Loves Guy Lombardo," 36.
18. Bergreen, *Louis Armstrong*, 128.
19. Meckna, "Louis Armstrong in the Movies," 359 and 367.
20. Armstrong, *Satchmo*, 194–95.
21. Armstrong, "Daddy, How the Country Has Changed!" 85.
22. Armstrong, *Satchmo*, 14.
23. Armstrong, *Satchmo*, 24.
24. Armstrong, *Satchmo*, 231.
25. Armstrong, *Satchmo*, 231.
26. Armstrong, *Satchmo*, 240.
27. Teachout, *Pops*, 330.
28. Merod, "Biography as Erasure," 180.
29. Gillespie, *To Be, or Not . . . to Bop*, 296.
30. Armstrong, "Daddy, How the Country Has Changed!" 88.
31. Gill and Hunter, *Tearing Down the Lost Cause*, 186.

2. TRUMAN CAPOTE'S QUEER CELEBRITY AND THE DECADENTLY SENTIMENTAL SOUTH

1. Capote, *Music for Chameleons*, 261.
2. Keith, *Slim*, 226.
3. Solomon, *So Famous and So Gay*, 79.
4. Brickell, *O. Henry Memorial Award*, xiv.
5. Newquist, *Counterpoint*, 77; Haskell Frankel, "The Author," 36.
6. Steinem, "A Visit with Truman Capote," 210.
7. Long, "In Cold Comfort," 128.
8. Brinnin, *Truman Capote*, 39.
9. Fleming, "The Private World of Truman Capote," 24.
10. *Mademoiselle*, "Truman Capote on Christmas, Places, Memories," 177.
11. Warhol, "Sunday with Mister C.," 43.
12. Capote, *The Dogs Bark*, 319. For Dyer's consideration of star personas, see the Introduction.
13. Rolo, "The New Bohemia," 118.
14. Clarke, *Too Brief a Treat*, 269.

15. Kostelanetz, *The End of Intelligent Writing*, 92.
16. Talley, "An Afternoon with Truman Capote," 8.
17. Clarke, *Too Brief a Treat*, 382.
18. Gill, *Here at "The New Yorker,"* 317.
19. Clarke, "The Art of Fiction L: Gore Vidal," 148.
20. Brinnin, *Truman Capote*, 172.
21. Norden, "*Playboy* Interview: Truman Capote," 51.
22. Capote, *Answered Prayers*, 15.
23. Keith, *Slim*, 230.
24. Brinnin, *Truman Capote*, 8, 121.
25. Brinnin, *Truman Capote*, 149.
26. Devlin, *Conversations with Tennessee Williams*, 301.
27. Grafton, *The Sisters*, 223.
28. Smith, "A Success Money Didn't Buy"; Fremont-Smith, "Literature-by-Consensus."
29. Plimpton, *Truman Capote*, 249.
30. Winn, "Capote, Mailer, and Miss Parker," 27.
31. Winn, "Capote, Mailer, and Miss Parker," 27.
32. *The Dick Cavett Show*, 25 Mar. 1971, disc 3, DVD.
33. Clarke, *Too Brief a Treat*, 441.
34. Grobel, *Conversations with Capote*, 143.
35. *The Tonight Show*, 27 Nov. 1973.
36. *The Dean Martin Show*, 24 Jan. 1974, on *The Dean Martin Celebrity Roasts* DVD.
37. Plimpton, *Truman Capote*, 412.
38. Grobel, *Conversations with Capote*, 174.
39. Plimpton, *Truman Capote*, 367.
40. Clarke, *Capote*, 475.
41. Canby, "Simon's Breezy *Murder by Death*."
42. Greenfeld, "Truman Capote, the Movie Star?" 17.
43. Capote, *Music for Chameleons*, 258. Capote contradicted himself on the issue of his remuneration for appearing in the film. When asked whether he received "a lot of money for his acting debut," he responded with a determined "Oh Lord no" (Josh Greenfeld, "Truman Capote, the Movie Star?" 17).
44. Krebs, "Notes on People," 34.
45. *The Stanley Siegel Show*, 18 July 1978.
46. Capote, *Answered Prayers*, xxi.
47. Burstein, "Tiny Yes, But a Terror?," 14.
48. Chambers, "Going Home: Truman Capote," 56.
49. Chambers, "Going Home: Truman Capote," 56 and 58.
50. Norden, "*Playboy* Interview: Truman Capote," 53.
51. Packer et al., "We Talk to . . . Truman Capote," 367.

52. Frost, "When Does a Writer Become a Star?" 23. P. B. Jones, the narrator of *Answered Prayers*, also voices this sentiment (48).

53. Wenner, "Coda: Another Round with Mr. C," 54.

54. Medwick, "Truman Capote: An Interview," 312.

55. Capote, "Elizabeth Taylor," 151; cf. *Portraits and Observations*, 319.

3. ELVIS PRESLEY, GRACELAND, AND CELEBRITY SHRINES

1. Katsilometes, "Amid Apathy and Dwindling Revenue."

2. Mims, "Ava Gardner Museum."

3. In researching this volume, I planned to visit the Kentwood Museum. Its website (kentwoodmuseum.tripod.com) is still functioning, but I received no responses to my email and phone queries about its operating hours.

4. Davidson, "Graceland: More Than a Hit Song," 58.

5. Landau, "Elvis: All the King's Splendor," 84.

6. *Elvis Presley's Graceland: The Official Guidebook*, 42.

7. McKeon and Everett, *The Quotable King*, 65.

8. *Elvis Presley's Graceland: The Official Guidebook*, 11.

9. William Henderson, qtd. in Perry, *Echoes of Elvis*, 101.

10. Vernon Presley, "Elvis," 161.

11. Ponce de Leon, *Fortunate Son*, 194.

12. McKeon and Everett, *The Quotable King*, 115.

13. King, "His Truth Goes Marching On," 98.

14. King, "His Truth Goes Marching On," 99.

15. *Elvis Presley's Graceland: The Official Guidebook*, 60.

16. Wilson, "Mississippi Rebels," 13.

17. For a full account of this song's journey from Big Mama Thornton to Presley, see Wynne, *A Hound Dog Tale*.

18. Garner, "Sam Phillips: The Man Who Invented Rock 'n' Roll, by Peter Guralnick."

19. Taylor, "Funky White Boys and Honorary Soul Sisters," 328.

20. Davis, "Beyond the White Negro," 226.

21. *Elvis Presley's Graceland: The Official Guidebook*, 2.

22. *Deseret News*, "Graceland Now Listed as National Historic Site."

23. Greene, "Greetings from Graceland," 54.

24. The Guest House at Graceland, https://guesthousegraceland.com/.

25. *Elvis Presley's Graceland: The Official Guidebook*, 15.

26. *Elvis Presley's Graceland: The Official Guidebook*, 15.

27. Kiely, "From Monticello to Graceland," 210.

28. *Graceland: The Living Legacy of Elvis Presley*, Foreword, v.

29. Davidson, "Graceland: More Than a Hit Song," 52 and 56.

30. Davidson, "Graceland: More Than a Hit Song," 51.

31. Marling, *Graceland*, 1.
32. Marling, *Graceland*, 155.
33. Wilson, "Foreword," xi.
34. *Elvis Presley's Graceland: The Official Guidebook*, 47.
35. *Graceland: The Living Legacy of Elvis Presley*, 207.
36. Marling, *Graceland*, 143.
37. Potter et al., *Remembering Enslavement*, 1.
38. Vernon Presley, "Elvis," 160.

4. GREAT ACTORS, SOUTHERN ACCENTS, AND TENNESSEE WILLIAMS'S STAR FACTORY

1. Kauffmann, "Movies: The Tennessee Williams Cycle," 21.
2. The other such film is *Everything Everywhere All at Once* (2022), with wins for Michelle Yeoh as Best Actress, Jamie Lee Curtis for Best Supporting Actress, and Ke Huy Quan for Best Supporting Actor.
3. Labov, Ash, and Boberg, *Atlas of North American English*, 125–30.
4. See Giles and Billings, "Language Attitudes"; and Labov, *Social Stratification*.
5. Kinzler and DeJesus, "Northern = Smart and Southern = Nice," 1156.
6. Bradley, "The Accent Whisperers."
7. Stead, *Reframing Vivien Leigh*, 64–65.
8. McCarten, "The Current Cinema: Way Down Yonder," 112.
9. Farber, "Films," 334.
10. *Time*, "The New Pictures: *A Streetcar Named Desire*," 105.
11. Williams, *Memoirs*, 226.
12. Although he mentions Mrs. Stone's years at "a boarding-school in Maryland" and refers briefly to "*The Tulsa Gazette*," Williams does not divulge much of Mrs. Stone's backstory in his novel *The Roman Spring of Mrs. Stone* (99 and 103).
13. Johnson, "Marlon Brando: Actor on Impulse," 75.
14. Hatch, "Movies: Old Hit, New Venture," 21.
15. Hine, "Polish Up an Oscar," 27.
16. Farber, "Films," 334.
17. Williams, *Memoirs*, 82–83.
18. Williams, "Five Fiery Ladies," 84.
19. Martin, "The Star Who Sneers at Hollywood," 32 and 33.
20. *Time*, "The New Pictures: *The Fugitive Kind*," 81.
21. McCarten, "The Current Cinema: Orpheus with a Hot Guitar," 147.
22. *McCall's*, "*The Fugitive Kind*," 179.
23. *Time*, "The $6,000,000 Method," 72.
24. Nugent, "Talk with the Star," 90.
25. *Life*, "Brando's Break into a New Field," 105.
26. MacDonald, "Three Years, Six Million," 24.

27. *Newsweek*, "No Four-Letter Words," 56.
28. Alpert, "SR Goes to the Movies: Fixed Cat," 58.
29. *Time*, "The New Pictures: *Cat on a Hot Tin Roof*," 92.
30. Williams, *Memoirs*, 83.
31. Alpert, "SR Goes to the Movies: Fixed Cat," 58.
32. McCarten, "The Current Cinema: Cotton-Belt Bedlam," 163.
33. *Vogue*, "People Are Talking About . . . ," 122.
34. Kauffmann, "Movies: The Outer Edges," 22.
35. *Look*, "From Tragedy . . . New Fame," 90.
36. *Time*, "The New Pictures: *Suddenly, Last Summer*," 84.
37. Williams, "Five Fiery Ladies," 86.
38. Devlin, ed., *Conversations with Tennessee Williams*, 154.
39. *Newsweek*, "Talk with the Star," 97.
40. Williams, "Five Fiery Ladies," 86.
41. Devlin, ed. *Conversations with Tennessee Williams*, 154.
42. Cowie, "They Called Her 'Box Office Poison,'" 23.
43. Crowther, "*Suddenly Last Summer*," 22.
44. *Newsweek*, "New Films: As It Should Be," 64.
45. McCarten, "The Current Cinema: Cotton-Belt Bedlam," 164.
46. Alpert, "SR Goes to the Movies: Orpheus Descended," 28.
47. Gill, "The Current Cinema: High Spirits and Low," 206.
48. *Time*, "New Film: *Baby Doll*," 61.
49. *Newsweek*, "Trying, as It Were," 106.
50. McCarten, "The Current Cinema: Life among the Lintheads," 60.
51. Alpert, "SR Goes to the Movies: Orpheus Descended," 28.
52. Brobst, "Why Does Every Southern Accent in a Movie Sound So Bad?"

5. ANDY GRIFFITH, *THE ANDY GRIFFITH SHOW*, AND THE PARADOX OF YOKEL STEREOTYPES

1. *Newsweek*, "Hillbilly's a Hit," 55.
2. Elliott, "Andy Griffith: Yokel Boy Makes Good," 107.
3. *Newsweek*, "Bumpkin to Big-Timer," 60.
4. Carr, *A Question of Class*, 5.
5. In addressing the intersection of rural southerners, yokel stereotypes, and their complicity with racism and racial violence in this chapter, I do not wish to imply that southern racism is solely connected with this subset of white southern citizens. White racism has long transcended social class barriers, and many middle-class and upper-class white southerners, whether living in urban, suburban, or rural regions, also actively perpetuate(d) racist ideologies.
6. *Time*, "What It Is, Is Talk," 77.
7. Elliott, "Andy Griffith: Yokel Boy Makes Good," 107.
8. Lerman, "The Male Attraction," 151.

9. Elliott, "Andy Griffith: Yokel Boy Makes Good," 108.
10. Millstein, "Strange Chronicle of Andy Griffith," 17.
11. Freeman, "I Think I'm Gaining on Myself," 70.
12. Millstein, "Strange Chronicle of Andy Griffith," 17.
13. Freeman, "I Think I'm Gaining on Myself," 70.
14. Millstein, "Strange Chronicle of Andy Griffith," 17.
15. *Life*, "Guitar-Thumping Demagogue," 68.
16. McCarten, "The Current Cinema: More TV Villainy," 86.
17. Knight, "*SR* Goes to the Movies: Monster on the Make," 23.
18. Elliott, "Andy Griffith: Yokel Boy Makes Good," 108.
19. McCarten, "The Current Cinema: Familiar, but Funny," 64; Earle Walbridge, "*No Time for Sergeants* Review," 1913; Philip T. Hartung, "The Screen: Beamish Boy," 280.
20. Scott, "Your Cosmopolitan Movie Guide," 16.
21. Freeman, "I Think I'm Gaining on Myself," 69.
22. Weeks, "Insider Q&A: Andy Griffith and Don Knotts," 18.
23. Schwed, "The Case of the Classic TV Sleuths," 36.
24. Weeks, "Insider Q&A: Andy Griffith and Don Knotts," 18.
25. Weeks, "Insider Q&A: Andy Griffith and Don Knotts," 18.
26. Weeks, "Insider Q&A: Andy Griffith and Don Knotts," 18.
27. Schwed, "The Case of the Classic TV Sleuths," 64.
28. Curtis, "Whistle if You Love Andy Griffith," 64.
29. Both *Petticoat Junction* and *Green Acres* are set in Hooterville, a fictional region first mentioned in *The Beverly Hillbillies*. Producer Paul Henning oversaw the creation and storylines of these three programs. Hooterville is, according to Barbara Moore and her coauthors, "located somewhere in the television version of rural America, a place simultaneously Southern and Midwestern, but in a vague sort of way" (*Prime-Time Television*, 124).
30. Kelly, *The Andy Griffith Show*, 8.
31. Kelly, *The Andy Griffith Show*, 8.
32. Jim Nabors's southern star persona merits a brief mention, as he leaned into tropes of southern rubedom for his role as Gomer Pyle, both in *The Andy Griffith Show* and its spinoff *Gomer Pyle, U.S.M.C.* (1964–69). This show mirrored the basic plot line of *No Time for Sergeants*, as an affable southern enlistee draws the ire and exasperation of his superiors. Nabors notably tweaked his southern persona, however, by his many singing performances, proving through his rich baritone that his southern antics were merely a shtick.
33. Kelly, *The Andy Griffith Show*, 4–5.
34. Morrison, "Andy Griffith: Sheriff of Mayberry," 80b.
35. Freeman, "I Think I'm Gaining on Myself," 69–70.
36. Freeman, "I Think I'm Gaining on Myself," 70.
37. Freeman, "I Think I'm Gaining on Myself," 70.
38. Leahy, "Case Closed," 2.
39. Schwed, "The Case of the Classic TV Sleuths," 37.

40. Leahy, "Case Closed," 3.
41. Freeman, "I Think I'm Gaining on Myself," 70.
42. Leahy, "Case Closed," 3.
43. Schwed, "The Case of the Classic TV Sleuths," 35.
44. Leahy, "Case Closed," 6.
45. Freeman, "I Think I'm Gaining on Myself," 69.
46. Freeman, "I Think I'm Gaining on Myself," 69.
47. Millstein, "Strange Chronicle of Andy Griffith," 17.
48. Elliott, "Andy Griffith: Yokel Boy Makes Good," 109.
49. Freeman, "I Think I'm Gaining on Myself," 69.
50. Eskridge, *Rube Tube*, 119.

6. TINA TURNER: SOUTHERN BY BIRTH, SWISS BY CHOICE

1. *Jet*, "Nina Simone Reveals: 'Mississippi Goddam' Song 'Hurt My Career,'" 54.
2. In this chapter I refer to Tina Turner and Ike Turner as Tina and Ike, despite the overarching stylistic decision to refer to the stars addressed in this volume by their last names. This decision was made to avoid unnecessary repetitiveness; no disrespect is intended to either Tina Turner or Ike Turner.
3. Turner, *My Love Story*, 159.
4. Turner, *I, Tina*, 110.
5. Dunbar, "Ike and Tina Turner: They're Too Much!," 62.
6. *Newsweek*, "Turning On," 92–93.
7. Turner, *I, Tina*, 146.
8. Turner, *My Love Story*, 91.
9. Mewborn, "Tina Turner: Raunchy, Rollin' and Back in the Rock of It," 49.
10. Mahon, *Black Diamond Queens*, 256.
11. Royster, *Black Country Music*, 41.
12. Collins, "Tina Turner: The *Rolling Stone* Interview," 47.
13. Johnson, "The Comeback Queen of Rock 'n' Roll," 45.
14. Hirshey, "Woman Warrior," 183.
15. *Ebony*, "Tina Turner: The Shocking Story," 34.
16. Turner, *I, Tina*, 219.
17. Turner, *I, Tina*, 216.
18. Sporkin, "Tina Turner: Her Most Candid Interview," 39.
19. Turner, *My Love Story*, 139.
20. Orth, "Tina: It Took a Grown-Up Woman to Save Rock and Roll," 318.
21. Johnson, "The Comeback Queen of Rock 'n' Roll," 44.
22. Rubenstein, "Tina Turner: Her Least Nostalgic Interview, Ever," 40.
23. Rubenstein, "Tina Turner: Her Least Nostalgic Interview, Ever," 41.
24. Gelman, "Tina's Triumph," 52.

25. Gelman, "Tina's Triumph," 54.
26. Sporkin, "Tina Turner: Her Most Candid Interview," 34.
27. Johnson, "The Comeback Queen of Rock 'n' Roll," 45.
28. Johnson, "The Comeback Queen of Rock 'n' Roll," 44.
29. Rubenstein, "Tina Turner: Her Least Nostalgic Interview, Ever," 40.
30. Rubenstein, "Tina Turner: Her Least Nostalgic Interview, Ever," 40.
31. Edwards, "What Becomes a Sex Goddess Most?" 52.
32. Orth, "The Lady Has Legs!" 171.
33. Turner, *My Love Story*, 26.
34. Hirshey, "Woman Warrior," 228.
35. Turner, *My Love Story*, 26.
36. Turner, "Tina Turner: The Queen of Rock 'n' Roll Riffs," 16.
37. Turner, *I, Tina*, 39.
38. Turner, *I, Tina*, 44.
39. Turner, *I, Tina*, 15.
40. Turner, *My Love Story*, 57.
41. Turner, *My Love Story*, 57.
42. Turner, *My Love Story*, 94.
43. Turner, *I, Tina*, 169.
44. Turner, *I, Tina*, 99.
45. Turner, *I, Tina*, 47.
46. Turner, *I, Tina*, 94.
47. Turner, *My Love Story*, 64.
48. *Jet*, "Tina Turner Considering Move from U.S.," 23.
49. *Ebony*, "Tina Sizzles at 60," 54.
50. Johnson, "The Comeback Queen of Rock 'n' Roll," 44.
51. Turner, *I, Tina*, 206.
52. Turner, *My Love Story*, 9.
53. Turner, *My Love Story*, 10.
54. Turner, *My Love Story*, 195.
55. Turner, *My Love Story*, 175.
56. Turner, *My Love Story*, 38.
57. Edwards, "What Becomes a Sex Goddess Most?" 52.
58. Gelman, "Tina's Triumph," 55.
59. Turner, *My Love Story*, 89.

7. DOLLY PARTON: THE HILLBILLY QUEEN OF CROSSOVER SELF-CENSORSHIP

1. Parton, *Dolly*, 317.
2. Cole, "The Original Steel Magnolia," 109.
3. Hoppe, "Icon and Identity," 50.

4. Parton, *Dream More*, 57.
5. Jahr, "Golly, Dolly!" 85.
6. Jefferson, "Dolly Parton: Bewigged, Bespangled . . . and Proud," 15.
7. Grobel, "*Playboy* Interview with Dolly Parton," 84.
8. Parton, *Dolly*, 2.
9. Parton, *Dolly*, 115.
10. Hurst, "You've Come a Long Way, Dolly," 122.
11. Pasternak, *Dolly Parton*, 10.
12. Berman, "Dolly Parton Scrapbook," 140+.
13. Parton, *Songteller*, 32.
14. *People* Staff, *Dolly!* 33.
15. Jahr, "Golly, Dolly!" 85.
16. Wilson, "Mountains of Contradictions," 109.
17. Parton, *Dolly*, 194.
18. Pasternak, *Dolly Parton*, 76.
19. Carson, "Dolly Parton Breaks a Heart," 92–93.
20. Coppage, "Dolly: Crossin' Over Is Hard to Do," 118.
21. Parton, *Dolly*, 228.
22. Flippo, "Dolly Parton," 40.
23. Hoppe, *Gone Dollywood*, 114.
24. *People* Staff, *Dolly!*, 55.
25. Nash, "Why Dolly Parton Is One Unsinkable Mountain Momma."
26. *People* Staff, *Dolly!*
27. Berman, "Dolly Parton Scrapbook," 140+.
28. Pew Research Center, "Religious Landscape Study," www.pewforum.org/religious-landscape-study.
29. Pasternak, *Dolly Parton*, 13.
30. Parton, *Dolly*, 70.
31. Parton, *Dolly*, 301.
32. Parton, *Songteller*, 8.
33. Grobel, "*Playboy* Interview with Dolly Parton," 82.
34. Jahr, "Golly, Dolly!," 84.
35. Jefferson, "Dolly Parton: Bewigged, Bespangled . . . and Proud," 14+.
36. Flippo, "Dolly Parton," 62.
37. Steinem, "Dolly Parton," 66.
38. Grobel, "*Playboy* Interview with Dolly Parton," 110.
39. Parton, *Dolly*, 134.
40. Parton, *Dolly*, 134.
41. Parton, *Dream More*, 5.
42. Jackson, "The United States of Dolly Parton," 62.
43. Moran, "Dolly Parton Rejected the Medal of Freedom."

Notes to Pages 106–120

44. Parton, *Dream More*, 112.
45. Parton, *Dream More*, 94.
46. Harris, "Springtime for the Confederacy."
47. Whitaker, "Dolly Parton Shares Why She Dropped the 'Dixie' from Her Stampede."
48. *People* Staff, *Dolly!*, 78.
49. Pasternak, *Dolly Parton*, 21.
50. Zoladz, "Is There Anything We Can All Agree On? Yes: Dolly Parton."

8. WHICH FLORIDIANS ARE SOUTHERNERS? TOM PETTY, GLORIA ESTEFAN, AND THE VAGARIES OF POP-STAR SOUTHERNNESS IN THE 1980S

1. Thomas, *Tom Petty*, 23.
2. Zollo, *Conversations with Tom Petty*, 9.
3. Thomas, *Tom Petty*, 24.
4. Zollo, *Conversations with Tom Petty*, 34.
5. Graff, "Tom Petty's New Tales of the Old South," 63. The quotation "one foot in the grave / and one foot on the pedal" is taken from Petty's song "Rebels."
6. Bauer and Gilad, "Fears, Frustrations, and Knowing How It Feels," 158.
7. Grayson, "Place, Race, and Mutability," 23.
8. Tannenbaum, "Steve Nicks Admits."
9. Washburn, *Southern Accents*, 5–6.
10. Washburn, *Southern Accents*, 25.
11. Graff, "Tom Petty's New Tales of the Old South," 63; cf. Michael Washburn, *Southern Accents*, 26.
12. Zollo, *Conversations with Tom Petty*, 34.
13. Washburn, *Southern Accents*, 27.
14. Greene, "Tom Petty on Past Confederate Flag Use."
15. Macherey, *A Theory of Literary Production*, 96.
16. Estefan, "Finding My Voice," 78.
17. Castro," "Little Glorita," 60.
18. *Teen Magazine*, "Miami Sound Machine: Nothing Gets in Their Way," 45.
19. *Teen Magazine*, "Miami Sound Machine: Nothing Gets in Their Way," 45.
20. Farley, "From a Cuban Heart," 68.
21. *Network*, "Music Meeting," 20.
22. Gerosa, "My Song of Love," 178.
23. DeGeneres, *Funny Thing*, 26.
24. Drummond, "Turning the Beat Around," 56.
25. Gloria Estefan Foundation, accessed 20 Sept. 2022.
26. Farley, "From a Cuban Heart," 68.
27. Berk, "Livin' la Vida Gloria," 50.
28. Palomino, *The Invention of Latin American Music*, 1.

29. Morales and Estefan, "Hey, Latin Lovers!," 102.

30. On the multiple waves of Cuban immigration since 1959, see Borland, *Cuban-American Literature of Exile*, 5.

31. Smith and Furuseth, *Latinos in the New South*, 2–3.

32. Florida Music Hall of Fame, "A Utopian Vision." It should be noted that the Florida Music Hall of Fame, at the time of this volume's publication, remains a vision, and it is difficult to ascertain whether it will ever become a reality.

33. For an overview of the expanding sense of the South in southern studies, see Cartwright, "Black Atlantic."

9. ON SOUTHERN WOMEN'S BOOK CLUBS: OPRAH WINFREY, REESE WITHERSPOON, JENNA BUSH HAGER, AND THE PERFORMANCE OF A LITERARY STAR PERSONA

1. For an overview of celebrity book clubs, see Jordan, "Inside the List."
2. Striphas, *The Late Age of Print*, 6.
3. Striphas, *The Late Age of Print*, 10.
4. Zoglin, "Lady with a Calling."
5. *Jet*, "Oprah Winfrey Reveals the Real Reason Why She Stayed on TV," 60.
6. Farr, *Reading Oprah*, 11.
7. Kinsella, "The Oprah Effect," 276–77.
8. Gray, "Oprah Winfrey's Winners," 84.
9. Max, "The Oprah Effect," 39.
10. Farr, *Reading Oprah*, 14.
11. Ulrich, "The Oprah Effect," 191.
12. Rooney, "Oprah Learns Her Lesson," 58.
13. Johnson, "Oprah Winfrey," 44.
14. Farr, *Reading Oprah*, 13.
15. Rooney, *Reading with Oprah*, 40.
16. Flamm and Valby, "He Stands Corrected."
17. Rooney, "Oprah Learns Her Lesson," 56.
18. Johnson, "Oprah Winfrey," 44.
19. Dr. Phil and Dr. Oz have endorsed a range of snake-oil products. For representative accounts, see Deardorff, "Dr. Phil Throws His Weight in the Wrong Direction," and Mutnick, "Senators Scold Dr. Oz."
20. Berk, "Reese Witherspoon: Blond Ambition," 40.
21. *Legally Blonde* first encourages audiences to see Elle Woods as an intellectual lightweight owing to her membership in a sorority and her obsessive interest in fashion, only to then upend these expectations, but does the film also encode a slight allusion to Woods's (and Witherspoon's) southern roots? While breaking up with her boyfriend at the film's beginning, she sputters, "Just because I'm not a Vanderbilt, suddenly I'm white trash?" The Vanderbilt name suggests the southern aristocracy whose name graces Vanderbilt University of Nashville and Biltmore Estate of Ashe-

ville, North Carolina. Still, if this line were intended to suggest that Elle was born a southerner, the following lines—"I grew up in Belair, Warner! Across the street from Aaron Spelling"—indicate that she was raised a Californian.

22. Smith, "Reese Witherspoon Lets Down Her Hair," 45.
23. Smith, "Reese Witherspoon Lets Down Her Hair," 102.
24. Berk, "Reese Witherspoon: Blond Ambition," 96. In another intriguing instance of the significations of the name Vanderbilt in Witherspoon's career, *Sweet Home Alabama* depicts Witherspoon's character ending her engagement to her fiancé Andrew, who then announces his impending nuptials to Erin Vanderbilt.
25. Puig, "Witherspoon's 'Sweet Home.'"
26. Willman, "Reese Witherspoon."
27. Portman, "Reese Faces Her Fears," 140.
28. Feldman, "Shifting the Narrative," 76.
29. Feldman, "Shifting the Narrative," 75.
30. Jordan, "Inside the List," 28, and Owens, *Where the Crawdads Sing,* back cover endorsement.
31. Feldman, "Shifting the Narrative," 76.
32. Reese's Book Club.
33. Parton, "The Story of Reese," 229.
34. DraperJames.com homepage; accessed 19 Apr. 2023.
35. Witherspoon, *Whiskey in a Teacup,* dedication page.
36. Witherspoon, *Whiskey in a Teacup,* 215.
37. Witherspoon, *Whiskey in a Teacup,* 219.
38. Witherspoon, *Whiskey in a Teacup,* 221–25.
39. Boone, "Reese Witherspoon Opens Up."
40. Bush Hager, "Reese on the Secrets of Southern Style," F28.
41. Jenna Welch Bush married Henry Chase Hager in 2008. I refer to her as Bush Hager throughout this chapter for stylistic consistency.
42. Canfield, "Getting Lit," 35.
43. Canfield, "Getting Lit," 35.
44. Hollandsworth, "Girl Gone Mild," 238.
45. McGrath, "First Book."
46. Hollandsworth, "Girl Gone Mild," 236.
47. McGrath, "First Book."
48. McGrath, "First Book."
49. Hollandsworth, "Girl Gone Mild," 236 and 148.
50. Argetsinger, "Jenna Bush, Author, Finds Eager Audience at Signing."
51. Laura Bush and Jenna Bush, *Read All about It!,* unpaginated, last page.
52. Laura Bush and Jenna Bush, *Read All about It!,* back cover.
53. Laura Bush and Jenna Bush Hager, *Our Great Big Backyard,* back cover.
54. Puente, "Jenna Bush Hager Gets *Southern Living* Job."
55. Puente, "Jenna Bush Hager Gets *Southern Living* Job."

56. Bush Hager, "Reese on the Secrets of Southern Style," "This One's for the Girls," and "Mom to Mom: Joanna's New Season."

57. Bush Hager, "A Texas Fiesta," "Holiday Glam, Texas Style," and "Go Wild for West Texas."

58. Bush Hager, "The Natural," "The Needlepointer," and "The Teacher."

59. Bruni, "The Bush Twins Want to Set the Record Straight."

60. Jenna Bush Hager and Barbara Bush, "Dear Sasha and Malia," 43.

61. Bush Hager, *Everything Beautiful in Its Time*, 33.

62. Bush Hager, *Everything Beautiful in Its Time*, 33.

63. Canfield, "Getting Lit," 34. The contents of this paragraph presented somewhat of an ethical challenge, in that I do not want to perpetuate the tired and demeaning "catfight" trope that pits two successful women as somehow engaged in a public battle for supremacy over the other—evident in such fake "feuds" as reported between Madonna and Cyndi Lauper in the 1980s, or between Britney Spears and Christina Aguilera in the early 2000s. I hope that I have presented the dueling visions of these book clubs and their hosts with sufficient context to support my thesis about the use of book clubs in the construction of celebrity personas.

64. Canfield, "Getting Lit," 35.

65. Canfield, "Getting Lit," 35.

66. Canfield, "Getting Lit," 35.

67. Kaiser, "How Jenna Bush Is Raising Three Readers."

68. "Read With Jenna Jr.," *Today.com*.

69. Nicolaou, "Jenna Bush Hager Recommends Five Things to Buy While Reading *Camp Zero*."

70. Diaz and Nicolaou, "Yes, Jenna Bush Hager Reads Every Book."

71. Eleven of the eighteen U.S. states with the lowest literacy rates are located in the South, including Tennessee, West Virginia, North Carolina, Arkansas, South Carolina, Alabama, Louisiana, Mississippi, Georgia, Texas, and Florida. See https://worldpopulationreview.com/state-rankings/us-literacy-rates-by-state.

10. ELLEN DeGENERES'S QUEER VOICE OF SOUTHERN (UN)KINDNESS

1. DeGeneres, *My Point . . . and I Do Have One*, 29.

2. DeGeneres, *My Point . . . and I Do Have One*, 30.

3. *Ellen* was originally titled *These Friends of Mine*; it was retitled *Ellen* for its second season, so as not to be confused with the blockbuster hit *Friends* (1994–2004).

4. Weber and Leimbach, "Ellen DeGeneres's Incorporate Body," 304.

5. Szczesiul, *The Southern Hospitality Myth*, 7.

6. DeGeneres, *My Point . . . and I Do Have One*, 5.

7. DeGeneres, *My Point . . . and I Do Have One*, 3.

8. Limon, "Spritzing, Skirting: Standup Talk Strategies," 114.

9. DeGeneres, *Seriously . . . I'm Kidding*, 119.

10. DeGeneres, *The Funny Thing Is . . .* , 195. The accuracy of DeGeneres's father's memory lies

beyond my expertise and research capabilities, but I can certainly testify to the prevalence of the locution "Pahdnah" in southern Louisiana.

11. DeGeneres, *Seriously . . . I'm Kidding*, 208.
12. DeGeneres, *Seriously . . . I'm Kidding*, 38.
13. DeGeneres, *My Point . . . and I Do Have One*, 135.
14. *Primetime Live*, "Delightful, Delovely, DeGeneres."
15. DeGeneres, *The Funny Thing Is . . .* , 3.
16. DeGeneres, *The Funny Thing Is . . .* , 116.
17. DeGeneres, *Seriously . . . I'm Kidding*, 79.
18. DeGeneres, *Seriously . . . I'm Kidding*, 85.
19. *Good Morning America*, "Ellen's Apology."
20. DeGeneres, *My Point . . . and I Do Have One*, 194.
21. For example, see Strachan, "When Ellen Came Out."
22. DeGeneres, *The Funny Thing Is . . .* , 144.
23. *Larry King Live*, "Ellen DeGeneres Discusses."
24. RottenTomatoes.com, "Mr. Wrong (1996)."
25. These interpretations of *Ellen* and *Mr. Wrong* are not intended to suggest that lesbians cannot play heterosexual characters convincingly, but that DeGeneres struggled to do so, with audiences to some degree discerning the disconnections among herself, her southern star persona of kindness, and her roles.
26. Handy, "He Called Me Ellen Degenerate?" 72.
27. Handy, "He Called Me Ellen Degenerate?" 72.
28. Handy, "He Called Me Ellen Degenerate?" 72.
29. *Ellen DeGeneres: All of Me.*
30. DeGeneres, *Seriously . . . I'm Kidding*, 5.
31. Mizejewski, *Pretty / Funny: Women Comedians and Body Politics*, 215.
32. Zinoman, "Ellen DeGeneres Isn't as Nice as You Think She Is."
33. DeGeneres, *Seriously . . . I'm Kidding*, 178.
34. *The Saturday Early Show*, "Comedian Ellen DeGeneres Discusses Her Personal Ties to New Orleans."
35. *CNN Showbiz Tonight*, "Ellen DeGeneres's Suicide Outrage."
36. Zinoman, "Ellen DeGeneres Isn't as Nice as You Think She Is."
37. Lee, "Ellen DeGeneres Sparks Backlash."
38. Ojomu, "'I thought she was bulletproof.'"
39. Stuever, "Ellen Becomes the If Girl."
40. DeGeneres, qtd. in Stuever, "Ellen Becomes the If Girl."
41. *Good Morning America*, "Ellen's Apology."
42. DeGeneres, *The Funny Thing Is . . .* , 101.
43. Moore, "Why 'Bless Your Heart' Is the Most Savage Insult in the Country."

11. TYLER PERRY: ATLANTA'S ENTREPRENEUR AND QUEER AUTEUR

1. Winfrey, "Tyler Perry: Empire Builder," 90. In addition to Winfrey herself, Perry honored Harry Belafonte, Halle Berry, Diahann Carroll, Whoopi Goldberg, Spike Lee, Sidney Poitier, Della Reese, Will Smith, Cicely Tyson, and Denzel Washington with eponymous soundstages.

2. Cole, "Tyler Perry Is Flying High."

3. *Forbes*, "The Rise and Rise of Tyler Perry."

4. Perry, *Higher Is Waiting*, 39–40.

5. For an overview of this theatrical tradition, see Henry Louis Gates, Jr., "The Chitlin Circuit." As he states, "the fact that the audience . . . is entirely black creates an essential dynamic" (142).

6. Jubera, "Tyler Perry Runs the Table," 125.

7. Turner, "Tyler Perry: Show Business His Way," 35.

8. *Forbes*, "The Rise and Rise of Tyler Perry."

9. Jubera, "Tyler Perry Runs the Table," 125.

10. *Forbes*, "The Rise and Rise of Tyler Perry."

11. Christian, "Becoming Tyler," 80.

12. Christian, "Becoming Tyler," 76.

13. Cole, "Tyler Perry Is Flying High."

14. D'Addario, "8 Questions: Tyler Perry," 60.

15. Barnes, "Tyler Perry Gets an Honorary Oscar."

16. Christian, "Tyler Perry: Sky Is the Limit," 33.

17. Christian, "Becoming Tyler," 74–76.

18. Hughes, "How Tyler Perry Rose from Homelessness to a $5 Million Mansion," 90.

19. Christian, "Becoming Tyler," 74.

20. Christian, "Tyler Perry: Sky Is the Limit," 38.

21. Gay, *Bad Feminist*, 238.

22. *The Chop Up*, qtd. in Shaw, "From the Margins to Center Stage," 47.

23. *The Chop Up*, qtd. in Shaw, "From the Margins to Center Stage," 47.

24. *Huffington Post*, "Tyler Perry to Spike Lee." By naming one of his soundstages after Lee, it would appear that Perry has moved past this artistic disagreement.

25. For example, the website Rotten Tomatoes, which aggregates film reviews, ranks *Diary of a Mad Black Woman* as scoring merely 16 percent favorable reviews, *A Madea Christmas* (2013) scoring 20 percent, and *The Single Moms Club* (2014) scoring 18 percent. *Boo! A Madea Halloween* (2016) registered with only 19 percent favorable reviews, and its sequel, *Boo 2! A Madea Halloween* (2017), earned a stunningly low 4 percent.

26. Scott, "Plus-Size Matriarch's Stretch in the Slammer."

27. Christian, "Tyler Perry: Meet the Man behind the Urban Theater Character Madea," 64.

28. Sarris, "Excerpt from 'Notes on the Auteur Theory in 1962,'" 64.

29. Christian, "Becoming Tyler," 74.

30. Doty, "Whose Text Is It Anyway?," 23.

31. Perry, *Don't Make a Black Woman Take Off Her Earrings*, xvi.

32. Millner, "The Unstoppable Tyler Perry," 154.
33. Morris, "The Year of Tyler Perry," 60.
34. Millner, "The Unstoppable Tyler Perry," 154.
35. Perry, *Don't Make a Black Woman Take Off Her Earrings*, ix.
36. Perry, *Don't Make a Black Woman Take Off Her Earrings*, x–xi.
37. Dreher, "Don't Slap Yo' Gran'Momma," 109–10.
38. Christian, "Hallelujer!!! Tyler Perry Aims to Lift Spirits," 44.
39. Reed, "Colorblind Melodrama: Tyler Perry's *For Colored Girls*," 160.
40. Dreher, "Don't Slap Yo' Gran'Momma," 113.
41. Story, "On the Cusp of Deviance," 369.
42. Patterson, "Do You Want to Be Well?" 49.
43. Perry, *Don't Make a Black Woman Take Off Her Earrings*, 92. Perry's book was published in 2006, long before Cosby's 2018 conviction of aggravated indecent assault. Cosby nonetheless provides a chilling example of the hypocrisy behind some advocates of respectability politics.
44. Perry, *Don't Make a Black Woman Take Off Her Earrings*, 98.
45. Cole, "Tyler Perry Is Flying High."
46. Petty, "'Old Folks at Home': Tyler Perry and the Dialectics of Nostalgia," 588.

12. MATTHEW McCONAUGHEY CROWNS HIMSELF TEXAS'S PHILOSOPHER KING

1. Daniels, *Matthew McConaughey*, 4.
2. Marchese, "Matthew McConaughey on Trying to Become Living Art."
3. McConaughey, *Greenlights*, 285.
4. Daniels, *Matthew McConaughey*, 21.
5. *Fresh Air*, "Matthew McConaughey: Getting Serious Again."
6. Heigl, "An Annotated Deep Dive."
7. Daniels, *Matthew McConaughey*, 132.
8. McConaughey, *Greenlights*, 293.
9. Travers, "*A Time to Kill*."
10. Ebert, "*A Time to Kill*."
11. McConaughey, *Greenlights*, 163.
12. Ansen, "*Contact*."
13. Koehler, "*The Wedding Planner*."
14. Christine Peters, qtd. in Daniels, *Matthew McConaughey*, 77.
15. Schwarzbaum, "*Failure to Launch*."
16. Stoynoff, "Matthew McConaughey Is on a Mission to Heal America."
17. *Fresh Air*, "Matthew McConaughey: Getting Serious Again."
18. *People* Staff, "2005's Sexiest Men Alive."
19. Daniels, *Matthew McConaughey*, 54.
20. Bargmann, "*G&G* Interview: Matthew McConaughey."
21. Bargmann, "*G&G* Interview: Matthew McConaughey."

22. McConaughey, *Greenlights*, 262.
23. Paiella, "Matthew McConaughey Is Thinking about His Eulogy."
24. Marchese, "Matthew McConaughey Is Not Afraid."
25. Marchese, "Matthew McConaughey on Trying to Become Living Art."
26. McConaughey, *Greenlights*, 3.
27. McConaughey, *Greenlights*, 13.
28. McConaughey, *Greenlights*, 137.
29. McConaughey, *Greenlights*, 144.
30. McConaughey, *Greenlights*, 284.
31. McConaughey, *Greenlights*, 7.
32. McConaughey, *Greenlights*, 192–93.
33. McConaughey, *Greenlights*, 154.
34. McConaughey, *Greenlights*, 194.
35. McConaughey, *Greenlights*, 223–24.
36. McConaughey, *Greenlights*, 85.
37. McConaughey, *Greenlights*, 276.
38. McConaughey, *Greenlights*, 292.
39. The full range of Peterson's viewpoints lie outside the scope of this chapter, but he certainly endorses a troubling view of violent masculinity with such statements as, "If you're talking to a man who wouldn't fight with you under any circumstances whatsoever, then you're talking to someone for whom you have absolutely no respect" (Lynskey, "How Dangerous Is Jordan B. Peterson?").
40. Mark, "Matthew McConaughey Rules Out Texas Governor Run."
41. Stoynoff, "Matthew McConaughey Is on a Mission to Heal America."
42. Langmann, "Matthew McConaughey Is Daring America to Meet in the Middle."
43. Stoynoff, "Matthew McConaughey Is on a Mission to Heal America."
44. Mark, "Matthew McConaughey Rules Out Texas Governor Run."

13. AZIZ ANSARI: COMIC STAR OF THE POSTSOUTHERN SOUTH

1. Yuan, "Aziz Ansari Is from a Red State, Too," 80.
2. For exemplary studies, see Washington, *Blasian Invasion*; Lawrence, *Indian Film Stars*; and Nishime, *Undercover Asian*.
3. For an account of the "model minority" myth, see Wu, *The Color of Success*.
4. Saran, *Navigating Model Minority Stereotypes*, 2.
5. Nishime, *Undercover Asian*, xi–xii.
6. Ansari, *Modern Romance*, back cover blurb.
7. Sanneh, "Funny Person."
8. *Parks and Recreation*, "Pilot."
9. *Parks and Recreation*, "Jerry's Retirement."
10. *Master of None*, "Nashville."
11. Sanneh, "Funny Person."

12. Smith, "Aziz Ansari: Buried Alive."
13. Grady, *The New South*, 145.
14. Haddox, "Literature," 257.
15. Haddox, "Literature," 262n1.
16. Bone, *The Postsouthern Sense of Place*, xii.
17. Zong and Batalova, "Indian Immigrants in the United States."
18. Ansari, *Madison Square Garden*.
19. Yuan, "How Aniz."
20. Ansari, *Buried Alive*.
21. Edwards, "21st-Century Joke Machine."
22. Sanneh, "Funny Person."
23. Sanneh, "Funny Person."
24. Ansari, *Buried Alive*.
25. Edwards, "21st-Century Joke Machine."
26. In asserting that racism is not funny, I neither overlook nor ignore the long history of racist humor but simply refuse to credit it as humorous. Furthermore, the stock figure of the redneck is also the subject of stereotyping, a topic ably explored in Carr's *A Question of Class: The Redneck Stereotype in Southern Fiction*.
27. Ansari, *Intimate Moments*.
28. Ansari, *Intimate Moments*.
29. *Master of None*, "Nashville."
30. Ansari, *Right Now*.
31. Ansari, *Right Now*.
32. Yuan, "Red State," 115.
33. *Parks and Recreation*, "Pilot."
34. *Parks and Recreation*, "Leslie's House."
35. *Parks and Recreation*, "The Stakeout."
36. Ansari, *Buried Alive*.
37. Ansari, *Modern Romance*, 12.
38. For the "gentlemen" citations, see Ansari, *Modern Romance*, e.g., 27, 52, 55, *passim*; for the "bozo" citations, see 42, 53, 89, *passim*.
39. On this mythic figure and its contradictions, see my *Queer Chivalry: Medievalism and the Myth of White Masculinity in Southern Literature*.
40. Way, "I Went on a Date with Aziz Ansari."
41. Ansari, *Right Now*.
42. Sanneh, "Funny Person."
43. Adams, "Aziz Ansari Becomes the Malcolm Gladwell of Stand-Up Comedy."
44. Abate, "The New Millennium Minstrel Show," 138.
45. Abate, "The New Millennium Minstrel Show," 141.
46. Yuan, "How Aniz."
47. Yuan, "How Aniz."

14. MILEY CYRUS'S QUEERLY AUTHENTIC SOUTHERN INNOCENCE

1. In this chapter I use "Cyrus" to refer to star Miley Cyrus, "Miley" for her character Miley Stewart, and "Hannah" for Stewart's alter ego Hannah Montana—while acknowledging the purposeful ambiguity between the actor and her roles.

2. Osgerby, "'So Who's Got Time for Adults!,'" 83.

3. As a relatively new term in the erotic lexicon, *pansexual* may require definition. Pansexuals are erotically attracted to people of any sex or gender identity, rejecting any erotic binary based on male and female. Furthermore, pansexuality is a sexual orientation inherently supportive of the transgender community, as pansexuals affirm their potential interest in partners regardless of whether their genitalia align with cisnormative conceptions of gender.

4. Littler, "Making Fame Ordinary," 14.

5. Kennedy, "Hannah Montana and Miley Cyrus," 227.

6. *Hannah Montana*, "Love That Lets Go."

7. Cyrus, *Miles to Go*, 5–6.

8. Ebenkamp, "Hannah and Her Boosters," M040.

9. Ebenkamp, "Hannah and Her Boosters," M040.

10. Memorable examples of this dialogue tic include "Melon-headed hottie say what?" ("The Test of My Love") and "Future of sleaze journalism say what?" ("Don't Stop 'til You Get the Phone").

11. *Hannah Montana*, "I Can't Make You Love Hannah If You Don't."

12. *Hannah Montana*, "Ooh, Ooh Itchy Woman."

13. Cyrus, *Miles to Go*, 13.

14. Cyrus, *Miles to Go*, 172.

15. Cyrus, *Miles to Go*, 164.

16. Ebenkamp, "Hannah and Her Boosters," M040.

17. *Hannah Montana: The Movie*.

18. *Hannah Montana*, "Oops! I Meddled Again."

19. Cyrus, *Miles to Go*, 112.

20. Larocca, "The Real Miley Cyrus."

21. *Hannah Montana*, "It's My Party and I'll Lie if I Want To."

22. For the cookie jar, see *Hanna Montana*, "He Could Be the One"; for the toy pig, see "California Screamin.'"

23. *Hannah Montana*, "More Than a Zombie to Me."

24. *Wizards on Deck with Hannah Montana*, "Double Crossed."

25. Cyrus, *Miles to Go*, 241.

26. *Hannah Montana*, "I Am Hannah, Hear Me Croak."

27. Wiltz, "The Latest Ingenue To-Do."

28. Toomey, "What Happened to Miley Cyrus?!"

29. Toomey, "What Happened to Miley Cyrus?!"

30. Larocca, "The Real Miley Cyrus."

31. Coscarelli, "Miley Cyrus on Nicki Manaj."
32. *Hannah Montana*, "Kiss It Goodbye."
33. Trebay, "Miley Cyrus's Style."
34. O'Connor, "Sinéad O'Connor's Open Letter to Miley Cyrus."
35. Trebay, "Miley Cyrus's Style."
36. de Casparis, "The Gender Debate," 240.
37. Coscarelli, "Miley Cyrus on Nicki Manaj."
38. The Happy Hippie Foundation.

CODA: SOUTHERN STARGAZING AS THE UNIVERSE EXPANDS

1. Royster, *Black Country Music*, 77–81.
2. RuPaul, *The House of Hidden Meanings*, 13.

WORKS CITED

9 to 5. Dir. Colin Higgins. Perf. Jane Fonda, Lily Tomlin, and Dolly Parton. 1980.
Abate, Michelle Ann. "The New Millennium Minstrel Show: Blackface Elements in *Seinfeld, Parks and Recreation,* and *Miranda Sings.*" *Journal of Popular Film and Television* 47.3 (2019): 132–51.
Adams, Erik. "Aziz Ansari Becomes the Malcolm Gladwell of Stand-Up Comedy (And That's a Good Thing)." *AV Club* 1 Nov. 2013. Web.
Alpert, Hollis. "SR Goes to the Movies: Fixed Cat." *Saturday Review* 13 Sept. 1958: 58.
———. "SR Goes to the Movies: Orpheus Descended." *Saturday Review* 23 Apr. 1960: 28.
Alvarez Borland, Isabel. *Cuban-American Literature of Exile: From Person to Persona.* University Press of Virginia, 1998.
Ansari, Aziz. *Aziz Ansari: Buried Alive.* New Wave Entertainment, 2013.
———. *Aziz Ansari: Live at Madison Square Garden.* 3 Arts Entertainment, 2015.
———. *Aziz Ansari: Right Now.* 3 Arts Entertainment, 2019.
———. *Intimate Moments for a Sensual Evening.* Comedy Central, 2010.
———, with Eric Klinenberg. *Modern Romance.* Penguin, 2015.
Ansen, David. "Contact." *Newsweek* 21 Jul. 1997: 68.
Argetsinger, Amy. "Jenna Bush, Author, Finds Eager Audience at Signing." *Washington Post* 30 Sept. 2007. Web.
Armstrong, Louis. *Louis Armstrong in His Own Words: Selected Writings.* Ed. Thomas Brothers. Oxford University Press, 1999.
———. *Satchmo: My Life in New Orleans.* Centennial edition. DaCapo, 1954.
Armstrong, Louis, as told to David Dachs. "'Daddy, How the Country Has Changed!' Satchmo Notes the Vast Improvement of U.S. Negro Musicians' Lot during His Career." *Ebony* May 1961: 81+.

Bargmann, Joe. "*G&G* Interview: Matthew McConaughey." *Garden & Gun* Feb./Mar. 2016. Web.

Barnes, Brooks. "Tyler Perry Gets an Honorary Oscar." *New York Times* 25 Apr. 2021. Web.

Bauer, Nate, and Shye Gilad. "Fears, Frustrations, and Knowing How It Feels: The Emotional Signifiers of Tom Petty's Songs." Sands 158–72.

Bergreen, Laurence. *Louis Armstrong: An Extravagant Life*. Broadway Books, 1997.

Berk, Sheryl. "Livin' la Vida Gloria." *McCall's* Nov. 1999: 50+.

———. "Reese Witherspoon: Blond Ambition." *Biography Magazine* Jun. 2002: 38+.

Berman, Connie. "Dolly Parton Scrapbook." *Good Housekeeping* Feb. 1979: 140+.

Bone, Martyn. *The Postsouthern Sense of Place in Contemporary Fiction*. Louisiana State University Press, 2005.

Boone, John. "Reese Witherspoon Opens Up about Religion and the Afterlife: 'I Think You Get an Angel and Wings and a Halo.'" *ETonline.com*. 3 Aug. 2016. Web.

Borshuk, Michael. "'So Black, So Blue': Ralph Ellison, Louis Armstrong, and the Bebop Aesthetic." *Genre* 36 (2004): 261–84.

Bradley, Ryan. "The Accent Whisperers." *New York Times Magazine* 20 Jul. 2017. Web.

Brickell, Herschel, ed. *O. Henry Memorial Award Prize Stories of 1946*. Doubleday, 1946.

Brinnin, John Malcolm. *Truman Capote: Dear Heart, Old Buddy*. Delacorte, 1986.

Brobst, Scout. "Why Does Every Southern Accent in a Movie Sound So Bad?" *New York Times* 26 Mar. 2024. Web.

Bruni, Frank. "The Bush Twins Want to Set the Record Straight." *New York Times* 19 Oct. 2017. Web.

Burstein, Patricia. "Tiny Yes, But a Terror? Do Not Be Fooled by Truman Capote in Repose." *People* 10 May 1976: 12–17.

Bush, Laura, and Jenna Bush. *Read All about It!* HarperCollins, 2008.

Bush, Laura, and Jenna Bush Hager. *Our Great Big Backyard*. Harper, 2016.

Bush Hager, Jenna. *Ana's Story: A Journey of Hope*. HarperCollins, 2008.

———. *Everything Beautiful in Its Time: Seasons of Love and Loss*. William Morrow, 2020.

———. "Go Wild for West Texas." *Southern Living* Jul. 2016: 60–67.

———. "Holiday Glam, Texas Style." *Southern Living* Dec. 2015: 60–67.

———. "Mom to Mom: Joanna's New Season." *Southern Living* Mar. 2019: 82–87.

———. "The Natural." *Southern Living* Aug. 2020: 98–101.

———. "The Needlepointer." *Southern Living* Dec. 2018: 140–42.

———. "Reese on the Secrets of Southern Style." *Southern Living* Sept. 2015: F28–F34.

———. "The Teacher." *Southern Living* May 2018: 63–64.

———. "A Texas Fiesta." *Southern Living* Sept. 2017: 17–22.

———. "This One's for the Girls." *Southern Living* Jul. 2019: 38–41.

Bush Hager, Jenna, and Barbara Pierce Bush. "Dear Sasha and Malia." *Time* 23 Jan. 2017: 43.

———. *Sisters First: Stories from Our Wild and Wonderful Life*. Grand Central Publishing, 2017.

Canby, Vincent. "Simon's Breezy *Murder by Death*." *New York Times* 24 Jun. 1976: 26.

Canfield, David. "Getting Lit." *Entertainment Weekly* 28 Jun. 2019: 32–35.

Capote, Truman. *Answered Prayers*. Random House, 1987.

———. *The Dogs Bark: Public People and Private Places*. Random House, 1973.

———. "Elizabeth Taylor." *Ladies' Home Journal* Dec. 1974: 72–78, 151.

———. *Music for Chameleons*. Random House, 1980.

———. *Portraits and Observations: The Essays of Truman Capote*. Modern Library, 2008.

Carr, Duane. *A Question of Class: The Redneck Stereotype in Southern Fiction*. Bowling Green State University Popular Press, 1996.

Carson, Tom. "Dolly Parton Breaks a Heart." *Rolling Stone* 19 Oct. 1978: 92–93.

Cartwright, Keith. "Black Atlantic." Romine and Greeson 73–87.

Castro, Peter. "Little Glorita, Happy at Last." *People* 12 Aug. 1996: 60+.

Chambers, Andrea. "Going Home: Truman Capote." *People* 26 Jan. 1981: 56–58.

Christian, Margena. "Becoming Tyler." *Ebony* Oct. 2008: 72–83.

———. "Hallelujer!!! Tyler Perry Aims to Lift Spirits with Laughter and Madea." *Jet* 23 Feb. 2022: 44–48.

———. "Tyler Perry: Meet the Man behind the Urban Theater Character Madea." *Jet* 1 Dec. 2003: 60–64.

———. "Tyler Perry: Sky Is the Limit." *Jet* 27 Feb. 2006: 32–38.

Clarke, Gerald. "The Art of Fiction L: Gore Vidal." *Paris Review* 15 (Fall 1974): 130–65.

———. *Capote: A Biography*. Simon & Schuster, 1988.

———, ed. *Too Brief a Treat: The Letters of Truman Capote*. Random House, 2004.

CNN Showbiz Tonight. "Ellen DeGeneres's Suicide Outrage." 1 Oct. 2010.

Cole, Harriette. "Tyler Perry Is Flying High and Enjoying the View." *AARP.org* 2 Aug. 2022. Web.

Cole, Jennifer V. "The Original Steel Magnolia." *Southern Living* Oct. 2014: 107–11.

Collins, Nancy. "Tina Turner: The *Rolling Stone* Interview." *Rolling Stone* 23 Oct. 1986: 46+.

Coppage, Neal. "Dolly: Crossin' Over Is Hard to Do." *Stereo Review* Sept. 1979: 118.

Coscarelli, Joe. "Miley Cyrus on Nicki Manaj and Hosting a 'Raw' MTV Video Music Awards." *New York Times* 27 Aug. 2015. Web.

Cowie, Peter. "They Called Her 'Box Office Poison' but She Was a Star They Couldn't Kill: Katharine Hepburn." *Films & Filming* Jun. 1963: 21+.

Crowther, Bosley. "*Suddenly Last Summer*: Movie from Williams Plays at Two Houses." Rev. of *Suddenly Last Summer*. *New York Times* 23 Dec. 1959: 22.

Curtis, Wayne. "Whistle if You Love Andy Griffith." *AARP: The Magazine* Jul./Aug. 2010: 46–47+.

Cyrus, Miley, with Hilary Liftin. *Miles to Go.* Disney Hyperion, 2009.

D'Addario, Daniel. "8 Questions: Tyler Perry." *Time* 4 Apr. 2016: 60.

Daniels, Neil. *Matthew McConaughey: The Biography.* John Blake Publishing, 2014.

Davidson, James. "Graceland: More Than a Hit Song—A Twentieth-Century Mecca." *Studies in Popular Culture* 10.1 (1987): 51–63.

Davis, Kimberly Chabot. "Beyond the White Negro: Eminem, Danny Hoch, and Race Treason in Contemporary America." *At Home and Abroad: Historicizing Twentieth-Century Whiteness in Literature and Performance.* Ed. La Vinia Delois Jennings. University of Tennessee Press, 2009. 221–54.

Davis, Miles, with Quincy Troupe. *Miles: The Autobiography.* Simon & Schuster, 1989.

The Dean Martin Celebrity Roasts: Man of the Hour, Truman Capote. Prod. Greg Garrison. 1973. Guthy-Renker Entertainment, 2003. DVD.

Deardorff, Julie. "Dr. Phil Throws His Weight in the Wrong Direction." *Knight Ridder Tribune News Service* 21 Oct. 2005.

de Casparis, Lena. "The Gender Debate: Miley Cyrus Gets the Conversation Started." *Elle UK* Oct. 2015: 236+.

DeGeneres, Ellen. *The Funny Thing Is . . .* Simon & Schuster, 2003.

———. *My Point . . . and I Do Have One.* Bantam, 1995.

———. *Seriously . . . I'm Kidding.* Grand Central, 2011.

Deseret News. "Graceland Now Listed as National Historic Site." 30 Dec. 1991.

Devlin, Albert J., ed. *Conversations with Tennessee Williams.* University Press of Mississippi, 1986.

Diaz, Anahy, and Elena Nicolaou, "Yes, Jenna Bush Hager Reads Every Book for Her Club. Here's How She Does It." *Today.com* 5 Jan. 2023. Web.

The Dick Cavett Show: Comic Legends. Perf. Dick Cavett, Groucho Marx, Truman Capote. Prod. Judy Englander. May 25, 1971. Daphne Productions, 2006. DVD.

Doss, Erika. *Elvis Culture: Fans, Faith, and Culture.* University Press of Kansas, 1999.

Doty, Alexander. "Whose Text Is It Anyway? Queer Cultures, Queer Auteurs, and Queer Authorship." *Queer Cinema: The Film Reader.* Ed. Harry Benshoff and Sean Griffin. Routledge, 2004. 19–33.

Dreher, Kwakiutl L. "Don't Slap Yo' Gran'Momma: Tyler Perry and Madea." *Screening Motherhood in Contemporary World Cinema.* Ed. Asma Sayed. Demeter Press, 2016. 108–31.

Drummond, Tammerlin. "Turning the Beat Around." *Time* 20 Oct. 2997: 56.

Dunbar, Ernest. "Ike and Tina Turner: They're Too Much!" *Look* 8 Sept. 1970: 62–64.

Dyer, Richard. *Heavenly Bodies: Film Stars and Society.* 2nd ed. 1986. Routledge, 2004.

———. *Stars*. British Film Institute, 1979.
Ebenkamp, Becky. "Hannah and Her Boosters." *Brandweek* 8 Sept. 2008: M040–M042.
Ebert, Roger. "A Time to Kill." Rogerebert.com 26 Jul. 1996. Web.
Ebony. "Tina Sizzles at 60." May 2000: 52–63.
———. "Tina Turner: The Shocking Story of a Battered Wife Who Escaped to Fame and Fortune." Nov. 1986: 31–42.
Edwards, Audrey. "What Becomes a Sex Goddess Most?" *Essence* Jul. 1993: 50–52+.
Edwards, Gavin. "21st-Century Joke Machine." *Rolling Stone* 8 Jul. 2010. Web.
Egan, Kate, and Sarah Thomas. "Introduction: Star-Making, Cult-Making and Forms of Authenticity." *Cult Film Stardom: Offbeat Attractions and Processes of Cultification*. Ed. Kate Egan and Sarah Thomas. Palgrave Macmillan, 2013. 1–17.
Ellen DeGeneres: All of Me. Films on Demand. 2013. Accessed 30 Jan. 2022. fod.infobase.com/PortalPlaylists.aspx?wID=150523&xtid=140195.
Elliott, Lawrence. "Andy Griffith: Yokel Boy Makes Good." *Coronet* Oct. 1957: 105–10.
Ellison, Ralph. *Invisible Man*. 1940. Vintage, 1980.
Elvis Presley's Graceland: The Official Guidebook. Updated and expanded 2nd ed. Elvis Presley Enterprises, 1996.
Eskridge, Sara. *Rube Tube: CBS and Rural Comedy in the Sixties*. University of Missouri Press, 2018.
Estefan, Gloria. "Finding My Voice." *Reader's Digest* Oct. 2007: 77–80.
Farber, Manny. "Films." *The Nation* 20 Oct. 1941: 334.
Farley, Christopher John. "From a Cuban Heart." *Time* 8 Jul. 1996: 68.
Farr, Cecilia Konchar. *Reading Oprah: How Oprah's Book Club Changed the Way America Reads*. State University of New York Press, 2005.
Feldman, Lucy. "Shifting the Narrative." *Time* 10–17 May 2021: 74–78.
Flamm, Matthew, and Karen Valby. "He Stands Corrected." *Entertainment Weekly* 2 Nov. 2001. Web.
Fleming, Anne Taylor. "The Private World of Truman Capote." *New York Times Magazine* 9 Jul. 1978: 22–25.
Flippo, Chet. "Dolly Parton." *Rolling Stone* 11 Dec. 1980: 39+.
Florida Music Hall of Fame. www.floridamusichall.com.
Forbes. "The Rise and Rise of Tyler Perry." Forbes.com. Oct. 2020. Web.
Frankel, Haskell. "The Author." *Saturday Review* 22 Jan. 1966: 36–37.
Freeman, Donald. "I Think I'm Gaining on Myself." *Saturday Evening Post* 25 Jan. 1964: 68–70.
Fremont-Smith, Eliot. "Literature-by-Consensus." *New York Times* 26 Jan. 1966: 28.
Fresh Air. "Matthew McConaughey: Getting Serious Again." 21 Feb. 2014. www.npr.org/2014/02/21/280711996/matthew-mcconaughey-getting-serious-again.

Works Cited

Frost, David. "When Does a Writer Become a Star? Truman Capote." *The Americans*. Stein & Day, 1970. 17–23.

Gardner, Ava. *Ava: My Story*. Bantam, 1990.

Garner, Dwight. "*Sam Phillips: The Man Who Invented Rock 'n' Roll*, by Peter Guralnick." *New York Times* 5 Nov. 2015.

Gates, Henry Louis, Jr. "The Chitlin Circuit." *African American Performance and Theater History: A Critical Reader*. Ed. Harry Elam and David Krasner. Oxford University Press, 2001. 132–48.

Gay, Roxane. *Bad Feminist: Essays*. Harper Perennial, 2014.

Gelman, Joan. "Tina's Triumph." *McCall's* Nov. 1997: 52–55.

Gerosa, Melina. "My Song of Love." *Ladies' Home Journal* Apr.1997: 118+.

Giles, Howard, and Andrew Billings. "Language Attitudes." *The Handbook of Applied Linguistics*. Ed. Alan Davies and Catherine Elder. Blackwell, 2004. 187–209.

Gill, Brendan. "The Current Cinema: High Spirits and Low." *New Yorker* 25 Nov. 1961: 204–6.

———. *Here at "The New Yorker."* Random House, 1975.

Gill, James, and Howard Hunter. *Tearing Down the Lost Cause: The Removal of New Orleans's Confederate Statues*. University Press of Mississippi, 2021.

Gillespie, Dizzy, with Al Fraser. *To Be, or Not . . . to Bop: Memoirs*. Doubleday, 1979.

Gloria Estefan Foundation. gloriaestefanfoundation.com.

Good Morning America. "Ellen's Apology: Host Addresses Behind-the-Scenes Allegations during the Show's Return." 22 Sept. 2020.

Graceland: The Living Legacy of Elvis Presley. Collins, 1993.

Grady, Henry W. *The New South*. Robert Bonner's Sons, 1890.

Graff, Gary. "Tom Petty's New Tales of the Old South." *Creem* Oct. 1985: 24+.

Grafton, David. *The Sisters: Babe Mortimer Paley, Betsey Roosevelt Whitney, Minnie Astor Fosburgh—The Life and Times of the Fabulous Cushing Sisters*. Villard, 1992.

Gray, Paul. "Oprah Winfrey's Winners." *Time* 2 Dec. 1996: 84.

Grayson, Mara Lee. "Place, Race, and Mutability: Everyman's Hillbilly Rhetoric." *Sands* 23–39.

Greene, Andy. "Tom Petty on Past Confederate Flag Use: 'It Was Downright Stupid.'" *Rolling Stone* 14 Jul. 2015. Web.

Greene, Bob. "Greetings from Graceland." *Esquire* Dec. 1987: 53+.

Greenfeld, Josh. "Truman Capote, the Movie Star?" *New York Times* 28 Dec. 1975, sec. II: 1, 17.

Greeson, Jennifer Rae. *Our South: Geographic Fantasy and the Rise of National Literature*. Harvard University Press, 2010.

Grobel, Lawrence. *Conversations with Capote*. New American Library, 1985.

Works Cited

———. "*Playboy* Interview with Dolly Parton: A Candid Conversation with the Curvaceous Queen of Country Music." *Playboy* Oct. 1978: 81+.
The Guest House at Graceland. guesthousegraceland.com/.
Haddox, Thomas F. "Literature." Romine and Greeson 250–63.
Handy, Bruce. "He Called Me Ellen Degenerate?" *Time International* 14 Apr. 1997: 72.
Hannah Montana Forever: Final Season. DVD. Walt Disney Studios, 2011.
Hannah Montana: Keeping It Real. DVD. Walt Disney Studios, 2009.
Hannah Montana: Life's What You Make It. DVD. Walt Disney Studios, 2007.
Hannah Montana: Miley Says Goodbye? DVD. Walt Disney Studios, 2010.
Hannah Montana: One in a Million. DVD. Walt Disney Studios, 2008.
Hannah Montana: Season 1. DVD. Walt Disney Studios, 2008.
Hannah Montana: The Movie. DVD. Walt Disney Studios, 2009.
Happy Hippie Foundation. happyhippies.org. Web.
Harris, Aisha. "Springtime for the Confederacy." *Slate* 24 Aug. 2017. Web.
Hartung, Philip T. "The Screen: Beamish Boy." *Commonweal* 13 Jun. 1958: 280.
Hatch, Robert. "Movies: Old Hit, New Venture." *New Republic* 8 Oct. 1951: 21–22.
Heigl, Alex. "An Annotated Deep Dive into the Majesty of Matthew McConaughey's 2005 Sexiest Man Alive Interview." *People* 11 Nov. 2015. Web.
Hine, Al. "Polish Up an Oscar." *Holiday* Oct. 1951: 25–28.
Hirshey, Gerri. "Woman Warrior." *Gentlemen's Quarterly* Jun. 1993: 180–83+.
Ho, Rodney. "Just a Southern Boy Coming Home: Ansari Brings His Act to Tabernacle." *Atlanta Journal Constitution* 15 Jun. 2012: D5.
Hollandsworth, Skip. "Girl Gone Mild." *Texas Monthly* Nov. 2007: 144+.
Hoppe, Graham. *Gone Dollywood: Dolly Parton's Mountain Dream.* Ohio University Press, 2018.
———. "Icon and Identity: Dolly Parton's Hillbilly Appeal." *Southern Cultures* Spring 2017: 49–62.
Huffington Post. "Tyler Perry to Spike Lee: 'Go Straight to Hell.'" 20 Apr. 2011. Web.
Hughes, Zondra. "How Tyler Perry Rose from Homelessness to a $5 Million Mansion." *Ebony* Jan. 2004: 86–92.
Hunt, Stacey Wilson. "Southerners Aren't Always at Home in Hollywood." *New York Times* 17 Aug. 2018. Web.
Hurst, Jack. "You've Come a Long Way, Dolly." *High Fidelity Magazine* Dec. 1977: 122–24.
Jackson, Lauren Michelle. "The United States of Dolly Parton." *New Yorker* 19 Oct. 2020: 62–66.
Jahr, Cliff. "Golly, Dolly! (What *Will* She Say Next?)." *Ladies' Home Journal* Jul. 1982: 83+.
Jefferson, Margo. "Dolly Parton: Bewigged, Bespangled . . . and Proud," *Ms.* Jun. 1979: 14+.

Jet. "Nina Simone Reveals: 'Mississippi Goddam' Song 'Hurt My Career.'" 24 Mar. 1986: 54–55.

———. "Oprah Winfrey Reveals the Real Reason Why She Stayed on TV." 24 Nov. 1997: 58–61.

———. "Tina Turner Considering Move from U.S." 9 Feb. 1987: 23.

Johnson, Brian D. "The Comeback Queen of Rock 'n' Roll." *Maclean's* 22 Jul. 1985: 44–45.

Johnson, Grady. "Marlon Brando: Actor on Impulse." *Coronet* Jul. 1952: 75–79.

Johnson, Marilyn. "Oprah Winfrey: A Life in Books." *Life* Sept. 1997: 44+.

Jordan, Tina. "Inside the List." *New York Times Book Review* 19 May 2019: 28.

Jubera, Drew. "Tyler Perry Runs the Table." *Men's Health* Nov. 2012: 125+.

Kaiser, Molly. "How Jenna Bush Is Raising Three Readers: Four Tips She Swears By." *Today.com* 30 May 2023. Web.

Katsilometes, John. "Amid Apathy and Dwindling Revenue, the Jewel Box That Is the Liberace Museum Closes Sunday." *Las Vegas Sun* 16 Oct. 2010.

Kauffmann, Stanley. "Movies: The Outer Edges." *New Republic* 29 Sept. 1958: 21–22.

———. "Movies: The Tennessee Williams Cycle." *New Republic* 2 May 1960: 21–22.

Keith, Slim, with Annette Tapert. *Slim: Memories of a Rich and Imperfect Life.* Simon & Schuster, 1990.

Kelly, Richard. *The Andy Griffith Show.* John F. Blair, Publisher, 1981.

Kennedy, Melanie. "Hannah Montana and Miley Cyrus: 'Becoming' a Woman, 'Becoming' a Star." *Celebrity Studies* 5.3 (2014): 225–41.

Kiely, Robert. "From Monticello to Graceland: Jefferson and Elvis as American Icons." *One Nation under God? Religion and American Culture.* Ed. Marjorie Garber and Rebecca Walkowitz. Routledge, 1999. 208–20.

King, Christine. "His Truth Goes Marching On: Elvis Presley and Pilgrimage to Graceland." *Pilgrimage in Popular Culture.* Ed. Ian Reader and Tony Walter. Macmillan, 1993. 92–104.

Kinsella, Bridget. "The Oprah Effect." *Publishers Weekly* 20 Jan. 1997: 276–78.

Kinzler, Katherine, and Jasmine DeJesus. "Northern = Smart and Southern = Nice: The Development of Accent Attitudes in the United States." *Quarterly Journal of Experimental Psychology* 66.6 (2013): 1146–58.

Knight, Arthur. "SR Goes to the Movies: Monster on the Make." *Saturday Review* 25 May 1957: 23.

Koehler, Robert. "The Wedding Planner." *Variety.com.* 18 Jan. 2001. Web.

Kostelanetz, Richard. *The End of Intelligent Writing: Literary Politics in America.* Sheed & Ward, 1974.

Krebs, Albin. "Notes on People." *New York Times* 15 Nov. 1977: 34.

Works Cited

Labov, William. *The Social Stratification of English in New York City.* 2nd ed. Cambridge University Press, 2006.

Labov, William, Sharon Ash, and Charles Boberg. *The Atlas of North American English: Phonetics, Phonology, and Sound Change.* Mouton de Gruyter, 2006.

Landau, Jon. "Elvis: All the King's Splendor." *Rolling Stone* 22 Sept. 1977: 84.

Landrieu, Mitch. *In the Shadow of Statues: A White Southerner Confronts History.* Viking, 2018.

Langmann, Brady. "Matthew McConaughey Is Daring America to Meet in the Middle." *Esquire* 18 Nov. 2020. Web.

Larocca, Amy. "The Real Miley Cyrus." *Harper's Bazaar* 6 Jan. 2010. Web.

Larry King Live. "Ellen DeGeneres Discusses the Conclusion of Her Groundbreaking Sitcom." 12 May 1998.

Lawrence, Michael, ed. *Indian Film Stars: New Critical Perspectives.* British Film Institute, 2020.

Leahy, Michael. "Case Closed: After Five Seasons of *Matlock,* Andy Griffith Says He's Leaving the Show." *TV Guide* 17–23 Nov. 1990: 2–6.

Lee, Alicia. "Ellen DeGeneres Sparks Backlash after Joking That Self-Quarantine Is Like 'Being in Jail.'" *CNN* 9 Apr. 2020.

Lerman, Leo. "The Male Attraction." *Mademoiselle* Feb. 1956: 150–53.

Life. "The Bitter Dispute over *Baby Doll.*" 7 Jan. 1957: 60–65.

———. "Brando's Break into a New Field." 4 Apr. 1960: 105+.

———. "Guitar-Thumping Demagogue." 27 May 1957: 68+.

Limon, John. "Spritzing, Skirting: Standup Talk Strategies." *Talk Talk Talk: The Cultural Life of Everyday Conversation.* Ed. S. I. Salamensky. New York: Routledge, 2001. 105–18.

Littler, Jo. "Making Fame Ordinary: Intimacy, Reflexivity, and 'Keeping It Real.'" *Mediactive* 2 (2004): 8–25.

Long, Barbara. "In Cold Comfort." *Esquire* Jun. 1966: 124+.

Look. "From Tragedy ... New Fame." 14 Oct. 1958: 90+.

Lynskey, Dorian. "How Dangerous Is Jordan B. Peterson, the Rightwing Professor Who 'Hit a Hornet's Nest'?" *The Guardian* 7 Feb. 2018. Web.

MacDonald, Dwight. "Three Years, Six Million, One Film." *Esquire* Oct. 1961: 24+.

Macherey, Pierre. *A Theory of Literary Production.* Trans. Geoffrey Wall. 1966. Routledge, 2006

Mademoiselle. "Truman Capote on Christmas, Places, Memories." Dec. 1971: 122+.

Mahon, Maureen. *Black Diamond Queens: African American Women and Rock and Roll.* Duke University Press, 2020.

Marchese, David. "Matthew McConaughey Is Not Afraid to Go down the Rabbit Hole." *New York Times* 29 Nov. 2021.

———. "Matthew McConaughey on Trying to Become Living Art." *New York Times Magazine* 5 Dec. 2021: 15–27.

Mark, Julian. "Matthew McConaughey Rules Out Texas Governor Run 'At This Moment.'" *Washington Post* 29 Nov. 2021. Web.

Marling, Karal Ann. *Graceland: Going Home with Elvis*. Harvard University Press, 1996.

Martin, Pete. "The Star Who Sneers at Hollywood." *Saturday Evening Post* 6 Jun. 1953: 32+.

Master of None. Perf. Aziz Ansari and Lena Waithe. 3 Arts Entertainment, 2015–21.

Max, D. T. "The Oprah Effect." *New York Times Magazine* 26 Dec. 1999: 36–41.

McCall's. "The Fugitive Kind." Jun. 1960: 179.

McCarten, John. "The Current Cinema: Cotton-Belt Bedlam." *New Yorker* 27 Sept. 1958: 163–64.

———. "The Current Cinema: Familiar, but Funny." *New Yorker* 7 Jun. 1958: 64–65.

———. "The Current Cinema: Life among the Lintheads." *New Yorker* 29 Dec. 1956: 59–60.

———. "The Current Cinema: More TV Villainy." *New Yorker* 8 Jun. 1957: 86–88.

———. "The Current Cinema: Orpheus with a Hot Guitar." *New Yorker* 23 Apr. 1960: 147–48.

———. "The Current Cinema: Way Down Yonder." *New Yorker* 29 Sept. 1951: 111–12.

McConaughey, Matthew. *Greenlights*. Crown, 2020.

McGrath, Ben. "First Book." *New Yorker* 8 Oct. 2017. Web.

McKeon, Elizabeth, and Linda Everett. *The Quotable King*. Cumberland House, 1997.

McPherson, Tara. *Reconstructing Dixie: Race, Gender, and Nostalgia in the Imagined South*. Duke University Press, 2003.

Meckna, Michael. "Louis Armstrong in the Movies, 1931–1969." *Popular Music and Society* 29.3 (2006): 359–73.

Medwick, Cathleen. "Truman Capote: An Interview." *Vogue* Dec. 1979: 263, 311–12.

Merod, Jim. "Biography as Erasure: Louis Armstrong's Radical Light." *boundary 2* 38.3 (2011): 165–215.

Mewborn, Brant. "Tina Turner: Raunchy, Rollin' and Back in the Rock of It." *Rolling Stone* 9 Jul. 1981: 48–49.

Millner, Denene. "The Unstoppable Tyler Perry." *Essence* Aug. 2007: 97+.

Millstein, Gilbert. "Strange Chronicle of Andy Griffith." *New York Times Magazine* 2 Jun. 1957: 17.

Mims, Bryan. "Ava Gardner Museum Closes Due to Flood Damage." *WRAL News* 15 Jan. 2021. Web.

Mizejewski, Linda. *Pretty / Funny: Women Comedians and Body Politics.* University of Texas Press, 2014.

Moore, Barbara, Marvin Bensman, and Jim Van Dyke. *Prime-Time Television: A Concise History.* Praeger, 2006.

Moore, Tracy. "Why 'Bless Your Heart' Is the Most Savage Insult in the Country." n.d. melmagazine.com/en-us/story/bless-your-heart.

Morales, Ed, and Gloria Estefan. "Hey, Latin Lovers!" *Interview* Jun. 1999: 98+.

Moran, Lee. "Dolly Parton Rejected the Medal of Freedom." *Huffington Post* 2 Feb. 2021. Web.

Morris, Wesley. "The Year of Tyler Perry. Seriously." *Film Comment* Jan.–Feb. 2011: 59–61.

Morrison, Chester. "Andy Griffith: Sheriff of Mayberry." *Look* 9 Apr. 1963: 80a-80e.

Mutnick, Ally. "Senators Scold Dr. Oz for Weight-Loss Scams." *USA Today* 17 Jun. 2014. Web.

Nash, Alanna "Why Dolly Parton Is One Unsinkable Mountain Momma." *Entertainment Weekly* 9 Aug. 2002. Web.

Network. "Music Meeting." 20 Jan. 1995: 20.

Newquist, Roy. *Counterpoint.* Rand McNally, 1964.

Newsweek. "Bumpkin to Big-Timer." 18 Jan. 1954: 60.

———. "Hillbilly's a Hit." 31 Oct. 1955: 55.

———. "New Films: As It Should Be." 28 Dec. 1959: 64

———. "No Four-Letter Words." 1 Sept. 1958: 56.

———. "Talk with the Star." 13 Jun. 1960: 97.

———. "Trying, as It Were." 20 Nov. 1961: 106.

———. "Turning On." 3 Nov. 1969: 92–93.

Nicolaou, Elena. "Jenna Bush Hager Recommends Five Things to Buy While Reading *Camp Zero.*" *Today.com* 19 Apr. 2023. Web.

Nishime, Leilani. *Undercover Asian: Multiracial Asian Americans in Visual Culture.* University of Illinois Press, 2014.

Norden, Eric. "*Playboy* Interview: Truman Capote." *Playboy* Mar. 1968: 51–53+.

Nugent, John. "Talk with the Star." *Newsweek* 3 Apr. 1961: 90–92.

O'Connor, Sinéad. "Sinéad O'Connor's Open Letter to Miley Cyrus." *The Guardian* 3 Oct. 2013. Web.

Ojomu, Nola. "'I thought she was bulletproof': Man behind 'Ellen DeGeneres Is Mean' Twitter Thread Never Expected Show to End as He Responds to Claims Attack Was 'Orchestrated.'" *The Metro* 14 May 2021. Web.

Orth, Maureen. "The Lady Has Legs!" *Vanity Fair* May 1993: 114–21+.

———. "Tina: It Took a Grown-Up Woman to Save Rock and Roll . . . and Soul to Save Herself." *Vogue* May 1985: 318+.

Osgerby, Bill. "'So Who's Got Time for Adults!': Femininity, Consumption, and the Development of Teen TV—from *Gidget* to *Buffy*." *Teen TV: Genre, Consumption, Identity*. Ed. Glyn Davis and Kay Dickinson. British Film Institute, 2004. 71–86.

Owens, Delia. *Where the Crawdads Sing*. G. P. Putnam's Sons, 2018.

Packer, Barbara, Laurie Deutsch, Barbara Bussmann, Ann Beattie, and Judi Silverman. "We Talk to . . . Truman Capote." *Mademoiselle* Aug. 1968: 366–67.

Paiella, Gabriella. "Matthew McConaughey Is Thinking about His Eulogy." *GQ* 21 Oct. 2020. Web.

Palomino, Pablo. *The Invention of Latin American Music: A Transnational History*. Oxford University Press, 2020.

Parks and Recreation. Perf. Amy Poehler, Aziz Ansari, and Rashida Jones. Deedle Dee Productions, 2009–20.

Parton, Dolly. *Dolly: My Life and Other Unfinished Business*. HarperCollins, 1994.

———. *Dream More: Celebrate the Dreamer in You*. G. P. Putnam's Sons, 2012.

———. *Songteller: My Life in Lyrics*. Chronicle, 2020.

———. "The Story of Reese." *InStyle* Dec. 2016: 226–31.

Pasternak, Judith Mahoney. *Dolly Parton*. MetroBooks, 1998.

Patterson, Robert J. "Do You Want to Be Well? The Gospel Play, Womanist Theology, and Tyler Perry's Artistic Project." *Journal of Feminist Studies in Religion* 30.2 (2014): 41–56.

People Staff. "2005's Sexiest Men Alive." People.com 3 May 2016. Web.

———. *Dolly! Nashville to '9 to 5' to Now: The Music Icon Who Brings the Country Together*. May 2022.

Perry, E. Warren, ed. *Echoes of Elvis: The Cultural Legacy of Elvis Presley*. Smithsonian Institution Scholarly Press, 2012.

Perry, Tyler. *Don't Make a Black Woman Take Off Her Earrings: Madea's Uninhibited Commentaries on Love and Life*. Riverhead, 2006.

———. *Higher Is Waiting*. Spiegel & Grau, 2017.

Petty, Miriam J. "'Old Folks at Home': Tyler Perry and the Dialectics of Nostalgia." *Quarterly Review of Film and Video* 34.7 (2017): 587–605.

Plimpton, George. *Truman Capote: In Which Various Friends, Enemies, Acquaintances, and Detractors Recall His Turbulent Career*. Doubleday, 1997.

Ponce de Leon, Charles. *Fortunate Son: The Life of Elvis Presley*. Hill & Wang, 2006.

Portman, Natalie. "Reese Faces Her Fears." *Harper's Bazaar* Nov. 2019: 136+.

Potter, Amy E., Stephen Hanna, Derek Alderman, Perry Carter, Candace Forbes Bright, and David Butler. *Remembering Enslavement: Reassembling the Southern Plantation Museum*. University of Georgia Press, 2022.

Presley, Vernon, as told to Nancy Anderson. "Elvis, by His Father Vernon Presley." *Good Housekeeping* Jan. 1978: 156+.

Primetime Live. "Delightful, Delovely, DeGeneres." 24 Nov. 1994.
Puente, Maria. "Jenna Bush Hager Gets *Southern Living* Job." *USA Today* 26 Nov. 2012. Web.
Pugh, Tison. *Queer Chivalry: Medievalism and the Myth of White Masculinity in Southern Literature.* Louisiana State University Press, 2013.
Puig, Claudia. "Witherspoon's 'Sweet Home.'" *USA Today* 18 Sept. 2002. Web.
Redmond, Sean. *Celebrity.* Routledge, 2018.
Reece, Gregory. *Elvis Religion: Cult of the King.* I. B. Tauris, 2006.
Reed, Alison Rose. "Colorblind Melodrama: Tyler Perry's *For Colored Girls* and the Absorption of Black Feminism." *Frontiers: A Journal of Women's Studies* 43.1 (2022): 151–84.
Reese's Book Club, https://reesesbookclub.com/litup.
Rolo, Charles. "The New Bohemia." *Flair* Feb. 1950: 27–29, 116–18.
Romine, Scott, and Jennifer Rae Greeson, eds. *Keywords for Southern Studies.* University of Georgia Press, 2016.
Rooney, Kathleen. *Reading with Oprah: The Book Club That Changed America.* University of Arkansas Press, 2008.
Rooney, Kathy. "Oprah Learns Her Lesson." *The Nation* 20 May 2002: 56–60.
RottenTomatoes.com. "*Mr. Wrong* (1996)." Web.
Royster, Francesca. *Black Country Music: Listening for Revolutions.* University of Texas Press, 2022.
Rubenstein, Hal. "Tina Turner: Her Least Nostalgic Interview, Ever." *Interview* Aug. 1993: 40–41.
RuPaul. *The House of Hidden Meanings.* HarperCollins, 2024.
Rushing, Wanda. "Region." Romine and Greeson 121–32.
Salamone, Frank. "Laughin' Louie: An Analysis of Louis Armstrong's Record and Its Relationship to African-American Musical Humor." *Humor* 15.1 (2002): 47–63.
Sanders, Charles L. "Louis Armstrong: The Reluctant Millionaire." *Ebony* Nov. 1964: 136+.
Sands, Crystal D., ed. *Tom Petty: Essays on the Life and Work.* McFarland, 2019.
Sanneh, Kelefa. "Funny Person: Can a Hardworking Cult Favorite Make It as a Mainstream Star?" *New Yorker* 1 Nov. 2010. Web.
Saran, Rupam. *Navigating Model Minority Stereotypes: Asian Indian Youth in South Asian Diaspora.* Routledge, 2016.
Sarris, Andrew. "Excerpt from 'Notes on the Auteur Theory in 1962.'" *Theories of Authorship: A Reader.* Ed. J. Caughie. Routledge & Kegan Paul, with the British Film Institute, 1981. 62–65.
Satchmo in East Berlin. 22 Mar. 1965. *YouTube.com.* Web.

Works Cited

The Saturday Early Show. "Comedian Ellen DeGeneres Discusses Her Personal Ties to New Orleans." 3 Sept. 2005.

Schwarzbaum, Lisa. "Failure to Launch." *Entertainment Weekly* 8 Mar. 2006. Web.

Schwed, Mark. "The Case of the Classic TV Sleuths." *TV Guide* 1–7 Feb. 1997: 34–37.

Scott, A. O. "Plus-Size Matriarch's Stretch in the Slammer." *New York Times* 20 Feb. 2009. Web.

Scott, Marshall. "Your Cosmopolitan Movie Guide." *Cosmopolitan* 16 May 1958: 16.

Shaw, Rashida. "From the Margins to Center Stage: Tyler Perry's Popular African American Theatre." *From Madea to Media Mogul: Theorizing Tyler Perry.* Ed. TreaAndrea Russworm, Samanth Sheppard, and Karen Bowdrie. University of Mississippi Press, 2016. 30–51.

Smith, Heather, and Owen Furuseth. *Latinos in the New South: Transformations of Place.* Ashgate, 2006.

Smith, Patrick. "Aziz Ansari: Buried Alive, Hammersmith Apollo, Review." *The Telegraph* 18 Jun. 2013. Web.

Smith, Sean M. "Reese Witherspoon Lets Down Her Hair." *Premiere* Aug. 2001: 44+.

Smith, William D. "A Success Money Didn't Buy: Capote's New Book Best-Seller Before It Was Written." *New York Times* 20 Feb. 1966: 16.

Solomon, Jeff. *So Famous and So Gay: The Fabulous Potency of Truman Capote and Gertrude Stein.* University of Minnesota Press, 2017.

Sporkin, Elizabeth. "Tina Turner: Her Most Candid Interview." *Ladies' Home Journal* Apr. 1987: 34+.

The Stanley Siegel Show. Guest Truman Capote. WABC-TV, New York, 18 Jul. 1978. Television. UCLA Film and Television Archive.

Stead, Lisa. *Reframing Vivien Leigh: Stardom, Gender, and the Archive.* Oxford University Press, 2021.

Steinem, Gloria. "A Visit with Truman Capote." *Glamour* Apr. 1966: 210+.

———. "Dolly Parton." *Ms.* Jan. 1987: 66+.

Story, Kaila Adia. "On the Cusp of Deviance: Respectability Politics and the Cultural Marketplace of Sameness." *No Tea, No Shade: New Writings in Black Queer Studies.* Ed. E. Patrick Johnson. Duke University Press, 2016. 362–79.

Stoynoff, Natasha. "Matthew McConaughey Is on a Mission to Heal America." *AARP* 26 May 2021. Web.

Strachan, Maxell. "When Ellen Came Out, She Didn't Just Change Lives. She Saved Them." *Huffington Post* 28 Apr. 2017. Web.

Strasbaugh, John. *E: Reflections on the Birth of the Elvis Faith.* Blast Books, 1996.

Striphas, Ted. *The Late Age of Print: Everyday Book Culture from Consumerism to Control.* Columbia University Press, 2009.

Stuever, Hank. "Ellen Becomes the If Girl." *Washington Post* 24 Sept. 2020. Web.

Szczesiul, Anthony. *The Southern Hospitality Myth: Ethics, Politics, Race, and American Memory.* University of Georgia Press, 2017.

Talley, Andre Leon. "An Afternoon with Truman Capote: Tales Told by the Tiny Terror." *W* 23–30 Jul. 1976: 8.

Tannenbaum, Rob. "Stevie Nicks Admits Past Pregnancy with Don Henley and More about Her Wild History." *Billboard* 26 Sept. 2014. Web.

Taylor, Paul C. "Funky White Boys and Honorary Soul Sisters." *Michigan Quarterly Review* 36.2 (1997): 320–35.

Teachout, Terry. *Pops: A Life of Louis Armstrong.* Houghton Mifflin Harcourt, 2009.

Teen Magazine. "Miami Sound Machine: Nothing Gets in Their Way." Jan. 1987: 45.

Thomas, Nick. *Tom Petty: A Rock and Roll Life.* Rev. ed. Guardian Express Media, 2018.

Time. "The $6,000,000 Method." 24 Mar. 1961: 72.

———. "New Film: *Baby Doll.*" 24 Dec. 1956: 61.

———. "The New Pictures: *A Streetcar Named Desire.*" 17 Sept. 1951: 105–6.

———. "The New Pictures: *Cat on a Hot Tin Roof.*" 15 Sept. 1958: 90–92.

———. "The New Pictures: *Suddenly, Last Summer.*" 11 Jan 1960: 84.

———. "The New Pictures: *The Fugitive Kind.*" 18 Apr. 1960: 81.

———. "What It Is, Is Talk." 18 Jan. 1954: 77.

The Tonight Show. Hosts Johnny Carson and Ed McMahon. Guests Truman Capote, Carl Reiner, and Jerry Van Dyke. NBC, 27 Nov. 1973.

Toomey, Alyssa. "What Happened to Miley Cyrus?! Her Biggest Controversies and Scandals." *Eonline.com* 27 Aug. 2013. Web.

Travers, Peter. "*A Time to Kill.*" *Rolling Stone* 24 Jul. 1996. Web.

Trebay, Guy. "Miley Cyrus's Style: An Exuberant Sexuality." *New York Times* 27 Aug. 2015. Web.

Turner, Miki. "Tyler Perry: Show Business His Way." *Jet* 18–25 Apr. 2011: 30–35.

Turner, Tina. "Tina Turner: The Queen of Rock 'n' Roll Riffs on Her Health, Karma, and Forgiveness." *AARP: The Magazine* Dec. 2020: 16.

Turner, Tina, with Deborah Davis and Dominik Wichmann. *My Love Story.* Atria, 2018.

Turner, Tina, with Kurt Loder. *I, Tina.* William Morrow, 1986.

Ulrich, Carmen Wong. "The Oprah Effect." *Essence* Oct. 2006: 190–92.

Vogue. "People Are Talking About . . ." May 1959: 122.

Walbridge, Earle. "*No Time for Sergeants* Review." *Library Journal* 15 Jun. 1958: 1913.

Wald, Elijah. "Louis Armstrong Loves Guy Lombardo." *Jazz / Not Jazz: The Music and Its Boundaries.* Ed. David Ake, Charles Hiroshi Garrett, and Daniel Goldmark. University of California Press, 2012. 31–48.

Warhol, Andy. "Sunday with Mister C.: An Audio-Documentary by Andy Warhol Starring Truman Capote." *Rolling Stone* Apr. 1973: 28+.

Washburn, Michael. *Southern Accents*. Bloomsbury Academic, 2019.

Washington, Myra S. *Blasian Invasion: Racial Mixing in the Celebrity Industrial Complex*. University Press of Mississippi, 2017.

Way, Katie. "I Went on a Date with Aziz Ansari. It Turned into the Worst Night of My Life." *Babe.net* 13 Jan. 2018. Web.

Weber, Brenda R., and Joselyn K. Leimbach. "Ellen DeGeneres's Incorporate Body: The Politics of Authenticity." *Hysterical! Women in American Comedy*. Ed. Linda Mizejewski and Victoria Sturtevant. University of Texas Press, 2017. 303–24.

Weeks, Janet. "Insider Q&A: Andy Griffith and Don Knotts." *TV Guide* 8–14 Nov. 2003: 18–19.

Wenner, Jann. "Coda: Another Round with Mr. C." *Rolling Stone* Apr. 1973: 50, 52, 54.

Whitaker, Sterling. "Dolly Parton Shares Why She Dropped the 'Dixie' from Her Stampede." *Taste of Country* 13 Aug. 2020. Web.

Williams, Tennessee. "Five Fiery Ladies." *Life* 3 Feb. 1961: 84+.

———. *Memoirs*. Doubleday, 1972.

———. *The Roman Spring of Mrs. Stone*. New Directions, 1950.

Willman, Chris. "Reese Witherspoon." *Entertainment Weekly* 2 Oct. 2006. Web.

Wilson, Charles Reagan. "Foreword." *The Tacky South*. Ed. Katharine Burnett and Monica Carol Miller. Louisiana State University Press, 2022.

———. "Mississippi Rebels: Elvis Presley, Fannie Lou Hamer, and the South's Culture of Religious Music." *Southern Quarterly* 50.2 (2013): 9–30.

Wilson, Pamela. "Mountains of Contradictions: Gender, Class, and Region in the Star Image of Dolly Parton." *South Atlantic Quarterly* 94.1 (1995): 109–34.

Wiltz, Teresa. "The Latest Ingenue To-Do." *Washington Post* 29 Apr. 2008. Web.

Winfrey, Oprah. "Tyler Perry: Empire Builder." *Time* 5–12 Oct. 2020: 90.

Winn, Janet. "Capote, Mailer, and Miss Parker." *New Republic* 9 Feb. 1959: 27–28.

Witherspoon, Reese. *Whiskey in a Teacup: What Growing Up in the South Taught Me about Life, Love, and Baking Biscuits*. Touchstone, 2018.

Wizards on Deck with Hannah Montana. DVD. Walt Disney Studios, 2009.

Wojcik, Pamela Robertson. "Typecasting." *Criticism* 45.2 (2003): 223–49.

Wu, Ellen D. *The Color of Success: Asian Americans and the Origins of the Model Minority*. Princeton University Press, 2013.

Wynne, Ben. *A Hound Dog Tale: Big Mama, Elvis, and the Song That Changed Everything*. Louisiana State University Press, 2024.

Yuan, Jada. "Aziz Ansari Is from a Red State, Too." *New York* 1–14 May 2017: 79+.

———. "How Aniz Ansari Started Working with His Brother on *Master of None* and What It Was Like to Grow Up with Aziz." *Vulture.com* 19 Jun. 2017. Web.

Works Cited

Zinoman, Jason. "Ellen DeGeneres Isn't as Nice as You Think She Is." *New York Times* 12 Dec. 2018. Web.

Zoglin, Richard. "Lady with a Calling." *Time* 8 Aug. 1988. Web.

Zoladz, Lindsay. "Is There Anything We Can All Agree On? Yes: Dolly Parton." *New York Times* 21 Nov. 2019. Web.

Zollo, Paul. *Conversations with Tom Petty*. Omnibus Press, 2005.

Zong, Jie, and Jeanne Batalova. "Indian Immigrants in the United States." Migration Policy Institute 31 Aug. 2017. www.migrationpolicy.org/article/indian-immigrants-united-states-2015.

INDEX

.38 Special, 109, 188
9 to 5 (1980), 100–101, 104–5
19 Kids and Counting (2008–15), 211
30 Rock (2006–13), 4, 149

Abrams, Stacey, 211
accents. *See* southern accents
African Queen, The (1951), 55, 65
Alice Adams (1935), 65
Allman Brothers, 109, 114, 122
Allyson, June, 20
American Idol (2002–), 148
Amistad (1997), 173, 175
Anderson, Judith, 66
Andy Griffith Show, The (1960–68), 4, 10, 70–71, 74–82, 219n32
Angelou, Maya, 127–28
Angels in the Outfield (1994), 172
Ansari, Aniz, 193–94
Ansari, Aziz, 3, 12, 181–94
Arbuckle, Roscoe "Fatty," 7
Armstrong, Louis, 3, 9, 12, 14–26, 211
Arnaz, Desi, 120
Atlanta, GA, 4, 11, 57, 80, 156–57, 166–68, 210
authenticity (of celebrity personas), 5–7, 83, 196–97; and Dolly Parton, 97–100, 105, 108; and Ellen DeGeneres, 144–45, 148–50, 152; and Elvis Presley, 48; and Matthew McConaughey, 169; and Miley Cyrus, 196–200, 205–7; and *The Andy Griffith Show,* 77–78; and Tina Turner, 91
Avedon, Richard, 29, 31

B-52s (band), 109
Baby Doll (1956), 55, 58, 67, 68
Baker, Carroll, 55, 67
Baldwin, Alec, 167
Basinger, Kim, 54
Bavier, Frances, 78
Beatles (band), 110, 117
Beatty, Warren, 60
Beaty, Daniel, 160
Begley, Ed, 56
Belafonte, Harry, 228n1
Beloved (1998), 126
Benitez, Jellybean, 120
Bergman, Ingrid, 54
Bernie (2011), 175–76
Berry, Halle, 228n1
Best Little Whorehouse in Texas, The (1982), 101, 104
Beverly Hillbillies, The (1962–71), 77, 82, 219n29
Beyoncé, 13, 209
Biden, Joseph, 106
Big Little Lies (2017–19), 135
Big Momma's House (2000), 165

Index

Blind Side, The (2009), 177
Bloodworth-Thomason, Linda, 81
Blue Lagoon, The (1980), 202
Bob the Drag Queen, 211
Bogart, Humphrey, 55
Bono, Sonny, 35
Boo! A Madea Halloween (2016), 228n25
Boo 2! A Madea Halloween (2017), 228n25
Boom! (1968), 55
Boys on the Side (1995)
Brando, Marlon, 10, 34, 55, 57, 60–62, 68
Breakfast at Tiffany's (1961), 58
Brooks, Garth, 6, 210
Brooks, Richard, 55
Brown v. Board of Education of Topeka (1954 U.S. Supreme Court decision), 25, 92
Bullock, Sandra, 177
Burke, Delta, 81
Burton, Richard, 56
Bush, Barbara Pierce, 137, 140, 141
Bush, George W., 137, 154, 211
Bush, Laura, 139
Bush Hager, Jenna, 3, 11, 12, 136–43
Butler, The (2013), 126
BUtterfield 8 (1960), 64

Cabin in the Sky (1943), 20–21
Capote, Truman, 3, 9, 27–40, 211–12, 215n43
Carroll, Diahann, 228n1
Carson, Johnny, 34, 35, 144
Carter, Dixie, 81
Carter, Jimmy, 46–47, 211
Cat on a Hot Tin Roof (1958), 55, 58, 62–64, 66
Cavett, Dick, 33–34
Change of Habit (1969), 42–43
Charles, Ray, 120
Charleston, SC, 57, 121
Cher, 89
Chicks (band) 209–10
Clift, Montgomery, 64
Clinton, Bill, 211
Clinton, Hillary, 106, 153
Clooney, George, 3

Coleman, Dabney, 100
Color of Money, The (1986), 63
Color Purple, The (1985), 89, 126
Connick, Harry, Jr., 146
Contact (1997), 172–73
Cool Hand Luke (1967), 63
Corden, James, 155
Cosby, Bill, 166, 229n43
Cox, Laverne, 211
Craig, Daniel, 68
Craven, Wes, 118
Crawford, Joan, 30
Crosby, Bing, 20–21
Cugat, Xavier, 120
Curtis, Jamie Lee, 217n2
Cyrus, Billy Ray, 197, 202
Cyrus, Miley, 3, 12–13, 183, 195–208, 212

D., Chuck, 48
Dallas Buyers Club (2013), 175
Daniels, Lee, 126, 175
Danny Thomas Show, The (1953–65), 75
Davis, Bette, 30, 35
Davis, Miles, 17
Davis, Viola, 3
Dazed and Confused (1993), 169–71
Dean Martin Celebrity Roast, The (1974–84), 34–35
DeGeneres, Ellen, 3, 11, 12, 118, 125, 144–55, 183, 211–12
Depp, Johnny, 7
Dern, Laura, 150–51
Designing Women (1986–93), 81
Diary of a Mad Black Woman (2005), 157, 162–64, 166, 228n25
Dickinson, Harris, 68
Dixie Chicks. *See* Chicks (band)
Dolly Parton's Mountain Magic Christmas (2022), 208
Dorfman, Tommy, 211
Doris Day Show, The (1968–73), 80
Driving Miss Daisy (1989), 3
Duck Dynasty (2012–17), 211
Dukes of Hazzard, The (1979–85), 81

Index

Dunnock, Mildred, 55
DuVernay, Ava, 126
Dyer, Richard, 5, 30

Edgar-Jones, Daisy, 68
EdTV (1999), 173
Election (1999), 132
Elise, Kimberly, 163
Ellen (1994–98), 144, 149–50, 226n3
Ellen DeGeneres Show, The (2003–23), 144, 152–55
Ellison, Ralph, 18
Endless Love (1981), 202
Erin Brockovich (2000), 177
Estefan, Gloria, 3, 10–11, 12, 109–10, 116–22, 211
Eureka, 211
Evening Shade (1990–94), 81
Everything Everywhere All at Once (2022), 217n2
Ex-Flame (1930), 20
Exposé, 120

Face in the Crowd, A (1957), 73–74, 81
Failure to Launch (2006), 173–74
Falwell, Jerry, 152
Fanatic, The (2019), 177
fans and fandom, 5–7, 120, 196; and Dolly Parton, 97–98, 104, 108; and Ellen DeGeneres, 145, 153–54; and Elvis Presley, 45–46, 49; and Louis Armstrong, 17, 24; and Miley Cyrus, 199–200, 203–6; and Oprah Winfrey, 125; and Tina Turner, 84, 90–91; and Tom Petty, 112; and Tyler Perry, 158–59
Father of the Bride (1950), 63
Father of the Bride (2022), 118
Faulkner, William, 63, 129
Fear (1996), 131
Fixer Upper (2013–18), 211
Follow That Dream (1962), 110
Fonda, Jane, 100, 106
Fool's Gold (2008), 173
Foster, Jodie, 172–73
Foxworthy, Jeff, 4
Foxx, Jamie, 7, 169
Franklin, Aretha, 86

Franzen, Jonathan, 130
Fraser, Brendan, 54
Frasier (1993–2004), 118
Freeman, Morgan, 3
Free State of Jones (2016), 177
Friedkin, William, 175
Fugitive Kind, The (1960), 55, 61, 66, 68
Furman, Brad, 175

Gable, Clark, 30
Gainesville, FL, 110–11
Gardner, Ava, 1–2, 41, 56, 213n1
Garner, Jennifer, 173
Gay, Roxane, 160
Georgia Satellites, 109
Ghosts of Girlfriends Past (2009), 173–74
Ghosts of Mississippi (1996), 167
Gibson, Mel, 89
Gillespie, Dizzy, 17, 25
Girl in the Empty Grave, The (1977), 80
Glass Menagerie, The (1950), 55, 60
Glee (2009–15), 118
Glenn Miller Story, The (1954), 20–21
Glenville, Peter, 55
Glory Alley (1952), 20
Godfather, The (1972), 62
Gold (2016), 177
Goldberg, Whoopi, 228n1
Golden Girls, The (1985–92), 81
Gomer Pyle, U.S.M.C. (1964–69) 4, 219n32
Gone with the Wind (1939), 59
Good Morning, Vietnam (1987), 16
Grace and Frankie (2015–22), 106
Graceland, 9, 12, 41–42, 48–53
Graham, Katharine, 32
Great Migration, 23, 167, 182
Green Acres (1965–71), 77, 219n29
Griffith, Andy, 3, 4, 10, 70–82, 149, 183

Hackman, Gene, 167
Hall, Grayson, 56
Hannah Montana (2006–11), 195–207
Hannah Montana: The Movie (2009), 197, 199

Index

Harrelson, Woody, 169, 172
Harris, Emmylou, 102
Harris, Steve, 163
Hart, Kevin, 4, 154
Harvey, Laurence, 67
Hawaii Five-O (1968–80), 80
Hello, Dolly! (1969), 20–22
Help, The (2011), 167
Hemsworth, Liam, 208
Hepburn, Katharine, 10, 54, 56, 57, 65–66
Here Comes Honey Boo Boo (2012–17), 211
Herndon, Ty, 210
Heston, Charlton, 58
High Society (1956), 20–21
Hill, George Roy, 55
hillbilly and redneck stereotypes, 2, 4, 7, 35, 63, 231n26; and Andy Griffith, 70–73, 78; and Aziz Ansari, 184, 188; and Dolly Parton, 96–97; and Miley Cyrus, 199; and Tyler Perry, 168
Holiday, Billie, 20
Horne, Lena, 21
Howard, Ron, 173
How to Get Away with Murder (2014–20), 3
How to Lose a Guy in 10 Days (2003), 173–74
Hud (1963), 63
Hudson, Kate, 173
Human Giant (2007–8), 182
Hunter, Kim, 55
Huston, John, 55

I Love Lucy (1951–57), 120
I Love You, Man (2009), 182
Immortal Life of Henrietta Lacks, The (2017), 126

Jacksonville, FL, 109
Jagger, Mick, 86
Jennings, Jazz, 211
Jim Crow South, 23, 167
Johnson, Dakota, 154
Johnson, Lyndon B., 211
Judge, Mike, 115
Julius Caesar (1953), 61

Kaling, Mindy, 189
Kaye, Danny, 20
Kazan, Elia, 55, 68, 73
Keith, Toby, 6–7, 210
Kelly, Grace, 20
Kennedy, John F., 105
Kerr, Deborah, 56
Kidman, Nicole, 135
Killer Joe (2011), 175–76
Killers, The (1946), 1
King of the Hill (1997–2010), 115
Knight, Shirley, 56
Knight, Ted, 34–35
Knotts, Don, 76–79
Kristofferson, Kris, 87

Landrieu, Mitch, 15, 26
Last Action Hero (1993), 89
Lawrence, Martin, 165
Lee, Harper, 31
Lee, Spike, 160–61, 228n1, 228n24
Legally Blonde (2001), 132, 224n21
Legally Blonde 2: Red, White, and Blonde (2003), 132
Leibovitz, Annie, 202–3
Leigh, Vivien, 10, 55, 57, 59–60
LeRoy, Mervyn, 72
Liberace, 41
Lil Nas X, 210
Lincoln Lawyer, The (2011), 175
Lindsey, George, 78
Linklater, Richard, 169, 173, 175
Lisa Lisa, 120
Lombardo, Guy, 19
Lone Star (1996), 172
Long, Hot Summer, The (1958), 63
Lopez, Jennifer, 173, 196
Los Lobos, 120
Losey, Joseph, 55
Louis Armstrong New Orleans International Airport, 14–15, 25–26
Love Me Tender (1956), 42
Lumet, Sidney, 55

Index

Lynn, Loretta, 6, 210
Lynyrd Skynyrd, 109, 122, 188

Madea Christmas, A (2013), 168, 228n25
Madea Goes to Jail (2009), 161
Mad Max: Beyond Thunderdome (1985), 89
Magic Mike (2012), 175–76
Magnani, Anna, 55, 66
Mailer, Norman, 33
Malden, Karl, 55, 67
Man in the Moon, The (1991), 131
Mankiewicz, Joseph L., 55, 65
Mann, Daniel, 55
Ma Rainey's Black Bottom (2020), 3
Marsalis, Wynton, 26
Martindale, Margot, 199
Martineé, Lewis, 120
Marx, Groucho, 33–34
Master of None (2015–21), 182–85, 188–89
Matlock (1986–95), 80
Matthau, Walter, 20
McAnally, Shane, 210
McBrayer, Jack, 4
McCarthy, Mary, 32
McCarthy, Melissa, 54
McClanahan, Rue, 81
McConaughey, Matthew, 3, 11, 12, 169–80
Meadows, Audrey, 34–35
Memphis, TN, 3, 41, 49, 52–53, 86
Merkel, Una, 56
Miami, FL, 81, 110, 116–18, 121
Mississippi Burning (1988), 167
Mod Squad, The (1968–73), 80
Mogambo (1953), 1
Moisant, John, 14
Mommie Dearest (1981), 162
Morning Glory (1931), 65
Morning Show, The (2019–), 135
Morrison, Toni, 126–28, 137
Mr. Wrong (1996), 149–50
Mud (2012), 175–76
Murder by Death (1976), 36–37
Murphy, Eddie, 54, 165

Murray, Anne, 41
Murray, Bill, 54
Music of the Heart (1999), 118

Nabors, Jim, 4, 78, 219n32
Nashville, TN, 14, 81, 98, 121, 131, 184, 210, 224n21
National Velvet (1944), 63
Native Son (1986), 126
New Andy Griffith Show, The (1971), 80
Newman, Paul, 10, 55, 57, 62–63
New Orleans (1947), 20
New Orleans, LA, 14–15, 24–26, 57, 60, 64–65, 121, 131; and Ellen DeGeneres, 144–47, 153; and Louis Armstrong, 15–16, 19–20, 23–26; and Truman Capote, 28, 38; and Tyler Perry, 160
New Orleans International Airport. *See* Louis Armstrong New Orleans International Airport
Newton Boys, The (1998), 173, 179
Nichols, Jeff, 175
Nicholson, Jack, 54
Nicks, Stevie, 110, 112
Night of the Iguana, The (1964), 55–56
No Time for Sergeants (play, television, and film), 72, 74, 76, 219n32
Nutty Professor, The (1996), 165

Obama, Barack, 166
Obama, Michelle, 141, 153
O Brother, Where Art Thou? (2000), 3
O'Connor, Sinéad, 207
Oliver, Joseph "King," 16, 24–25
One Day at a Time (2017–20), 118
One Touch of Venus (1948), 1–2
On Her Majesty's Secret Service (1969), 17
On the Waterfront (1954), 61
Oprah Winfrey Show, The (1986–2011), 125–31
Orlando, FL, 14, 81

Page, Geraldine, 56, 67
Paperboy, The (2012), 175
Parker, Sarah Jessica, 173
Parks and Recreation (2009–15), 182–85, 190–91

Parton, Dolly, 3, 10, 12–13, 87, 96–108, 109, 118, 135, 197, 206–8, 209, 211
Patterson, James, 102
Pavan, Marisa, 55
People (magazine), 38, 103, 174
Period of Adjustment (1962), 55–56
Perry, Tyler, 3, 11, 12, 156–68, 211
Peterson, Jordan, 179, 230n39
Petticoat Junction (1963–70), 77, 219n29
Petty, Tom, 3, 10–11, 12, 109–16, 122, 211
Philadelphia Story, The (1940), 21, 65
Philippe, Ryan, 133
Pleasantville (1998), 132
Poehler, Amy, 190
Poitier, Sidney, 228n1
Porter Wagoner Show, The (1960–81), 99
"postsouthern" South. *See* South, as postsouthern
Potts, Annie, 81
Presley, Elvis, 3, 9, 12, 41–53, 110, 131
Presley, Lisa Marie, 48–49, 52
Presley, Priscilla, 44, 48–49
Presley, Vernon, 45, 52, 53
Pullman, Bill, 150

Qualley, Margaret, 68
Quan, Ke Huy, 217n2
Quintero, José, 55, 60

Rainmaker, The (1956), 65
Raintree County (1957), 63
Real Housewives of Atlanta (2008–), 211
Real McCoys, The (1957–63), 77, 82
Rebecca (1941), 66
redneck stereotype. *See* hillbilly and redneck stereotypes
Reese, Della, 228n1
Reign of Fire (2002), 174, 178
R.E.M., 109
Reno 911! (2003–), 182
Reynolds, Burt, 81
Rhinestone (1984), 101
Ritt, Martin, 63
Roberts, Julia, 7, 118, 177

Rock, Chris, 4, 181
Rogers, Kenny, 101, 109
Rolling Stones, 85, 86, 111
Roman Spring of Mrs. Stone, The (1961), 55–56, 59–60
Ronstadt, Linda, 102, 103
Room at the Top (1959), 56
Rooney, Mickey, 58
Rose Tattoo, The (1955), 55
Ross, Herbert, 172
RuPaul, 210–11

Sahara (2005), 174
Santana, 120
Sayles, John, 172
Sayonara (1958), 61
Schafer, Hunter, 211
Schneider, John, 81
School for Scoundrels (2006), 182
Schumacher, Joel, 172
Schwarzenegger, Arnold, 37, 89
Scorsese, Martin, 175
Scrubs (2001–10), 182
Sea of Trees, The (2015), 177
Selma (2014), 126
Serenity (2019), 177
Shangela, 211
Shields, Brooke, 201–2
Showboat (1951), 1
Signoret, Simone, 56
Simon, Neil, 36
Simon, Paul, 50
Simone, Nina, 83–84
Sinatra, Frank, 20
Sing (2016), 177
Sing 2 (2021), 177
Single Moms Club, The (2014), 228n25
Smith, Will, 228n1
Smokey and the Bandit, 81
Smoky Mountain Christmas, A (1986), 101
Soderbergh, Steven, 175
Sophie's Choice (1982), 58
South, as imaginary space, 8–9

Index

South, as postsouthern, 181, 185–86, 189, 191
southern accents, 12, 57–58, 63–64, 67–68; and Aziz Ansari, 185; and Ellen DeGeneres, 147; and Matthew McConaughey, 170, 174; and Tom Petty, 112–15
southern geography, 7–8
southern hospitality myth, 11, 145
southern literacy rates, 12, 143, 226n71
southern stars versus stars from the South, 1–3
southern stereotypes. *See* stereotypes and southern stereotypes
Spears, Britney, 41, 226n63
Spector, Phil, 85
Spielberg, Steven, 89, 126, 173
stars and star personas, 4–6
Steel Magnolias (1989), 101, 118
Steinem, Gloria, 105
stereotypes and southern stereotypes, 2, 5–6, 56–58, 70–71, 81, 218n5; and Andy Griffith, 72–72, 74, 78; and Asian Americans, 182–83; and Aziz Ansari, 181, 184–85, 188–90, 193; and Black Americans, 193; and Louis Armstrong, 17, 19; and Matthew McConaughey, 169, 175–76; and southern women, 124, 136–37; and Truman Capote, 28, 36; and Tyler Perry, 165
Stewart, Jimmy, 20
Stone, Emma, 167
Straight Talk (1992), 102
Streep, Meryl, 58
Streetcar Named Desire, A (1951), 55–56, 58, 59–61
Streisand, Barbra, 20–22, 212
Suddenly, Last Summer (1959), 55–56, 58, 64–66
Sullivan, Ed, and *The Ed Sullivan Show* (1948–71), 44, 70, 70
Summer and Smoke (1961), 55–56, 67
Summertime (1955), 65
Susann, Jacqueline, 34–35
Sweet Bird of Youth (1962), 55–56
Sweet Home Alabama (2002), 134, 225n24
Sykes, Wanda, 4

Taylor, Elizabeth, 39, 55–56, 57, 62–65
Texas Chainsaw Massacre: The Next Generation (1994), 172
Thelma and Louise (1991), 89
Thicke, Robin, 203–4
Thomas, Danny, 75–76
Thornton, Big Mama, 47
Thornton, Billy Bob, 7, 150
Time to Kill, A (1996), 172, 175
Tomei, Marisa, 54
Tomlin, Lily, 4, 100, 106
Touch of Evil (1958), 58
Tracy, Spencer, 30
Trading Paint (2019), 177
Traveling Wilburys, 115
Travolta, John, 177
True Detective (2014), 175
Trump, Donald, 106, 179
Turner, Ike, 10, 84–88, 95
Turner, Tina, 3, 10, 12, 83–95, 109, 209, 211
typecasting, 2, 5–7; and Andy Griffith, 10, 72–73, 79–80; and Gloria Estefan, 116; and Matthew McConaughey, 174; and Reese Witherspoon, 134
Tyson, Cicely, 166, 228n1

Valens, Ritchie, 120
Vallée, Jean-Marc, 175
Van Dyke, Dick, 80
Vidal, Gore, 31, 32
Viva Zapata! (1952), 61

Wagoner, Porter, 99–100
Waithe, Lena, 182
Walk the Line (2005), 134
Warner, Malcolm-Jamal, 160
Washington, Denzel, 228n1
Waters, Ethel, 21
Wedding Planner, The (2001), 173–74
We're Here (2020–24), 211
White Boy Rick (2018), 177
Williams, Tennessee, 3, 9–10, 32, 54–69, 212
Williams, Vanessa, 199

Wilson, August, 161
Wilson, Flip, 165
Winfrey, Oprah, 3, 11, 12, 123–31, 143, 150, 156, 228n1
Winter Kill (1974), 80
Witherspoon, Reese, 3, 11, 12, 123–25, 131–36, 140–41, 143, 211
Wolfe, George C., 126
Wolf of Wall Street, The (2013), 175
Woman of the Year (1942), 65
Women of Brewster Place, The (1989), 126

Wopat, Tom, 81
Wright, Chely, 210

Yang, Alan, 182
Yearwood, Trisha, 210
Yeoh, Michelle, 217n2

Zellweger, Renée, 7, 169
Zemeckis, Robert, 172
ZZ Top, 109

www.ingramcontent.com/pod-product-compliance
Lightning Source LLC
Chambersburg PA
CBHW030532230426
43665CB00010B/862